# THE LIBERTY LINE

# THE
# LIBERTY LINE

*The Legend of the
Underground Railroad*

LARRY GARA

THE UNIVERSITY PRESS OF KENTUCKY

Original publication of this book was aided by a grant
from The Ford Foundation.

Published by The University Press of Kentucky
Scholarly publisher for the Commonwealth,
serving Bellarmine University, Berea College, Centre College of Kentucky,
Eastern Kentucky University, The Filson Historical Society, Georgetown
College, Kentucky Historical Society, Kentucky State University, Morehead
State University, Murray State University, Northern Kentucky University,
Transylvania University, University of Kentucky, University of Louisville,
and Western Kentucky University.

*Editorial and Sales Offices:* The University Press of Kentucky
663 South Limestone Street, Lexington, Kentucky 40508–4008

06 05 04 03   5 4 3

**Library of Congress Cataloging-in-Publication Data**

Gara, Larry.
The liberty line : the legend of the underground railroad / Larry Gara.
p.     cm.
Originally published: Lexington : University of Kentucky Press.
1961. With new pref.
Includes bibliograhical references and index.
ISBN 0-8131-0864-0 (alk. paper)
1. Underground railroad.  2. Fugitive slaves—United States.  I. Title.
E450.G22     1996
973.7'115—dc 20       95-26336

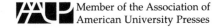

Member of the Association of
American University Presses

# CONTENTS

*for Lenna Mae*

# PREFACE

Few Americans are unfamiliar with the romantic saga of the underground railroad, for its combination of righteous behavior and high drama are deeply imbedded in many minds. Though this story is compounded of both fact and fancy, its legendary character has not been recognized or investigated. Yet as a popular legend it certainly deserves serious study. This book is mainly the story of that legend and of the elements—fact and fancy—which contributed to its growth. Where possible, discrepancies between the legendary version and the historical events have been examined.

For reconstructing the history of the legend, I have drawn from as wide as possible a variety of sources. Materials used to supplement and often to correct accounts found in the more frequently used postwar abolitionist memoirs include abolitionist correspondence and propaganda writings, the letters and other papers of people who had a vested interest in slavery, and newspapers. I learned a great deal about the subject from the mass of materials accumulated by Professor Wilbur H. Siebert. Although my conclusions differ from his, I am extremely grateful for his collection and his pioneer writings. I have also tried to place the history of the legend in the setting provided by more recent scholarship on the institution of slavery itself.

Many people have given assistance to me at various stages of the collecting of material and the writing of this book. I have gained insight and knowledge from the works of others and can acknowledge only a few of the numerous obligations that such a study entails.

I am extremely grateful to the American Philosophical Society for a grant from its Penrose Fund which made possible a summer's research trip and enabled me to collect a wide variety of materials that would otherwise have been unavailable to me.

Professor William B. Hesseltine of the University of Wisconsin and Miss Hazel C. Wolf of Peoria, Illinois, read the entire manuscript, and Professor Holman Hamilton of the University of Kentucky read the portion relating to the Fugitive Slave Law. They gave many suggestions and generous criticism which I have taken into account in revising the study. The final product is much improved for their kind efforts, though, of course, errors in fact or judgment which may still remain are solely my responsibility. Merton Dillon and Joel Goldfarb shared with me notes from their own research which had bearing on some phases of this study. Professor D. Ray Wilcox of Geneva College kindly lent me a copy of a chapter of his thesis treating the underground railroad and the Covenanters.

With the generosity so common among their profession, librarians have time after time gone out of their way to accommodate a visitor who wished to make the most of a brief stay. I want especially to thank Miss Eleanor Weir Welch, formerly the librarian of the Milner Library of Illinois State Normal University, Miss Mattie Russell of the Manuscripts Division of the Duke University Library, and Miss Frances L. Goudy of the Henry Buhl Library of Grove City College. Miss Welch opened the library's resources to me when I was teaching in a neighboring institution, and as a result I was able to do much of the groundwork research at the Milner Library. Miss Russell gave me leads to many items which I might not otherwise have found in the superbly cataloged manuscript collections of the Duke Library. Miss Goudy located materials, borrowed books from other libraries, and shared with me her own knowledge of American history with a patience and understanding for which I am grateful. Staffs of the following libraries were also extremely helpful: the Boston Public Library, the Chester County (Pennsylvania) Historical Society, the Chicago Historical Society, the Library of Congress, the Delaware Historical Society, the Friends Historical Library at Swarthmore College, the

Haverford College Library, the Houghton Library of Harvard University, the Kansas Historical Society, the Library of the University of Kentucky, the Mercantile Library of St. Louis, the Newberry Library, the Oberlin College Library, the Ohio Historical Society, the Historical Society of Pennsylvania, the Virginia State Library, the Western Reserve Historical Society, and the State Historical Society of Wisconsin.

Finally, even though this study is dedicated to my wife, Lenna Mae Gara, it would be grossly unfair to omit mention here of her constant help as research assistant, editor, and typist. While her own interest in the subject may have lightened the burden somewhat, the thousand and one tasks she performed so well deserve more than the usual final reference to which destiny has assigned the wives of historians.

LARRY GARA

*Grove City, Pennsylvania*

# PREFACE TO THE 1996 EDITION

MY LONG journey on the underground railroad began nearly fifty years ago when I was a student in Paul Miller's United States history class at William Penn College in Iowa. For that class I wrote a paper on the underground railroad, based on secondary source material and full of the usual stereotypes and oversimplified stories. Four years later, in a graduate seminar with William B. Hessletine at the University of Wisconsin, my reexamination of the underground railroad began. For the seminar I wrote a paper on the propaganda function of the underground railroad. My use of original source materials convinced me that the traditional version rested on shaky ground. I put the topic aside while completing work for my degree, then returned to it as the subject of my first postgraduate research. The result was *The Liberty Line: The Legend of the Underground Railroad,* originally published more than thirty years ago.

After examining the traditional sources, I concluded that the underground railroad legend was a mixture of fact and fiction. Research for most earlier histories had relied on memoirs of white abolitionists. Wilbur H. Siebert based his pioneer monograph, *The Underground Railroad from Slavery to Freedom* (1898), for example, on the reminiscences of descendants and friends of abolitionists. Several things became clear to me as my research continued. While assistance was available to fugitive slaves in the North, it was quite different from the legendary accounts. As I studied the narratives or autobiographies of former slaves, I was struck with their active roles in their own escapes. These records contrasted with their passive roles in the legendary accounts, when, indeed, those accounts mentioned them at all. Discovering William Still's classic *The Underground Rail Road* strengthened my view. Here was a work written by an African American who had devoted years to working with the Philadelphia Vigilance Committee to help fugitive slaves. Still preserved and published contemporary records, yet he had been overlooked as a source for underground railroad history. Placing the fugitive slaves at the center of their struggle for freedom was the major contribution of *The Liberty Line.*

Of course, white abolitionists played a significant role, and I had no intention of overlooking them. Were I to write the book again, I would give more recognition to the abolitionists, many of whom risked a great deal to help escaping slaves. Yet it remains undeniable that the slaves themselves actually planned and carried out their runs for freedom. Any aid they received came after they had left the slave states and were in territory where they still faced return under terms of the Fugitive Slave Law.

More often than not, their destination was Canada, where they became refugees from an oppressive society. In this light the underground railroad became an instrument of colonization, even though most abolitionists had rejected the colonization idea. African Americans in Canada became refugees from oppression just as had other groups who emigrated to new lands in order to escape tyranny. Recognizing this contradiction, some abolitionists tried to convince fugitives that they could safely remain in the United States. Yet ever-present race discrimination in the North, coupled with the threat of kidnapping or legal return to slavery, made Canada an attractive haven. Consequently, despite their opposition to the colonization idea, many abolitionists actually assisted in such a program.

Another theme that I would develop were I to rewrite *The Liberty Line* is the important example of successful nonviolent action the underground railroad provided. Much has been written about the relatively few open slave rebellions, and about Nat Turner in particular. Those were heroic uprisings, but all of them failed and resulted in terrible retribution. On the other hand, with few exceptions the slave escapes were a nearly perfect model of nonviolent action, action that often succeeded without loss of life.

Moreover, abolitionists who helped the former slaves were also nonviolent activists, openly violating federal and state laws as they practiced nonviolent civil disobedience. While only a few were arrested under the Fugitive Slave Law, their ordeal resulted directly from adherence to what they considered a higher law than the United States Constitution. Carleton Mabee's important *Black Freedom: The Nonviolent Abolitionists from 1830 through the Civil War* (1970) discusses many other examples of nonviolent action practiced by slaves and abolitionists.

Much of this history becomes lost in the many legendary accounts that continue to appear today in newspapers and popular magazines. Recent scholars have begun to question the traditional stories, some of which are too fantastic to be taken seriously. Benjamin Quarles made a major contribution with his *Black Abolitionists* (1969), calling attention to the "Black Underground" that supplemented and sometimes worked independently from the traditional underground railroad of the white abolitionists. Other scholars have made use of the slave narratives and of Still's writing. Yet elements of the legend persist, describing a well organized national network with imaginative hiding places and tunnels, and painting an oversimplified picture of helpless fugitives being carried, literally, to freedom.

The legend has become part of the American psyche, for the story it tells is both fascinating and admirable. Indeed, I was naive to consider my work finished when *The Liberty Line* was published. That was only the beginning. Requests for talks and articles began shortly after publication, and they continue to the present. Moreover, the concept of an underground railroad has been applied to situations as diverse as getting draft resisters to Canada during the Vietnam War and, more recently, assisting refugees from an oppressive government in El Salvador.

Each year Black History Month seems to spawn stories about the underground railroad, but proof of the railroad's importance in American history is not confined to February. Wilmington, Delaware, and Ripley and Cincinnati, Ohio, are just a few of the places where underground railroad history is being preserved. In Cincinnati, plans are under way for an underground railroad museum and learning center. In 1995, public television station WXXI in Rochester, New York, produced a two-hour documentary entitled "Flight to Freedom." Addison Thompson, an archi-

tectural photographer, has spent several years photographing underground railroad sites for a proposed book. In 1991 Byron
Fruehling, a graduate student in archaeology at the University
of Akron, conducted an archaeological search of seventeen Ohio
houses said to have been connected with the underground railroad. His conclusion was that none of the homes he examined
had contained tunnels or secret places of concealment. "If such
constructions existed at all, they must be extremely rare," he
wrote.

Part of the resurgence of interest in the underground railroad
must be credited to Charles L. Blockson, curator of the African
American Collection of Temple University, chair of the National
Underground Railroad Advisory Committee, and descendant of
an escaped slave. With a major article in *National Geographic* and
two books—*The Underground Railroad* and *Hippocrene Guide to the
Underground Railroad* (1994)—Blockson has devoted much of his
time and energy to promoting underground railroad history.

That history is especially relevant today, when once again
pseudoscience is being used to question the intelligence and abil-
ity of African Americans. In the winter of 1980, five Oberlin College students simulated a flight from slavery, walking from
Greensburg, Kentucky, to Oberlin, Ohio. They based "Rediscov-
ering the Underground Railroad" on careful research. Their experience, they said, allowed them to look through the eyes of
fugitive slaves, "illustrating what it was like to run for freedom."
In 1983 a group of NAACP marchers made similar use of the
underground railroad story, retracing a route from Kentucky to
Michigan. They marched, they said, to "shake the apathy in the
North" by registering thousands of black voters along their route.
Blockson has drawn up the route for a similar journey from Atlanta to Canada. Called "Trek a Mile in My Shoes," the project
enables descendants of fugitive slaves to travel the ground their
ancestors had traveled in their flight to freedom. The historical
record of the underground railroad and the legend that grew
from it do indeed have relevance for our time, and it is good to
have *The Liberty Line* once more back on track.

*Chapter One*

# THE LEGENDARY RAILROAD

THOUSANDS WHO attended the Columbian World's Fair in Chicago in 1893 saw a painting by Charles T. Webber entitled "The Underground Railroad"; this dramatic picture showed a large family of fugitives arriving at the home of Levi Coffin of Cincinnati, who, with his wife and friends, was guiding the shivering and frightened Negroes through the snow to shelter. Obviously these poor fugitives from southern slavery had had a difficult trip, but the central characters in the painting—the heroic figures—were the Quaker friends of the fleeing bondsmen. The picture portrayed two of the most familiar stereotypes in the legend of the underground railroad: valiant Quaker conductors and their helpless, grateful passengers.

One of the visitors who saw the Webber painting was Wilbur H. Siebert, a young instructor from Ohio State University, who was deeply moved by the subject and its treatment. He had already begun to collect material for a history of the underground railroad, and the emotional impact of the painting further inspired his efforts.[1] Five years later, Professor Siebert published his exhaustive book on the underground railroad and thereby gave scholarly sanction to a great mass of material that was partly legend and partly fact.

Few other legends in American history have gained the almost universal acceptance and popularity of the underground railroad. The romance and glamour of the institution have helped endear it to Americans, especially in the North. The legend of the underground railroad tells of intrepid abolitionists sending multitudes of passengers over a well-organized transportation system to the Promised Land of freedom. The fugitives often were hotly pursued by cruel slave hunters, and nearly always they eluded capture because of the ingenuity and daring of the conductors. All was carried on with the utmost secrecy. It was, to quote the dust jacket of a popular history, "an urgent whisper, a quickly extinguished light, flight over dark roads and quiet rivers with hidden cargo." There were "courageous people [who] moved in silent, spontaneous revolt against a monstrous injustice. The wheels of the Underground Railroad were turning and 'Make Free' was the password to freedom."[2]

Although the underground railroad was a reality, much of the material relating to it belongs in the realm of folklore rather than history. The writer was not amiss who suggested that perhaps it was a Paul Bunyan "equipped with a frontier magic" who "scooped up the earth with his fist and shot out his arm in tunnels" and laid the Underground Railroad.[3] The "Storyteller's Map of American Myths," published in the August 22, 1960, issue of *Life* magazine, rightly includes the fictional Eliza Harris, best known of all the underground railroad passengers. Fantastic exaggerations of the exploits of such real persons as Harriet Tubman, Thomas Garrett, and Levi Coffin make them as much a part of our folklore as of our national history.

Most legends have many versions, and the story of the underground railroad is no exception. Few people can provide details when asked about the institution. Specific information is usually crowded out by vague generalizations. The underground railroad is accepted on faith as a part of America's heritage. The picture it brings to mind differs from person to

[1] "The Webber Fund," a printed circular in scrapbook "The Underground Railroad in Ohio, vol. 7," Wilbur H. Siebert Papers, Ohio Historical Society.

[2] Dust jacket of William Breyfogle, *Make Free: The Story of the Underground Railroad* (Philadelphia, 1958).

[3] Henrietta Buckmaster, *Let My People Go: The Story of the Underground Railroad and the Growth of the Abolition Movement* (Beacon paperback ed., Boston, 1959), 11.

person, but there are certain ideas which are nearly always associated with it.

One of the assumptions usually associated with the concept of the underground railroad is that people, including those who were slaves, have an inherent yearning for freedom. "The slaves are men," wrote an abolitionist in 1831. "They have within them that unextinguishable thirst for freedom, which is born in man." The idea is still popular today, and the legend takes little account of the practical situation in which the slave found himself or the very limited alternatives which that situation offered. "There were hundreds of thousands of black men and women who thought of freedom by day and dreamed of it by night," wrote the author of a popular account of the underground railroad.[4]

Strangely, however, the hero of the legendary struggle for freedom was not the slave who panted for release from his chains. Indeed, the slave often received only a secondary role in the exciting drama. All he had to do was to leave the land of whips and chains and wend his way to the nearest underground line. His role was largely passive. It may have required courage to risk a long and dangerous trip from slavery, but whatever was demanded of him was as nothing compared to the bravery and daring of his white abetters. Without abolitionist aid, the legend goes, few if any slaves could ever have found their way to the North or to Canada. With such aid, fugitives successfully eluded their vindictive pursuers and safely reached their objective. And the hero of the dramatic flight is clearly the abolitionist.

The legend is a melodrama. The villains are the slave catchers with their vicious bloodhounds; occasionally the master himself is depicted as the slave hunter. The abolitionists, on the other hand, are idealists of fortitude and courage. "Splendid men and women were those ardent operators on the Underground Railroad," who possessed "traits of character which enobled and

---

[4] Samuel J. May, *A Discourse on Slavery in the United States, Delivered in Brooklyn, July 3, 1831* (Boston, 1832) , 16; Breyfogle, *Make Free*, 16–17.

dignified human nature," wrote a daughter of one of them.[5]

This, of course, is a vastly oversimplified interpretation. Abolitionists, after all, were human, with the ambitions, drives, and mixed motives common to the race. Not all those who considered themselves abolitionists spent their waking hours helping the allegedly helpless fugitive slave on his way to Canada; some of the most uncompromising opponents of slavery considered such activity useless or even immoral. But it is the idealized stereotype of the abolitionist—a pure-hearted knight in shining armor—who plays the heroic role in the underground railroad drama. The actual men and women of the abolition movement, like the slaves themselves, are far too complex to fit into a melodrama.

The villain, too, is a stereotype. He is a mean Southerner, a term synonymous in the popular legend with slaveholder or defender of the slave system. He, too, is something other than human, in this case something less. The whole ante bellum South was a dismal swamp of slavery—a cesspool of vice—and the inhabitants lacked ethical principles or the rudiments of human decency. The great majority of Southerners who had no direct interest in slavery are overlooked, as is the benevolent slaveowner. The yeoman farmer of the Old South, who usually worked his acreage without the help of slave labor, is the forgotten man of this legend as he is of that other tradition which depicts the southern plantation as the home of a graceful aristocratic culture.[6]

To some the drama is a struggle between the God-fearing and righteous New Englanders on the one side and the wicked Southerners on the other. In this version of the legend, New England is the source of morality and civilization and the underground railroad work is in part illustrative of the superiority of the character of New England emigrants to the West. Ober-

[5] Emma Julia Scott, "The Underground Railroad," prepared for the Woodford County (Ill.) Historical Society and read at the society's annual picnic, August 30, 1934.
[6] For the plantation legend, see Francis P. Gaines, *The Southern Plantation: A Study in the Development and Accuracy of a Tradition* (New York, 1925).

lin, one of the most famous of the underground railroad stations, was, according to its historian-president James H. Fairchild, "a product of New England ideas and culture and life. The founders, the colonists, the students, and the teachers, were all from New England, most of them directly, the rest indirectly." New England pioneers formed the backbone of the American character in the West, and their educational institutions and their churches helped to save the various frontiers from the evil influences of the South. In part this legendary role is symbolized by the long struggle of the New England reformers against slavery, the nineteenth century relic of barbarism. It was an extension of Jonathan Edwards' crusade against sin. In 1931 an Ohio newspaper story about the underground railroad around Coshocton pointed out that though some people living there had brought with them southern notions, there were others "with whom New England ideas prevailed." The Yankees' "aggressive stand against slavery promoted a sentiment ready to support the fleeing slaves."[7]

Other groups, too, provided participants for the legendary institution. The Quakers—perhaps because of their very early and consistent stand against slavery—are often thought of as underground railroad conductors. Members of the Society of Friends were known before the Civil War, as they have been since, as people of strong convictions and firm purpose. Some antislavery workers among them became symbols by which the entire generation of their religious group has been evaluated. Years after the war, Thomas Garrett was described in a popular magazine as a "Quaker whose principal object in life was to assist fugitive slaves."[8] Stories are legion of fugitive slaves who found aid and guidance from the people of soft language and strong ideals. Simeon Halliday, the Quaker abolitionist in *Uncle Tom's Cabin,* helped to popularize the type. The legend tells of former

[7] James H. Fairchild, *Oberlin: The Colony and the College* (Oberlin, 1883), 42; clipping from *Coshocton* (Ohio) *Tribune,* May 3, 1931, in scrapbook "The Underground Railroad in Ohio, vol. 4," Siebert Papers, Ohio Historical Society.
[8] Lillie B. Chace Wyman, "Harriet Tubman," *New England Magazine,* n.s. 14:112 (March, 1896).

slaves seeking out men with broad-brimmed hats as those who would invariably aid them in their flight to freedom; such stories imply that a fugitive who was fortunate enough to find a Quaker was almost sure to be successful. Sometimes the underground railroad is considered primarily a Quaker institution. The daughter of an Illinois abolitionist alleged that the "Quakers always opposed to the institution [of slavery] were the most active in the U.G.R.R. work. Any negro who came for aid was never turned away."[9] Certainly in the popular legend, Quakers are people who would always risk life, limb, and fortune, if necessary, for the cause of the helpless slave.

The risks were great. Abolitionists faced the calumny of their proslavery neighbors as well as the danger of court action should their activities on behalf of the fugitive slaves be uncovered. Though the legendary version of the underground railroad story pays little attention to the problems faced by former slaves in the North, there is plenty of recognition given to the tribulations of their friends, the abolitionists. The Fugitive Slave Law, according to legend, was designed especially to ensnare abolitionists and to check their benevolent enterprise. "Generally the train masters kept no dispatch books or records of train schedules or of passengers," lest such material be used as evidence against them, said a local Iowa historian.[10]

If the risks were great, the rewards were worth it, for according to the popular legend the mysterious line carried a great mass of passengers to the land of freedom. Although actual figures are seldom brought to mind, most people think that large numbers of the slaves availed themselves of the services of the underground railroad. The existence of Negro populations in northern towns and cities is often cited as evidence of an underground terminal. In 1932 an Ohio newspaper published a story about an old mill supposed to have been a station on the underground railroad. It was reputed to be among the last of the

[9] Scott, "The Underground Railroad."
[10] Jacob Van Ek, "Underground Railroad in Iowa," *The Palimpsest*, 2:142–43 (May, 1921).

noted stations. The elderly owner recalled having heard relatives tell about the operations of the underground railroad. He said "as many as 50 slaves would be housed under the wheel until officers and owners would pass by with their bloodhounds." In 1954 a series of underground railroad stories in a Pennsylvania paper mentioned "thousands of slaves" who passed through the underground railroad stations for thirty years. When J. C. Furnas asked some of his friends to guess the number of fugitive slaves who escaped from the South in the decade preceding the Civil War, the average answer was 270,000, or 74 every day. Several said a million.[11] Clearly there is in the legend the impression of great numbers. The exodus of fleeing slaves from the South is pictured as a flood rather than a trickle.

Furthermore, the popular legend assigns an importance to the underground railroad which reaches beyond the narrow objective of transporting runaway slaves to Canada. There is an impression of the mysterious railroad as a major factor working toward the emancipation of the slaves through the Civil War. The significance of the underground railroad has been greatly magnified in the same way that the popular concept of the amount of traffic on the road has been magnified. A biography of Harriet Tubman describes the underground railroad as an institution which was "so much at the core of the American problem that it called forth an ignominious Fugitive Slave Law," and "was one of the greatest forces which brought on the Civil War, and thus destroyed slavery."[12]

The underground railroad carried its slave passengers to the Promised Land of freedom. Like a Hollywood movie, the legend implies a happy ending when the fugitives reached a haven of free soil, though, as with other aspects of the legend, there is some disagreement about the facts. Sometimes the Promised Land is placed in the North. Thousands of fugitives "found

[11] Clipping from *Cleveland Press*, February 20, 1932, in scrapbook "The Underground Railroad in Ohio, vol. 1," Siebert Papers, Ohio Historical Society; clipping from *Upper Darby News*, August 5, 1954, in the Chester County (Pa.) Historical Society; J. C. Furnas, *Goodbye to Uncle Tom* (New York, 1956), 239.

[12] Earl Conrad, *Harriet Tubman* (Washington, D.C., 1943), 43.

Delaware County their haven," wrote a Pennsylvania journalist in 1959. A local Pennsylvania history told of the underground railroad which passed runaway slaves from station to station "at night in closed wagons, on their way to New England or to freedom in Canada." It is Canada which is most frequently mentioned as the road's terminus, and popular folksingers sometimes assume that to the slaves the North or Canada was obviously the Promised Land. The most scholarly study of slave songs, however, reveals that though the desire to escape was a major theme of the songs, Canaan, the New Jerusalem, or the Promised Land was most often Africa rather than the North or Canada.[13]

The time setting of underground railroad activities is probably vague in the thinking of most people, but in popular accounts there is an idea of continuity, sometimes extending back to the colonial era. Professor Siebert cited George Washington's complaints about Quakers who helped runaways as proof that the institution had an early origin. He maintained further that widescale organization of such activities was begun before 1840. Writers of memoirs could not agree. An Indiana abolitionist wrote that the "system was organized in an early day and grew as rapidly as the public sentiment became educated on the subject." A Vermonter believed that the "period of activity must have declined in the forties"; another abolitionist wrote for a newspaper that the "obnoxious" Fugitive Slave Law brought the underground railroad into existence; a third thought that "passage of the National Fugitive Slave Law made business very dull on the U.G.R.R." in his locality in Ohio; and a fourth, remembering the impact of Mrs. Stowe's novel, claimed that "the appearance of *Uncle Tom's Cabin* brought public feeling up to white heat and promiscuous running away developed into the system known as the Underground Railroad."[14] Such disparities indicate the need for a very critical use

[13] *Chester* (Pa.) *Times,* February 12, 1959; Everett G. Alderfer, *The Montgomery County Story* (Norristown, Pa., 1951) , 163; Miles Mark Fisher, *Negro Slave Songs in the United States* (Ithaca, N.Y., 1953) , 108, 111–12, 146.

[14] Wilbur H. Siebert, *The Underground Railroad from Slavery to Freedom* (New York, 1898) , 33, 43; Marvin Benjamin Butler, *My Story of the Civil War*

of memoir material. However, it is safe to say that the majority of those familiar with the popular legend place the underground railroad in a pre-Civil War setting without regard for the actual years involved.

The road continued its humanitarian work right up to the Civil War itself. The grand minority who existed in every community perfected its organization and carried on its service. In the popular view of the legend, every abolitionist's home was an underground railroad station on a very busy line. In 1936 an article in the *Cincinnati Enquirer* described the underground railroad which "flourished in a number of states before the Civil War." According to the newspaper, it was "the most successful secret organization that ever existed in this country," and Ohio, because of its location, "was by far the most highly successful of all the states involved."[15]

Such a conspiracy inevitably demanded intricate plans for carrying on its activity. It was not just a group of stations but a series of well-forged links in an endless chain which, said an underground railroad novelist, not only spanned the North but also worked "like a ferment beneath the surface of Southern society." According to the legend, the road had many lines. Each conductor, wrote a popular historian, "had to know the friends of liberty" in his area and how to reach them "in the quickest and safest manner whenever he had freight to deliver."[16]

According to tradition, the conductors were usually ignorant of the workings of the mysterious organization beyond their own locale, for only the road's officials were trusted with such

---

*and the Under-ground Railroad* (Huntington, Ind., 1914), 179; Rowland E. Robinson to Siebert, August 19, 1896, in scrapbook "The Underground Railroad in Vermont," Siebert Papers, Ohio Historical Society; clipping from *Fulton* (N.Y.) *Times*, November 28, 1906, in scrapbook "The Underground Railroad in New York, vol. 3," Wilbur H. Siebert Papers, Houghton Library of Harvard University; account of Ira Thomas, October 29, 1895, in scrapbook "The Underground Railroad in Ohio, vol. 11," and Elijah Huftelen, *The Underground Railroad*, a pamphlet in scrapbook "The Underground Railroad in New York, vol. 1," Siebert Papers, Ohio Historical Society.

[15] *Cincinnati Enquirer*, March 8, 1936.

[16] Philip Van Doren Stern, *The Drums of Morning* (New York, 1942), 95.

vital and dangerous information. "All the work had to be done under the cover of utmost secrecy," said an Illinois author. Even the conductor's children were kept in the dark. Apparently only the fugitives knew the location of the underground stations. The conductors were pledged to secrecy and strict obedience, and all transactions were carried on orally through the use of an underground code of secret "signs and signals" which were well understood. "Without them," commented a writer of local history, "the operation of the system of running slaves into free territory would not have been possible."[17] Traditional stories of tokens with secret significance to the underground workers are common.[18] Associated with this is the idea that there was no mention of the activity in the contemporary press. As one student of local underground railroad history said, "publicly there was no Underground Railway. Had the existence of it been even suspected, the Government or the kidnappers would have wiped it out."[19] To this need for secrecy has been attributed the dearth of underground railroad records. The abolitionists had to abide by a "policy of silence which governed everything and everybody concerned in the work," alleged a Sunday feature article in a New England newspaper.[20] As a result, the legend has it, few details of the work were ever placed on record.

Working in secret, the abolitionists of legendary fame devised ingenious hiding places where a hotly pursued fugitive could be safely concealed while the hunt was on. Stories of houses with secret rooms and passageways persist. Chimneys marked with a special row of white or variously colored bricks assured the fugitive that the home beneath was really an underground railroad depot. Sometimes the house itself was a veritable laby-

---

[17] George Owen Smith, *The Lovejoy Shrine, The Lovejoy Station on the Underground Railroad* (2d ed., Princeton, Ill., 1949) , 15; Ora Williams, "Underground Railroad Signals," *Annals of Iowa*, 3d ser. 27:300 (April, 1946) .

[18] Richard W. Phillips to John H. Ryan, September 15, 1915, in scrapbook "The Underground Railroad in Ohio, vol. 9," Siebert Papers, Ohio Historical Society.

[19] William H. Smith to Siebert, December 28, 1933, in scrapbook "The Underground Railroad in Pennsylvania, vol. 2," Siebert Papers, Ohio Historical Society.

[20] *Providence Sunday Journal*, January 13, 1918.

rinth of hidden passageways and rooms known only to the initiated. When underground or hidden storage places, tunnels, and even air shafts are found in older houses, there are always individuals who quickly conclude that these places were built and used for hiding fugitive slaves.[21] Myths about secret hiding places and underground tunnels inevitably grew up about the homes of well-known abolitionists.[22]

Writers of fiction, from Harriet Beecher Stowe to the historical novelists of the present generation, have borrowed from the legend and have also added to it and helped to popularize it. A recent novel which repeats all the stereotypes of the underground railroad tradition is Philip Van Doren Stern's *The Drums of Morning*. Stern places his hero in the mainstream of antislavery history. Orphaned in 1837 when his father was murdered with Elijah Lovejoy in Alton, Illinois, Bradford in the course of his adventures is jailed and branded on the hand for trying to run slaves from Florida, witnesses the rendition of Anthony Burns in Boston, and establishes a thriving underground railroad depot on a farm near Chambersburg, Pennsylvania.

The novel depicts a highly organized underground railroad system, with stations and agents in the South as well as in the free states, and apparently masterminded by an elderly invalid Quaker lady. The conductors undertook "a dangerous and thankless task" as well as an arduous one. The underground operators were always well informed of all ferment among the slaves in the South because of the "grapevine system that was even more mysterious in its operations than the Underground itself." The underground railroad as Stern portrays it deprived Southerners of fifty thousand slaves worth thirty million dollars.[23]

[21] Many such stories can be found in newspaper accounts. For example, see *Columbus* (Ohio) *Dispatch,* July 9, 1923, December 10, 1927.

[22] The late Professor Robert S. Fletcher of Oberlin College told the author about persistent but entirely unfounded stories of a secret passageway in James H. Fairchild's home.

[23] Stern, *The Drums of Morning.* See Book Five, "The Road to Freedom; Pennsylvania, 1854–59," 325–432.

Two popular histories of the underground railroad, Henrietta Buckmaster's *Let My People Go* and William Breyfogle's *Make Free,* also repeat some of the best known traditional material and indicate rather clearly the current status of the legend. Both authors write with an emotional bias which apparently has influenced their acceptance of the melodramatic legendary version. In a preface to a paperback edition of her book, Henrietta Buckmaster admits to a "slight partisanship on the side of freedom," but claims that this helped her "in setting forth the moral climate of that time in relation to ours."[24]

Both volumes repeat traditions concerning the naming of the mysterious institution, and both portray an extremely busy organization. According to Breyfogle, the "conductors proved as brave as they were close-mouthed." The work was dangerous, often accompanied by the "rattle of gunfire." Both books contain legendary incidents about terrified fugitives hotly pursued by slave catchers who are outsmarted by the abolitionists and their underground train. There are the usual ingenious hiding places, secret codes, and the underground grapevine that kept the slaves informed of escape opportunities. As described in these volumes, the underground reached deep into the South. Those who spirited slaves from bondage are pictured as leading figures in the abolition movement.[25]

Both writers describe their heroes in terms more appropriate to legend than history. There was Harriet Tubman, the "Moses of her people," with her numerous slave-running expeditions "into the enemy's country"; the saintly Levi Coffin, President of the Road, whose station received batches of fugitives "from operators in the South," the East, and the West; Thomas Garrett, the doughty Quaker "miracle worker" of Wilmington, who flouted the Fugitive Slave Law and paid a bitter price for his convictions; and the wily scientist Dr. Alexander Ross, whose private underground line took slaves from the deep South to

---

[24] Buckmaster, *Let My People Go,* preface, and 8–9.
[25] Breyfogle, *Make Free,* 35, 38, 95–96; Buckmaster, *Let My People Go,* 111–12, 199.

freedom. There were others, too, including Calvin Fairbank, Frederick Douglass, Isaac Hopper, Josiah Henson, and, of course, John Brown. All of them had "greatness within them," and all did much to assist the fugitives to reach the Promised Land, which these authors identify as Canada.[26]

The underground railroad conductors, according to Breyfogle, were "the muscles and nerves and the brain" of the abolition movement at work, and the railroad, by siphoning off the "worst malcontents and the most enterprising and courageous" of the slaves, was a safety valve which prevented an epidemic of horrible insurrections in the South. Henrietta Buckmaster also gives a prominent role to the institution within the abolition movement and in ante bellum history. She claims that by 1852 the underground railroad "was one of the greatest powers in the country." It made property in slaves insecure and "allowed no slave master to relax." It helped keep alive the necessary agitation which led to the inevitable war for freedom.[27]

Professional scholars as well as popular writers have been influenced by the romantic material of the underground railroad legend. Some traditional matter has found its way into monographs dealing with the abolition crusade or events relating to it. Albert Bushnell Hart wrote that the underground railroad was "not a route, but a net-work; not an organization, but a conspiracy of thousands of people banded together for the deliberate purpose of depriving their southern neighbors of their property and of defying the fugitive-slave laws of the United States." A historian of slavery in Illinois wrote of the underground railway which had been "instituted by the anti-slavery sympathizers in order to aid the negroes to escape to the North in safety." The road had to operate in "absolute secrecy" in order to "facilitate the escape of the negroes" and also to protect the lives and property of the conductors, who everywhere "displayed an

[26] Buckmaster, *Let My People Go*, 77, 151–52, 248–49; Breyfogle, *Make Free*, 35, 177–78, 190–93.
[27] Breyfogle, *Make Free*, 36, 104, 162, 173; Buckmaster, *Let My People Go*, 216, 267.

indomitable courage backed by a will not to be balked or thwarted."[28]

Another historian drew heavily on traditional material for his description of the underground railroad in Pennsylvania. He maintained that since 1800 a "mysterious organization" had been in operation, which irritated the South and "to a great extent made it possible for such a steady stream of fugitives to find permanent freedom." He claimed that in Pennsylvania the "shadowy railroad" had its origin and received its name. A recent study of slavery also describes the underground railroad "which absorbed the energies of numerous individuals" as a "well-articulated network of routes and stations, especially thick in the Middle West, for speeding fugitives on their way to the Canadian border." The author placed the road's origin in the early 1820's, but claimed that there was greatly increased activity after 1840. Imposing twentieth century terminology on the long-defunct institution, he called it "a 'fellow-traveler' movement par excellence."[29]

Some of the source material used by Wilbur H. Siebert, the foremost authority on the underground railroad, is also of traditional origin. For example, his latest work on the subject, *The Mysteries of Ohio's Underground Railroad,* quotes a song about the "railroad undergroun'," which is said to have been sung by a family of fugitives who crossed Lake Erie in 1858. As authority for this story, Siebert cites a semifictional account by H. U. Johnson.[30]

Some historians have sought by a process of deductive reasoning to give the status of scholarship to underground railroad tradition. A pioneer work on fugitive slaves alleged that "no such numbers as are known to have fled could possibly have es-

---

[28] Albert Bushnell Hart, *Slavery and Abolition, 1831–1841* (New York, 1906), 228; N. Dwight Harris, *The History of Negro Servitude in Illinois and of the Slavery Agitation in That State, 1719–1864* (Chicago, 1904), 57–61.

[29] Edward R. Turner, *The Negro in Pennsylvania, 1639–1861* (Washington, 1911), 239–41; Stanley M. Elkins, *Slavery: A Problem in American Institutional and Intellectual Life* (Chicago, 1959), 188.

[30] Wilbur H. Siebert, *The Mysteries of Ohio's Underground Railroad* (Columbus, 1951), 278.

caped . . . had they depended solely upon their own exertions." From the start of antislavery agitation around 1830, the account continued, "a mysterious organization made it a business to receive, forward, conceal, and protect fugitives." More recently, a historian of Kentucky slavery said much the same thing. Assuming that large numbers of slaves had escaped, he commented that it was "plainly evident that no such numbers could have escaped from Kentucky masters had they relied solely on their own efforts." He described the underground railroad as "an elusive and shadowy transportation system" with codes and rigid discipline characteristic of a "vast secret service." The illegal "system grew from an obscure trickle of private humanitarianism into a powerful interstate organization."[31]

College textbooks of American history usually include a brief description of the underground railroad, and some of these accounts are colored by the romantic legend. A recent, widely used text says that the grapevine telegraph "carried news to the blacks of an 'Under Ground Railroad' to liberty." After reaching the northern shore of the Ohio River, the Negroes were "transferred from one abolitionist household to another, hidden by day in cocklofts or haystacks or shocks of Indian corn; piloted by night through the woods, or concealed in farm wagons; sometimes driven in a Friend's carriage, disguised in women's clothes and a deep Quaker bonnet." The number thus rescued was small, but the activity gave stimulus to the abolitionist cause and aroused the rage of Southerners. Running the underground was dangerous, "pursuit was often hot and ruthless," and in some parts of southern Illinois and Indiana those "suspected of harboring runaways were apt to have their houses burned, their persons tarred and feathered." Another textbook claims that many fugitives went north on the underground railroad "which the anti-slaveryites were operating at full steam."

[31] Marion Gleason McDougall, *Fugitive Slaves (1619–1865)* (Boston, 1891), 60; J. Winston Coleman, Jr., *Slavery Times in Kentucky* (Chapel Hill, N.C., 1940), 220–21.

The railroad "consisted of a chain of stations (anti-slavery homes), through which thousands of passengers (runaway slaves) were spirited by conductors (usually abolitionists) from the slave states to the free-soil sanctuary of Canada."[32]

Illustrative of the acceptance of the traditional underground railroad description is its inclusion in a number of standard reference works. The 1953 edition of the *Encyclopedia Britannica* describes it as an "organized system" in the North which assisted slaves to reach Canada, and attributes the name to "exaggerated use" of such railway terms as lines, stations, conductors, and packages or freight. It names Levi Coffin and Robert Purvis as presidents and cites the Pennsylvania Quakers as the probable organizers of the system. "Estimates of the number of slaves who reached freedom through the system vary from 40,000 to 100,000," the article states.

The *Encyclopedia Americana* (1954) refers to the underground railroad as a "secret method of conducting negro slaves" from the South to the northern free states and Canada. Abolitionists "between the Ohio River and the Great Lakes" furnished "shelter and assistance," and their homes were called stations. The *Americana* also lists William Lloyd Garrison, Wendell Phillips, Josiah Grinnell, Gerrit Smith, Theodore Parker, Thomas Garrett, Charles Torrey, Samuel May, Levi Coffin, T. W. Higginson, and F. B. Sanborn as "patrons of the 'underground' system." The *Columbia Encyclopedia* (1956) depicts the railroad as an "irregular secret system," which possibly stemmed back to 1804. It says the slaves were guided from station to station "over generally fixed routes," with the stationmasters "ever on the lookout for the next 'train.' " It was not thoroughly organized, because of its illegality, "and secrecy was absolutely essential." The Quakers started the work. Leaders were Levi Coffin, John Brown, and some Negroes, including Harriet Tubman. The underground railroad, according to this

---

[32] Samuel Eliot Morison and Henry Steele Commager, *The Growth of the American Republic* (4th ed., 2 vols., New York, 1950), 1:529; Thomas A. Bailey, *The American Pageant: A History of the Republic* (Boston, 1956), 378.

work, existed in every northern state, with "particularly extensive networks throughout Ohio, Indiana, and Illinois." The activity provided "an active outlet for the bursting moral energy of the abolitionists," though it freed only an estimated 75,000 slaves.

The articles all present a somewhat restrained but romanticized description of the underground railroad. Such material is partly of a nature that cannot be proved without reliance on traditional sources. Its presence in such reliable reference works indicates the widespread acceptance of the legend.

Legends are usually compounded of both fact and fancy, and the legend of the underground railroad is no exception. Few writers have exercised critical discrimination in dealing with the institution, and some of the scholars have accepted unprovable assertions and questionable data as a basis for their statements. In some instances it is impossible to distinguish fact from fancy. There is probably at least a germ of truth in most of the stories concerning the mysterious institution, though the scattered seeds of historical fact which mature into legends have a way of multiplying beyond belief. Although it is doubtful that any amount of critical scholarship will modify the legend in the popular mind, a study of available materials uncovers quite a different version of the underground railroad. Perhaps the legend itself reveals something of the American character and aspirations, and as such is worthy of its own history.

The facts, insofar as they can be discovered, show that the slaves were not presented with the neat arrangement pictured in the legend for spiriting them to Canada. For most it was necessary, and to some it probably seemed preferable, to adjust themselves to the realities of the slave system. The slave was not in a position to choose between the simple alternatives of slavery and freedom; in the urgent human terms in which these things presented themselves, the matter was much more complicated. The Promised Land was not as close as the northern states or Canada, though for some these places provided an environment far more congenial than that of slavery.

The relatively few slaves who did escape were primarily dependent on their own resources. The abolitionists play a less important part and the escaping slaves a more important one in the revised presentation. Evidence for a nationwide conspiratorial network of underground railroad lines is completely lacking; the nationally organized railroad with its disciplined conductors, controlling directors, and planned excursions into the South did not exist. The abolitionists had no centralized organization, either for spiriting away slaves or for any other of their activities. There was a semblance of organized underground railroad activity in certain localities, but not all the abolitionists participated in or even condoned such work. Free Negroes contributed much more to such enterprises than they have usually been given credit for, and fugitives who rode the underground line often did so after having already completed the most difficult and dangerous phase of their journey alone and unaided.

For the abolitionists, the use of the fugitive issue in their propaganda assumed a more important role than the actual assistance given to the fugitives. The road is significant in history, not for its practical effect on the operation of southern slavery, but for the part it played in the verbal battles which preceded the Civil War. Much that has previously been accepted as fact is in truth no more than a repetition of one variety or another of partisan polemic.

The legend of the underground railroad had its origin in the ante bellum period, when an image of the mysterious institution, based in part on propaganda statements of abolitionists and their southern opponents, began to take shape. However, the great bulk of material on the underground railroad appeared after the war. In reminiscences and histories, elderly abolitionists told of the institution and their part in it. They tended to enlarge its scope and exaggerate its importance, and thus contributed much to one of America's best known but least examined legends.

## Chapter Two

# SLAVERY AND FREEDOM

THE LEGENDARY underground railroad carried its passengers "from Slavery to Freedom." The phrase, quoted from the title of Professor Siebert's history of the underground railroad, implies a simple and dramatic contrast. According to this pattern of thinking, the slaves were all straining under their bonds, yearning to be free; their inherent love of freedom inspired their escapes. Yet seldom did the bondsmen act from such clearcut motives. The desirability of freedom for its own sake was apparently not nearly so obvious to those born in slavery as to Professor Siebert. In actual fact, many additional considerations, far more prosaic than a search for freedom, influenced those slaves who made a break from slavery. Motives for running away, whether instinctive or practical, were usually more than balanced for the slave by a variety of circumstances which made it far easier not to do so. Furthermore, there were other ways to leave bondage; not all slaves who entered the ranks of the freedmen did so by running away, nor did they all prefer life in the North to life in the South.

After all, the slaves were people and every individual was unique. Each viewed life somewhat differently from his companions, and each had his own ideas about slavery. Even the conditions of servitude varied considerably according to the time, the location, and the immediate circumstances. But to the great majority, slavery meant hard work and severe restrictions on one's personal mobility. A Maryland slaveholder who voluntarily freed his slaves found that when they were free, they remained around his home but refused to work or even to make a gesture at paying rent. And when freedom finally came to all the southern slaves, many of them celebrated their emancipation by refraining from all work and by moving about, sometimes at random. An aged former slave recalled that only one family remained on the plantation where he had lived; "the rest was just like birds, they just flew."[1]

Other freed slaves remained where they had been and continued to labor for their former masters. Many years later, some of the former bondsmen expressed their reaction to freedom when it had first come upon them. One said, "We knowed freedom was on us, but we didn't know what was to come with it. We thought we was going to get rich like the white folks. . . . But it didn't turn out that way." Another explained that when his master told him and his fellow slaves that they were free, "We didn't hardly know what he means, . . . didn't many of us go, 'cause we didn't know where to of went." A Texas slave who also continued to work for his former master said, "Freedom wasn't no difference I knows of." Some even missed the security which the more paternalistic slaveholders had provided. An Alabama Negro reported that he had had "a harder time" since emancipation. Another from the same state recalled the "happy days" of the past, when the Negroes lacked the advantages they have enjoyed since the Civil War, but when they had someone to go to when they were in trouble and a security that they never again regained.[2] To some few slaves at least, that security, which provided a modicum of food and shelter, was more meaningful than an abstract freedom.

Others disagreed. One former slave admitted that he had had less security and more "worriment" since emancipation, but still he preferred freedom. Another woman who had lived

[1] J. T. Mason to Gerrit Smith, January 21, 1850, abstracted in *Calendar of the Gerrit Smith Papers in the Syracuse University Library* (*General Correspondence*, vol. 2, Albany, N.Y., 1942), 357; Henderson H. Donald, *The Negro Freedman* (New York, 1952), 1–3; B. A. Botkin, *Lay My Burden Down: A Folk History of Slavery* (Chicago, 1945), 229.
[2] Botkin, *Lay My Burden Down*, 93, 152, 223, 238; Charles S. Johnson, *In the Shadow of the Plantation* (Chicago, 1934), 19.

through both slavery and freedom admonished her interviewer not to believe anyone who said he would rather be a slave. "We all had freedom in our bones," said still another, who had been very young at the time of the Civil War.[3] A reported interview with a fugitive in an abolitionist newspaper indicates that there were those who felt the same way before the war. After the interviewee had listed his former benefits—he had been well clothed, well fed, treated kindly, and not overworked—a reporter suggested that he should return to slavery, since he would be better off there. "Gentlemen," he replied, "the place I left, with all its advantages, is open to any one of you that want to fill it."[4]

One of his contemporaries attempted to find freedom in another way. A free Negro in Louisville, Kentucky, he voluntarily sold himself into slavery. Before long he was apprehended for committing petty larceny. A Louisville editor suggested that his object in selling himself had been "to better enable him to pursue an idle life, and to be personally irresponsible for his own acts." Apparently the court agreed, for not only was he punished by whipping, but it was decreed that since he had originally been a free Negro, he "was bound to stay free."[5]

To many slaves a temporary relief from the daily toil was a type of "freedom" in itself, and the great majority of fugitive slaves were seeking such temporary relief. Running away for short periods of time was a common problem in the South. In most cases planters assumed that missing slaves were only taking a short break. For the planter such short-term leaves presented a problem in management, at worst a nuisance; for the slave it was a psychological safety valve and a control device.[6]

---

[3] Botkin, *Lay My Burden Down*, 267; Johnson, *Shadow of the Plantation*, 20; *Unwritten History of Slavery: Autobiographical Accounts of Negro Ex-Slaves* (Fisk University, *Social Science Source Documents* no. 1, Nashville, 1945) , 295.

[4] Chicago *Western Citizen*, August 11, 1845.

[5] Louisville *Daily Courier*, August 17, 1852.

[6] Charles S. Sydnor, "Pursuing Fugitive Slaves," *South Atlantic Quarterly*, 28:152 (April, 1929) ; John Spencer Bassett, *Slavery in the State of North Carolina* (Baltimore, 1899) , 32; Frederick Law Olmsted, *A Journey in the Seaboard Slave States in the Years 1853-1854, with Remarks on Their Economy* (2 vols., New York, 1904) , 1:111–13.

Plantation records abound in references to running away. The habit was more popular during the hot summer months when work was heavy than in other seasons. In some cases slaves took turns at running to the woods or swamps. A South Carolina planter found two slaves missing on May 22, 1828. These two women returned on June 1, but two weeks later three others ran off, and they were soon joined by four more. Another planter suspected one of his slaves of shirking by feigning illness. After an examination the planter told him "to go and work it off," but the slave decided "to woods it off" instead.[7] Sometimes the example of one or more slaves running off seemed to put similar ideas into the minds of others. There were veritable epidemics of slave escapes from time to time.[8] "I never heard of as many runaways as at this time," lamented a planter in 1839.[9] Southern papers referred to group escapes as "stampedes" of Negroes.

In Alabama a slave could absent himself for two full days before he was even considered a runaway under the law.[10] Many came back in less time than that. Often temporary fugitives returned voluntarily to their familiar homes and work routines, even though they faced severe punishment. Slaves who habitually ran away risked the fate of being sold to a new master. But those who were addicted to running away constituted a relatively small percentage of the total slave population. In general, runaways had specific reasons for their behavior, both in leaving and in returning. One slave girl who ran away because she was threatened with an undeserved punishment returned home after spending some time in a nearby swamp. When asked why she returned, she replied that she was "most dead

[7] Rockingham Plantation Journal, entries for May 22, June 1, 14, 17, 19, 1828, in Duke University Library; Edwin Adams Davis, ed., *Plantation Life in the Florida Parishes of Louisiana, 1836–1846, as Reflected in the Diary of Bennet H. Barrow* (New York, 1943), 157.

[8] Carrolton, Ky., *Family Mirror*, November 20, 1852; *Maysville* (Ky.) *Eagle*, September 22, 1857; New Orleans *Daily Picayune*, March 2, 1850; William Read to Samuel S. Downey, August 18, 1848, Downey Papers, Duke University Library; *Liberator*, September 11, 1857.

[9] Davis, ed., *Barrow Diary*, 161, 341.

[10] James B. Sellers, *Slavery in Alabama* (University, Ala., 1950), 266.

with hunger."[11] Lack of food probably drove many runaways back to their plantations.

Many escapes, then, were unpremeditated and afforded only a temporary relief from routine labor; but some slaves had other reasons, not directly related to an abstract love of freedom, for attempting to free themselves. Slaves often found security in the familiar and, after having become adjusted to and even fond of a particular master and the home he provided, they dreaded the possibility of suddenly facing a new master, new tasks, and a new set of slave acquaintances. Even the independent individualist Frederick Douglass admitted years after his escape that the prospect of leaving his friends was "decidedly the most painful thought" with which he had to contend. Fear of change for the worse caused a slave in Virginia to run away from his master, who was "a very good old man." Many years afterward he admitted, "I never would a left him, but he was gittin old and I didn't know into whose hands I'd fall into."[12] Fear of being sold was common and often provided a reason for running away. Sometimes slaves escaped after they were threatened with sale or learned of plans to sell them, though in many cases the sale plans were imaginary.[13] The owners of ten slaves who escaped from Kentucky could only explain the exodus by a rumor that two of them were to be sold to a Louisiana cotton planter. The slaves, of course, may have had other reasons.[14]

It was not uncommon for slaves who had been sold or hired out to return to their former masters and homes. Newspaper

---

[11] Frances Anne Kemble, *Journal of a Residence on a Georgian Plantation in 1838–1839* (New York, 1863), 174–75.

[12] Frederick Douglass, *Narrative of the Life of Frederick Douglass, . . . Written by Himself* (Boston, 1845), 106; transcript of interview between Wilbur H. Siebert and Isaac White in Windsor, Ontario, August 3, 1895, in scrapbook "The Underground Railroad in Ohio, vol. 6," Wilbur H. Siebert Papers, Ohio Historical Society.

[13] Robert C. Smedley, *History of the Underground Railroad in Chester and the Neighboring Counties of Pennsylvania* (Lancaster, Pa., 1883), 270; William Still, *The Underground Rail Road* (Philadelphia, 1872), 210; Benjamin Drew, *The Refugee: or the Narratives of Fugitive Slaves in Canada* (Boston, 1856), 52–54; Marion J. Russell, "American Slave Discontent in Records of the High Courts," *Journal of Negro History*, 31:427 (October, 1946).

[14] Louisville *Daily Courier*, October 27, 1852.

advertisements for runaways often were inserted in the area
where a slave had previously served, and it was common to assume that a fugitive would head for his place of former residence. Planters were sometimes genuinely concerned about the
welfare of slaves whom they had sold or hired out, and there
were instances of such individuals giving protection to their
former slaves. The owner of two Alabama slaves whose time
had been hired out prevented one of them from returning to
the employer, saying "that he had no right to retain them if he
treated them cruelly; or if they were dissatisfied."[15]

Desire to be with a husband or wife also prompted some escapes. In 1815 a North Carolina woman ran away to her husband's master; another slave from Virginia set foot for Richmond, three hundred miles from his home, to see his wife whom
he could not otherwise have seen for a year. When a St. Louis
slave learned that his wife was to be sold, he induced her to run
to Canada with him; and a Louisville family did the same.[16] A
Georgia slaveowner suggested that a friend would do well to pay
fifty dollars more than usual prices for a Negro whose wife he
already owned, for "one good Negro having a wife at home is
worth much more than one with a wife out."[17]

While some slaves ran away to be with their mates, others
ran away to be freed from them. Escape was in certain instances
a form of divorce. Occasionally escapes were motivated in part
at least by a sexual attraction between a free person and a slave.
When a young white woman was caught with a fugitive slave
in Virginia, it seemed to observers that "her object was not so
much to convey a slave to a free State as to obtain license for herself."[18] In another case a young white man succeeded in getting
his disguised slave paramour across the river from Kentucky

[15] Sellers, *Slavery in Alabama*, 267; Helen T. Catterall, ed., *Judicial Cases Concerning American Slavery and the Negro* (5 vols., Washington, D.C., 1926–1937),
3:34, 144, 150, 156.
[16] Catterall, *Judicial Cases*, 2:27; Richmond *Daily Dispatch*, March 9, 1852;
Drew, *The Refugee*, 175–76, 180–82.
[17] Mat. Whitfield to Gabriel T. Spearman, December 9, 1849, E. A. Nisbet Papers, Duke University Library.
[18] *Liberator*, February 14, 1851.

into Indiana, but the fellow's enthusiasm got the better of him. When he raised the lady's veil, her color was revealed and both were arrested. A young married Virginian got into similar difficulties when, after spending a night in a hotel with Eliza, a slave, he tried unsuccessfully to leave the state in her company. A highly respected grocer in Louisville became enamored of a young slave girl, whom he helped escape to Canada. Later he sent her "letters of a very affectionate nature," which were the cause of his being apprehended by the law.[19] A teenage slave girl in Baltimore listened to the entreaties of an enamored swain who promised to marry her and remove her to Pennsylvania. The escapade ended quickly when the couple was discovered about twenty-two miles from Baltimore "in a hay loft, laying quite cosily together."[20]

Some slaves ran away to avoid punishment for crime. Those who were guilty of murder, theft, rape, or other serious offenses usually ran away.[21] Martin Posey, a cruel and ruthless slave-owner in South Carolina, promised freedom to his slave if he would murder Posey's wife. After the slave had fulfilled his part of the bargain, he ran away in fear and was tracked down with bloodhounds to be murdered in turn by the husband, who sought to protect himself. Posey, however, was convicted of both crimes.[22] A more refined though nonetheless startling crime led a New Orleans slave to decamp. The trusted servant was sent by John R. Shaw and Company to cash a check for more than four thousand dollars and to deposit the money in another bank. When the servant fled with the cash, police believed he must have had an accomplice; it was difficult for them to acknowledge that a slave could have carried through successfully such a very large operation.[23]

[19] Catterall, *Judicial Cases*, 1:202–203, 3:414; Baltimore *Sun*, February 25, 1856; Frankfort, Ky., *Tri-Weekly Commonwealth*, August 31, 1857.
[20] Richmond *Daily Dispatch*, May 7, 1852.
[21] *Maysville* (Ky.) *Eagle*, November 7, 1857; Catterall, *Judicial Cases*, 3:419; A. M. Reed Diary, entry for April 26, 1861, typewritten copy in Duke University Library; Richmond *Daily Dispatch*, May 18, 1852.
[22] Catterall, *Judicial Cases*, 2:413–14.
[23] St. Louis *Daily Union*, August 4, 1851.

Crimes which led to slave escapes were sometimes the direct result of criticism, censure, or punishment. Isaac, a Mississippi slave, resented being reproved by an overseer for bad plowing, and when the overseer attempted to chastise him, Isaac plunged a knife into the man's abdomen and fled. Two other bondsmen whipped a young master, nearly killed a loyal slave who tried to defend the planter, and then left.[24]

Cruel treatment, severe and unjustified punishment, abuse, and overwork were also reasons for some to leave slavery. As a slave in Virginia, Christopher Nichols was beaten severely and often. He finally decided to escape. "My master was killing me as fast as he could when I got away," he said after reaching Canada. A Louisiana slave named David ran away after his master broke his finger. James, a Maryland slave who was an expert blacksmith, was one day severely beaten by his master. Disgraced by the punishment, he decided to escape to the North.[25]

Though the true motives for escape were endlessly varied, it was commonly believed by slaveholders that the problem of running away could be minimized by good treatment, and many planters took pride in the fact that their slaves did not run off. When slaves did run off, planters were inclined to blame someone other than themselves, and on occasion even issued explanations to the newspapers. In 1853 a Missouri slaveowner answered charges made by Canadian abolitionists that ten of his slaves had fled because two daughters of one of them had been sold. He denied that the sale had ever taken place and claimed instead that he had actually purchased the slave and her two children when he moved from Kentucky in order to keep the family together. Another slaveowner from the same state alleged that his favorite servant, who had disappeared while attending his child on a trip to the East, had been stolen by

[24] New Orleans *Daily Picayune* (California ed.) , March 14, 1850.
[25] Frankfort *Tri-Weekly Kentucky Yeoman*, June 8, 1858; Drew, *The Refugee*, 67–72; Catterall, *Judicial Cases*, 3:57, 405, 5:297–98; [A. Mott and M. S. Wood], *Narratives of Colored Americans* (New York, 1882) , 55–56.

abolitionists in Pittsburgh. The master said that "such was the affection of his child for this servant, and such the regard which the whole family had for her, that had he been offered five thousand dollars in gold for her it would have been no temptation to him to part with her."[26] A Nashville woman, on the other hand, whose favorite servant had run away after being hired out to a merchant, gave the fugitive his freedom instead of accepting his offer to pay for himself. But this was the exception. "I had rather a negro would do any thing Else than runaway," wrote Bennet H. Barrow in his diary, expressing a common attitude among the slaveholding class. In his will a Maryland slave-owner left all his slaves to his wife, at whose death they were to be freed, but it was provided also that if any of the slaves ran away, they would forfeit their freedom and be sold for life.[27] In view of the sensitivity of slaveholders on this point, their attribution of slave escapes to the intervention of abolitionists should not always be taken as strong evidence of underground railroad activity.

Today's legend of the underground railroad assumes, as no doubt the northern abolitionists of the ante bellum period also assumed, that any slave who succeeded in eluding his captors set forth as a matter of course for free territory. A great number of escaping slaves, however, did not head for the North at all but for parts of the South. Some went into Mexico, but probably most fugitives sought refuge in the very section that abolitionists were labeling "the charnel house of Slavery." For instance, six slaves who tried unsuccessfully to escape from North Carolina in 1817 were aided by two white men, but insisted that they be taken southward before they would consent to go along with their abetters. When owners advertised for slaves in southern papers and when professional slave traders seriously hunted runaways, they seldom assumed that the people they were seek-

[26] St. Louis *Republican*, May 2, 1853; St. Louis *Intelligencer*, November 29, 1850.
[27] Horace Cowles Atwater, *Incidents of a Southern Tour; or, the South, as Seen with Northern Eyes* (Boston, 1857), 45–46; Davis, ed., *Barrow Diary*, 165; Catterall, *Judicial Cases*, 4:100–101.

ing had gone north. They looked instead in likely places in the land that was familiar to the slave. They hunted the runaways in the areas where they were well acquainted or had relatives, former masters, friends, or something else that would attract them. Southern ship captains used fugitives as deckhands, cooks, engineroom workers, and sailors. Such employment enabled them to elude pursuers and to remain in the region with which they were familiar.[28] After locating two fugitives hired as stewards on a steamer running between Charleston and Palatka, Florida, a slave trader was advised that the captain would probably "object to giving them up," as they had become "quite valuable to him."[29]

Owners of runaways frequently assumed that they had headed for the nearest swamp, for southern swamps did provide refuge for many fugitive slaves. Such havens might become more than temporary hiding places, and the larger swamps attracted some runaways who lived in them permanently.[30] In 1819 a slave captured in a South Carolina swamp told his captors about a party of thirty armed Negroes in swamps forming "a regular chain" from one town to another.[31] These permanent fugitives were often armed, and one group had even made extensive plans to construct a fort. Such groups, led by determined runaways, could live by stealing their food, using deserted buildings, and getting help from less daring slaves. The Great Dismal Swamp, stretching from Virginia into North Carolina, housed a large group of escaped slaves who built huts, farmed on hidden islands, and made staves and shingles which they traded for salted provisions, coarse cloths, and tools pro-

---

[28] Sydnor, "Pursuing Fugitive Slaves," 156; *Liberator*, November 10, 1854; Catterall, *Judicial Cases*, 2:30; *Richmond Enquirer*, December 28, 1858.

[29] William Wright to Ziba B. Oakes, October 25, 1853, Ziba B. Oakes Papers, Boston Public Library.

[30] A. J. McElveen to Ziba B. Oakes, August 30, 1856, W. O. Prentis to Oakes, March 30, 1854, Oakes Papers; *Charleston Observer*, July 21, 1827, cited in Ulrich B. Phillips, ed., *Plantation and Frontier (A Documentary History of American Industrial Society*, ed. by John R. Commons and others, vol. 2, Cleveland, 1910), 90–91.

[31] Henry Ravenel Diary, entry for July 12, 1819, cited in Phillips, ed., *Plantation and Frontier*, 91.

vided to them by a rough set of Norfolk traders known as
"swamp merchants."[32] In the summer of 1849, heavy floods
around New Orleans forced runaways living in the nearby
swamps to emerge and hide out by day and to pilfer city homes
at night, causing considerable loss by their depredations.[33]

Some Indian tribes frequently befriended fugitives. Towns
made up of fugitives inside Indian territory in the Carolinas
and Georgia were established before 1812. Seminole slaveholders had a reputation for good treatment of their chattels,
and the advantages of such benevolent slavery attracted some
runaways to Indian territory. The Seminoles of Florida had
a type of slavery which resembled the sharecropping system of
later times. Such semifreedom was preferable to serving a
white master, and some escaping slaves headed for Indian
country in order to put themselves under the protection of a
chieftain. The towns were virtually independent communities
and the inhabitants, for all practical purposes, were free. Although many of the southern Indian tribes attempted to check
marriages between the Indians and the fugitives, there was
considerable intermarriage. A British author and traveler explained to his English readers that the propinquity of the Indians in Florida was a "nuisance to the planter, not only on
account of danger from attacks, but from the facilities it af-
fords to the escape of slaves."[34]

Southern cities were favorite hiding places for fugitives.
There the slaves could often find employment, and by min-
gling with the general population and the free Negroes, they
frequently managed to avoid detection for long periods of
time. One runaway slave lived five months in a Washing-

[32] Edmund Jackson, "The Virginia Maroons," in *The Liberty Bell: By
Friends of Freedom* (Boston, 1852), 146–49; Olmsted, *A Journey in the Seaboard
Slave States*, 1:177–78.

[33] *Liberator*, August 10, 1849.

[34] Kenneth Wiggins Porter, "Negroes and the Seminole War, 1817–1818," *Jour-
nal of Negro History*, 36:252–53 (July, 1951); Catterall, *Judicial Cases*, 1:313;
*Liberator*, September 12, 1851; Austin Willey, *The History of the Antislavery
Cause in State and Nation* (Portland, Maine, 1886), 174; J. C. Hamilton, "Slavery
in Canada," *Magazine of American History*, 25:238 (March, 1891); James Stirling,
*Letters from the Slave States* (London, 1857), 225.

ton, D.C., Methodist church attic before he was discovered.[35] Slaves frequently expressed a preference for city life. Mary ran away when her mistress left New Orleans; she would willingly stay with anyone who would purchase her in the city, she maintained, but she would not return to the country. A slave woman who had been hired out in Frankfort, Kentucky, decided to leave her employer and live with a free Negro barber. She liked the city and the barber; so she wrote a letter to her master stating that she had safely reached Canada. But her letter carried a Frankfort postmark, and she was captured and the barber was jailed.[36]

By no means all those who left slavery left as fugitives; manumission of slaves was far more common than is generally assumed, especially in the context of the underground railroad legend. Census reports for 1850 and 1860 indicate that more slaves were manumitted than ran away in either of the years preceding those reports. Southern states reported a total of 1,011 slaves missing and presumed to be fugitives in 1850, and a total of 1,467 manumissions; in 1860 the difference was even greater, with 803 fugitives and 3,078 manumitted Negroes.[37]

If the slaves held diverse views about slavery, so did slaveholders. Some, for one reason or another, decided to give up all of their human property. Often it was the large plantation owner who freed his slaves. In the winter of 1849 more than eighty manumitted slaves passed through Virginia on their way to Pennsylvania. A Cass County, Michigan, settlement of Negroes was made up of about fifty freed slaves, and a former slave in Canada testified that his master had freed all of his three hundred slaves at the time of his death. In 1861 Frederick Douglass, the abolitionist and former slave, called attention to ninety thousand freedmen then living in Maryland,

---

[35] *Liberator*, August 27, 1858.

[36] Catterall, *Judicial Cases*, 3:654; Lexington, Ky., *Observer and Reporter*, May 14, 1851.

[37] J. D. B. DeBow, *Statistical View of the United States, . . . Being a Compendium of the Seventh Census* (Washington, 1854), 64–65; Joseph C. G. Kennedy, *Population of the United States in 1860; Compiled from the Original Returns of the Eighth Census* (Washington, 1864), xv.

many of whom had been "freed for conscience sake by their owners."[38]

Slaveholders sometimes went to considerable trouble and expense to free their bondsmen. In Louisiana each case was submitted to a jury of twelve slaveholders, who had to be satisfied that manumission was a voluntary act of the owner and that the slave was of good character and capable of self-support. Many southern states restricted or forbade manumission within their borders, but such laws were frequently evaded. In 1848 a South Carolina judge declared that the twenty-seven-year-old law forbidding manumission in that state should be repealed. "A law evaded as it is," he said, "and against which public sentiment, within and without the State, is so much arrayed, ought not to stand."[39]

The terms of manumission sometimes required the slave to agree to go to Liberia. Of the approximately twelve thousand Negroes reported sent to Africa by the American Colonization Society, nearly half were voluntarily freed by their masters. Once in a while pressure was applied to slaveholders and the manumission was only voluntary in a technical sense. In 1859 the Presbyterian Board of Missions approved a Negro lad— even though his master had not offered him—for education and work in Africa. Though the young man's owner was sympathetic to the cause of colonization, he said he could not afford to give up the slave and was angered by the Board's offer of only six hundred dollars for him. One of the colonizationists feared that if the young slave were not educated and freed, "the matter would be eagerly laid hold of by our abolition friends at the North and turned to our disadvantage; and with good reason."[40]

[38] Salem, Ohio, *Anti-Slavery Bugle,* December 8, 1849; *Liberator,* March 8, 1850; Drew, *The Refugee,* 136–37; Philip S. Foner, ed., *The Life and Writings of Frederick Douglass* (3 vols., New York, 1950), 3:150.

[39] *National Anti-Slavery Standard,* March 15, 1856; Catterall, *Judicial Cases,* 2:404–405.

[40] Sumner Eliot Matison, "Manumission by Purchase," *Journal of Negro History,* 33:157 (April, 1948); John Wilson to Rev. N. M. Gordon, October 27, 1849, Gordon Papers, University of Kentucky Library.

But despite the efforts of the colonizationists, a great many of the slaves who were manumitted remained in the United States. Owners whose principles inspired them to reject further use of unpaid labor sometimes made provision in this country for their former chattels. A Virginian who had emancipated his forty-eight slaves personally conducted them to Ohio, where he purchased a farm, settled them on it, and stayed long enough to get them started in their new life. A Missourian provided his estate and plantation for his slaves in his will, in such terms that they could never dispose of the land or be cheated of it by others. A wealthy South Carolinian left a hundred and fifty thousand dollars to seven of his manumitted slaves. One skilled bondsman was willed his master's blacksmith shop and all his tools, rentfree, for his natural life. After setting his ten slaves free, a Missourian took them to Cedar Township, Iowa, where he bought land for them and entered into bonds for their good behavior.[41]

A smaller number of slaves were freed by self-purchase. Of 1,129 Negroes in Cincinnati in 1835 who had once served as slaves, 476 had bought themselves. A poll of the Negro population in Philadelphia in 1837 revealed that of the more than eighteen thousand freedmen there, two hundred and fifty had purchased their own emancipation. Two hundred and eighty-one Negroes living in two Maryland counties had obtained freedom in the same manner.[42] Often it was the highly skilled urban dweller who entered into an arrangement with his master for eventually paying the full purchase price of his freedom. Slaves who were hired out as shoemakers, tailors, blacksmiths, masons, carpenters, and even as manual laborers and porters were obligated to pay their masters a stated sum. Earnings above that amount belonged to the slave and were sometimes applied to a manumission fund. To some bondsmen, the freedom which they purchased with their own toil was

[41] Salem, Ohio, *Anti-Slavery Bugle*, November 13, 1852; *Liberator*, June 21, 1850, August 1, 1851, June 1, 1855; Catterall, *Judicial Cases*, 1:129.
[42] Matison, "Manumission by Purchase," 167.

preferable to the precarious lot of a fugitive, though the slaves who bought their freedom did so at considerable sacrifice.

Pay for Negro workers was low, and it was not easy for a bondsman to earn enough to equal his purchase price. It took a North Carolina slave eighteen years, working at night, to raise the nearly a thousand dollars his master required of him. Working as a mason, another slave saved eighteen hundred dollars for his freedom. A runaway in Kentucky surrendered to the trader who had purchased him with the understanding that he would have a chance to buy himself. It took half a dozen years of labor as a steward on a steamboat to pay the trader the sixteen hundred dollars stated in a contract.[43] Noah Davis worked a dozen years to buy himself and his five children, paying more than four thousand dollars in all. He dictated and sold an autobiography to raise the sum needed to buy two more children who were still in bonds.[44] On occasion, free Negroes held members of their own families in benevolent bondage. A young man in Kentucky purchased first his own freedom, then his underage brother's. He hired his youthful brother to work for others, and when the youngster died, the freedman sued the company who had hired him for the wages due him as his brother's owner.[45] Some masters took advantage of slaves who desired to purchase their own or their family's freedom and charged excessive prices. Peter Still bought his own freedom for five hundred dollars but found it nearly impossible to raise the much larger sum asked for his wife and children.[46]

Although some slaves made use of the various methods of ob-

[43] Drew, *The Refugee*, 239–48, 251–54, 271–73.
[44] *A Narrative of the Life of Rev. Noah Davis, a Colored Man, Written by Himself, at the Age of Fifty-four* (Baltimore, 1859).
[45] Wilmington *Delaware Gazette*, December 28, 1858.
[46] Kate E. R. Pickard, *The Kidnapped and the Ransomed. Being the Personal Recollections of Peter Still and his Wife "Vina," After Forty Years of Slavery* (Syracuse, N.Y., 1856), 372. This situation aroused the ire of William Lloyd Garrison, who believed that such a man as Still should certainly be permitted to buy his family at "fair market value," or about twenty-five hundred dollars instead of the five thousand asked for and eventually paid. William Lloyd Garrison to Samuel J. May, May 31, 1853, Garrison Papers, Boston Public Library.

taining freedom, most of them apparently adjusted to their lot. For despite the drudgery and humiliation, slavery had its own system of rewards and punishments, and it was to the immediate advantage of the slave to make the best of his condition or to better it within the slave system itself. House servants had unusual privileges and some status in the slave society. Some were glad to exchange work in the hot fields for the special jobs of butler, coachman, cook, or child servant. There were even some slaves who were overseers. But with the improved status went increased time demands and a closer adjustment to the life of the white masters, and there were those slaves who preferred fieldwork. Fieldwork, as a New Englander put it, was "task work and when the task is done, the rest of the day is play time." Furthermore, slaves felt more at ease with their fellow bondsmen than with their white owners.[47]

In some locations the line between slavery and freedom was a thin one at best, and many Negroes were in a condition of semislavery or semifreedom, depending on how it was interpreted.[48] In 1856 three mulatto slaves ran away from South Carolina when their owner's business failed. These three were all musicians, and two of them had other skills as well; one was a barber and one a housepainter. They had lived in their own house and were, as slaves, virtually free. In this case it was probably the uncertainty of their future after their owner's business lapse rather than independence of spirit that led to their escape.[49]

[47] Carter G. Woodson, *The Negro in Our History* (9th ed., Washington, 1947), 235–36; Sidney W. Martin, ed., "A New Englander's Impressions of Georgia in 1817–1818: Extracts from the Diary of Ebenezer Kellogg," *Journal of Southern History*, 12:258–59 (May, 1946); Kenneth M. Stampp, *The Peculiar Institution: Slavery in the Ante-Bellum South* (New York, 1956), 330.

[48] For a provocative article concerning the semifree status of both Negro and white workers in the ante bellum South, see Richard B. Morris, "The Measure of Bondage in the Slave States," *Mississippi Valley Historical Review*, 41:219–40 (September, 1954). Professor Morris concludes that "a portion of the laboring population of both races in the ante-bellum slave states dwelt in a shadowland enjoying a status neither fully slave nor entirely free." See also Clement Eaton, "Slave-Hiring in the Upper South: A Step Toward Freedom," *Mississippi Valley Historical Review*, 46:663–78 (March, 1960).

[49] Catterall, *Judicial Cases*, 2:448–49.

But for most slaves, security was to be found in adjustment to slavery rather than in a hazardous escape to an unfamiliar way of life. The slave system operated in a way not designed to prepare the slaves for life in a nonslave society. Although the observant traveler Frederick Law Olmsted believed that slaves generally would have liked to be free and that they were never "really contented or satisfied with slavery," he was also confident that "having been deprived of the use of their limbs from infancy, as it were," they would not wish "suddenly to be set upon their feet, and left to shift for themselves." James Redpath, an abolitionist who traveled throughout the slave states, reported after speaking with hundreds of slaves in Alabama that he had never yet met one "contented with his position." He went on to admit, however, that neither had he met with many slaves who were "actively discontented with involuntary servitude." Their discontent was passive only.[50]

The ignorance of most slaves about the free states made it more unlikely that such discontent would be translated into action. They knew of the existence of free territory through talking with whites, free Negroes, and other slaves who had been there. For border-state residents, this kind of knowledge was probably universal, and it was not unusual in the lower South. But for the most part such knowledge was based on vague hearsay. Slaveholders sometimes deliberately circulated stories about the severity of winters in the northern states and Canada.[51] Frederick Law Olmsted talked with a North Carolina slave who had heard about New York as a free state and who commented that it was probably a good thing for all the Negroes there to be free. A Louisiana slave confided to Olmsted that all the slaves he knew discussed the prospects of freedom and would have preferred it to slavery. But apparently

---

[50] Olmsted, *Journey in the Seaboard Slave States*, 1:146; James Redpath, *The Roving Editor, or, Talks With Slaves in the Southern States* (New York, 1859), 171–72.

[51] Samuel Ringgold Ward, *Autobiography of a Fugitive Negro: His Anti-Slavery Labours in the United States, Canada, and England* (London, 1855), 161.

they did not consider escaping. Even some slaves who ran away northward were ignorant of geography and distance and had little idea of how to get to their destination. "The real distance was great enough," said Frederick Douglass, "but the imagined distance was, to our ignorance, much greater. Slaveholders sought to impress their slaves with a belief in the boundlessness of slave territory, and of their own limitless power. Our notions of the geography of the country were very vague and indistinct." An abolitionist reported in 1843 that he had talked with a man who had escaped from slavery but who "was so ignorant that he did not know for sure where he had been raised, or what territory he had covered in his escape." Canada, apparently, was almost unknown as a possible haven. "We had heard of Canada," continued Douglass, "then the only real Canaan of the American Bondman, simply as a country to which the wild goose and the swan repaired at the end of winter to escape the heat of summer, but not as the home of man."[52]

Under those circumstances the number of slaves who escaped from southern bondage was not large. The exact number, of course, can never be determined. The legend puts it high, but in actual fact the proportion of runaways to the entire slave population was small. They were numbered in the thousands, and only a small percentage of the millions of slaves in the South.[53] In twenty-five years the Woodville, Mississippi, *Republican* carried advertisements of a hundred and sixty-five slaves who had run off. This came to about twenty-two a year. Many fugitives, of course, were not advertised, and some advertisements were carried for fugitives who were not in the area it was supposed by the claimants. Some were advertised in several papers, and the advertisements sometimes ran for as long as thirty weeks.[54]

---

[52] Olmsted, *Journey in the Seaboard Slave States*, 2:17, 343–44; Drew, *The Refugee*, 50, 72–76; Chicago *Western Citizen*, November 16, 1843; Frederick Douglass, *Life and Times of Frederick Douglass* (Hartford, 1884), 198, 199.

[53] Francis Butler Simkins, *A History of the South* (New York, 1953), 128.

[54] Sydnor, "Pursuing Fugitive Slaves," 163; Sellers, *Slavery in Alabama*, 292.

In reply to arguments of a North Carolina congressman which were based on the assumption that Delaware had lost $100,000 worth of slaves a year, Representative John Van Dyke of New Jersey asked: "But where are the slaves all gone to? . . . They are not to be found in Canada—that great supposed gathering place—nor are they to be found in the free States, nor anywhere else."[55] Census takers in 1860 found that the free Negro population in the North had increased by less than 13 percent in the previous decade, while the slave population in the South had increased by 23.5 percent.[56] Free Negro population in the New England states tended to be stable after 1840, although some towns in New England had a large Negro population.[57] Flight from the northern states to Canada because of a wave of terror among the free Negroes after the passage of the Fugitive Slave Law may have accounted for the decrease of 2,583 in the New York State free Negro population noted in the census of 1860. A decade earlier, almost fourteen thousand Negroes lived in New York City alone; of these, 2,120 had been born in the South. How many were fugitives and how many had been manumitted was not recorded.[58]

The Canadian picture was also unclear. Samuel R. Ward, himself a fugitive slave, said in 1855 that it was "a matter of great difficulty" for slaves to reach Canada. "It follows, that *but few* comparatively can come."[59] The Canadian census bore out Ward's statement, though the statistics were confusing. Both 4,669 and 8,000 were given as the total Negro population in Canada West in 1850. In 1860 the figure stood at slightly more than eleven thousand.[60] The census records did not reveal what percentage of these people had run away from

[55] *Congressional Globe,* 31 Cong., 1 sess. (1850), App., pt. 1, 326.
[56] Kennedy, *Population of the United States,* xvi.
[57] E. Franklin Frazier, *The Free Negro Family: A Study of Family Origins before the Civil War* (Nashville, 1932), 9.
[58] Leo H. Hirsch, Jr., "New York and the Negro, from 1783 to 1865," *Journal of Negro History,* 16:415 (October, 1931).
[59] Ward, *Autobiography,* 157–58.
[60] Extracts from Samuel Gridley Howe, *The Refugees from Slavery in Canada West* (Boston, 1864), copied in scrapbook "Fugitive Slaves in Canada, vol. 3," Siebert Papers, Ohio Historical Society.

slavery and what percentage had been freed or born in Canada. Unofficial contemporary estimates around the time of the Civil War varied from twenty thousand to seventy-five thousand Negroes in Canada, and usually those making estimates assumed that all in Canada were fugitives or their descendants.[61]

Census statistics on such matters as fugitive slaves were by no means complete or wholly accurate either in Canada or in the United States. At best the United States figures gave an indication of how many fugitives had been *reported* by their owners to have run away permanently within a one-year period preceding the census. These official statistics indicated that the South lost approximately a thousand slaves a year by running away.

Even though the number was unquestionably low, at least some people of the ante bellum era accepted the impression given by the census as more or less correct. Early in February, 1852, the Salem, Ohio, *Anti-Slavery Bugle* commented that it had learned from the synopsis of the recent census report that 1,011 fugitives had escaped in a one-year period. The number was not questioned. The *Liberator* also published the census figures without comment. Writing in the Washington, D.C., *National Era,* its editor, Gamaliel Bailey, seemed to think the census figures substantially correct. Answering a pamphlet by one who called himself "Randolph of Roanoke," who estimated that 61,624 slaves had escaped from the South between 1810 and 1850, Bailey said he had "seldom witnessed a more absurd or ridiculous perversion of facts." Bailey admitted that he was unable to estimate the number of fugitive slaves but thought it evident "that the calculations of Randolph [were] at least *ten times* too large." He pointed out that in New York, for instance, the free Negro population showed an excess of females over males. Since most fugitives were males, it would have been just the opposite if the freed-

<hr>

[61] Fred Landon, "Canada's Part in Freeing the Slave," reprint from *Ontario Historical Society Papers and Records,* 17:78, in scrapbook, "Fugitive Slaves in Canada, vol. 3," Siebert Papers, Ohio Historical Society.

man population were made up mostly of fugitives, he reasoned. The abolitionist editor called attention to the hundred and fifty-one slaves which an antislavery society claimed to have assisted in escaping during the past year. Randolph had used the figure to prove that abolitionists were effectively organized to help slaves escape; Bailey used it to prove that they did not succeed in helping many to run off. Whatever the implications, the fact is that Bailey and some other abolitionists accepted the low figures of the census of 1850.[62]

The census of 1860 showed even fewer fugitive slaves reported for the year preceding than had been the case a decade earlier. Furthermore, of the 803 fugitives reported in 1860, a larger percentage came from the lower South and a smaller from the border states than had been indicated by the earlier count. Once again the abolitionists based their arguments on the assumption that the official figures were substantially correct. In 1862 the New York *National Anti-Slavery Standard* reprinted an item from another paper which said: "The last census report shows how groundless were the complaints made by the South about the loss of a great number of fugitive slaves, and particularly how false was the assertion that the number of fugitives to the North was increasing, and was so great as to constitute a formidable grievance in the list which they presented as a justification for their act in assailing the government by force." The *Standard* also carried a complete table showing the numbers of fugitives in the two census reports, and commented: "The falling off in the last decade *may* be owing to the imperfection of the returns; but if not, it is doubtless to be ascribed in part to the operation of the Fugitive Slave law, and in part to the fact that the slave population near the line of

---

[62] Salem, Ohio, *Anti-Slavery Bugle*, February 27, 1852; *Liberator*, September 6, 1850, February 16, 1855; Washington *National Era*, August 22, 1850, June 19, 1851; *The Friend*, December 20, 1851. *The Friend*, a Quaker journal, carried similar statistics for 1851 and commented that the number of Negroes who had escaped or had been liberated was much smaller than they would wish. *The Friend* took this as an occasion for suggesting a different abolitionist strategy, emphasizing an appeal to the southern slaveholders rather than efforts to convince hearers in the North.

Mason and Dixon was much less numerous during the latter than in the former period." In its twenty-eighth annual report, the American Anti-Slavery Society commented on escape statistics, asserting that the migration of fugitives from the South during 1859 had equaled the average of former years, though they conceded that no one had the means of accurately determining that average. The report cited the New Orleans *Commercial Bulletin,* which estimated that fifteen hundred slaves had escaped annually for the past fifty years. That estimate, they said, was "much exaggerated; doubtless through its desire to embitter, as much as possible, the Southern feeling against the North." They agreed, however, that probably 98 percent of all Negroes native of the South then in the North were fugitive slaves when they left the slave states. But the abolition society could hardly believe that, excluding all the fugitives who had gone through to Canada, as many as seventy-five thousand slaves had made good their escape within the preceding fifty years.[63]

It is obviously an oversimplification, then, to assume that all slaves in the ante bellum South dreamed constantly of escaping to the North. Though their lives were difficult, often cruelly burdensome, still many of them preferred immediate and tangible relief to the uncertainties of an abstract freedom. Thus slaveowners and overseers faced the constant problem of absenteeism of slaves who ran off in anger, in fear, or simply in the desire to avoid work. Besides those who, by various means, achieved at least partial respite from the drudgery of slave life, there were also some few fortunate enough to have generous masters who either freed them outright or allowed them to purchase themselves.

Given the conditions of their time, most of the bondsmen had little alternative to some kind of adjustment within the slave society. Very few of them allowed any hope of freedom

[63] *National Anti-Slavery Standard,* March 16, May 25, 1861, September 27, 1862; *Twenty-eighth Annual Report of the American Anti-Slavery Society, by the Executive Committee, for the Year Ending May 1, 1861* (New York, 1861), 158.

they may have harbored to lead to deeds. The chances of a successful escape from the South were indeed remote, and few would risk the ordeal of a flight to the North. Indistinct and false notions of geography, together with the uncertainty of a future in an unknown environment, undoubtedly contributed to the fact that a majority of slaves resigned themselves to their condition.

There was a minority, however, more sensitive to its bondage than the rest. If the average slave adjusted to slavery and to his place in it, there were always some who did not. For them, running away was a logical solution. They were the misfits in the system, and their best adjustment was to leave it altogether. The decision to leave was not to be taken lightly. The chances of being recaptured were high. But there were those who were motivated in running away not by a desire to gain new privileges, or to return to a former and more benevolent master, or to enjoy a temporary respite from a difficult and monotonous work routine, but rather by a determination to leave the world of slavery forever. It was a small minority who had the courage to implement the idea. Some even would have died rather than return to slavery, and records of a few desperate struggles with fugitives testify to this.[64] Often they arrived independently at the decision to run away. "It always appeared to me that I wanted to be free, and could be free," said a fugitive slave who had reached Canada. "No person ever taught me so,—it came naturally in my mind."[65]

Such unusual individuals clung desperately to their independence, however precarious. They were the ones who were fugitives, not from the irksome aspects of the southern labor system, but from human slavery itself. Those who successfully escaped from bondage, made their way to free soil, and took up a new life in a strange land must have little resembled the helpless and trembling fugitives of the legendary melodrama.

---

[64] *Louisville Daily Courier,* May 5, 1853, August 31, 1859; St. Louis *Republican,* February 24, May 22, 1855; *Richmond Enquirer,* June 8, 1860; *Liberator,* August 30, 1850.

[65] Drew, *The Refugee,* 344–46.

*Chapter Three*

# THE ROAD TO THE NORTH

THIRTY YEARS after the Civil War an aged Illinois abolitionist recalled "I do not know of any fugitives ever being transported by anyone, they always had to pilot their own canoe, with the little help that they received."[1] His statement rightly called attention to the fugitives' own exertions in the interest of their freedom. A mass of reminiscences and articles have emphasized the importance of abolitionist aid to fugitive slaves, but in many cases it was the slaves themselves who took things into their own hands, planned their escapes, and during the greater part of their journeys arranged for or managed their own transportation, without the assistance of the legendary underground railroad. Occasionally the abolitionists gave recognition to the self-reliance of the fugitives. In 1858 a Syracuse meeting, called to celebrate the rescue of the fugitive Jerry, resolved: "That from the renowned Frederick Douglass down to the obscurest fugitive slave, there is not one who deserves not our praise for the skill with which he contrived his escape, and the courage with which he accomplished it."[2]

Such self-reliance developed in spite of the ignorance of most slaves about the free states, and the tendency of the slave system to stifle individual initiative and confidence. Frequently such fugitives had not been badly treated in slavery at all. Instead, they were sometimes the highly privileged ones. They served as house servants, barbers, highly skilled mechanics, candlemakers, factory hands, druggists, carpenters, and other trained workers. Some were entertainers and musicians. Often they had been hired out and as hired workers had enjoyed near-freedom even while still in slavery.[3] It was the gifted and highly intelligent slave who enjoyed the semifreedom of a hired laborer and, having greater sophistication and more freedom of movement, was better qualified than most bondsmen to conceive and put into action a plan of escape. Though, no doubt, some fugitives were stupid, these were not so likely to succeed, even if determined and courageous. In 1850 a North Carolina planter advertised for his slave Solomon, who, since he had left without "having the slightest difficulty" with his owner or overseer, was presumed to be heading for a free state. Solomon, the planter advised, "may attempt to pass as a free negro, but he is not intelligent, and if questioned particularly, may be easily detected in inconsistencies and falsehoods."[4]

It was often, as an abolitionist wrote in her memoirs and as many other witnesses of different viewpoints agreed, "the brightest and best who were capable of surmounting all the dangers and difficulties of escape."[5] They were, as a fugitive himself put it, "men of mark," and as a New England paper reported, "strong, shrewd and intelligent, superior to their class." A Scottish clergyman commented on the former slaves who had migrated to his native land. He found all the fugitives he knew to be "persons of superior talents." William Still, a Negro abolitionist in Philadelphia who was active in work with refugees from slavery, described some of the people he dealt with as of "marked intellectual features," "quite smart," "of more than ordinary shrewdness," and "possessed

---

[1] W. H. Lyford to Wilbur H. Siebert, March 27, 1896, in scrapbook "The Underground Railroad in Illinois, vol. 3," Wilbur H. Siebert Papers, Houghton Library of Harvard University.

[2] *National Anti-Slavery Standard*, October 23, 1858.

[3] Helen T. Catterall, ed., *Judicial Cases Concerning American Slavery and the Negro* (5 vols., Washington, 1926–1937), 2:208–209, 341, 418, 536, 5:156, 183; printed broadside, William H. Noble Papers, Duke University Library.

[4] *Richmond Enquirer*, August 20, 1850.

[5] Elizabeth Buffum Chace, "My Anti-Slavery Reminiscences," in *Two Quaker Sisters* (New York, 1937), 164.

of more than average common sense."⁶ Planters who inserted advertisements in newspapers frequently described the runaways as "uncommonly bright," "free spoken and intelligent," "talented and wily." One was "an artful cunning fellow" who could play the fiddle and "read tolerably well." Many if not most of the successful fugitives could read, and some of them knew two or three languages. Versatility also extended to other areas. A Louisiana runaway was "by trade a painter, glazier and ship-carpenter," and another from South Carolina had experience as a manager of both rice and saw mills.⁷

Self-reliance was also evident in the methods of escape used by slaves who ran away. Despite legendary tales about an underground telegraph, those former slaves who dictated or wrote their own memoirs revealed no knowledge of such a system of communication. Many bondsmen knew nothing about abolitionist assistance; very few had accurate information. It is unlikely that such knowledge prompted the majority of slave escapes. In 1841 Joseph Sturge, a British abolitionist traveler, met a fugitive couple on a boat going from New York to Albany. They had escaped by railway and steamboat, carrying forged passes. Sturge learned that they had never heard of the vigilance committees that existed "to facilitate the escape of runaway slaves."⁸ Such ignorance was not uncommon.

Assuming that they could not expect any help, many slaves made careful plans for their journeys, and some escapes were

⁶ Samuel Ringgold Ward, *Autobiography of a Fugitive Negro: His Anti-Slavery Labours in the United States, Canada, and England* (London, 1855), 164–65; item from a Scottish newspaper reprinted in William Wells Brown, *The Black Man, His Antecedents, His Genius, and His Achievements* (New York, 1863), 29; William Still, *The Underground Rail Road* (Philadelphia, 1872), 191, 213, 229, and *passim*.

⁷ *Richmond Enquirer*, June 20, 1851; *Louisville Daily Courier*, September 14, 1853; Ulrich B. Phillips, ed., *Plantation and Frontier* (*A Documentary History of American Industrial Society*, edited by John R. Commons and others, vol. 2, Cleveland, 1910), 82–83; printed broadside dated October 27, 1802, in folder, "Miscellany on Runaway Slaves," in box in the Pennsylvania Abolition Society Papers, Pennsylvania Historical Society; St. Louis *Daily Missouri Republican*, August 7, 1858; New Orleans *Daily Picayune*, April 5, 1850; Charleston *Courier*, January 2, 1854; James B. Sellers, *Slavery in Alabama* (University, Ala., 1950), 278–80.

⁸ Joseph Sturge, *A Visit to the United States in 1841* (Boston, 1842), 71.

contemplated and planned over a long period of time. In some instances, slaves from several plantations would work out escape plans together, occasionally finding either the courage or the opportunity for these connivings in religious gatherings. More than once, Negro camp meetings encouraged running away. A Missouri slave woman who had contemplated escape for several years finally left for Canada with her husband and son after attending such a service, "and made a long camp-meeting of it," she reported afterward.[9]

Some individuals, however, plotted and executed their own escapes without consulting anyone, even members of their own families. Many fleeing slaves did not trust others, and those who had attempted escape several times before making good their aim had sometimes learned from bitter experience that it was best to keep such plans to themselves. When William Wells Brown escaped in the winter of 1834, he traveled at night, slept in barns, and stole corn and food from fields along his way. He supposed every person to be his enemy, and "was afraid to appeal to any one, even for a little food, to keep body and soul together." "I had long since made up my mind not to trust myself in the hands of any man, white or colored," he later reported. Although Brown received refuge from an Indiana Quaker whose name he adopted as his own, and later got some help from Ohio abolitionists, he wrote a letter to an abolitionist newspaper in 1855 in which he said, "When I escaped, there was no Underground Railroad. The North Star was, in many instances, the only friend that the weary and footsore fugitive found on his pilgrimage to his new home among strangers, and consequently, the means of getting away from slavery was not as easy then as now."[10]

Brown's method was used by many others who literally

---

[9] Benjamin Drew, *The Refugee: or the Narratives of Fugitive Slaves in Canada* (Boston, 1856), 299–301.

[10] Brown, *The Black Man*, 23–24; William Wells Brown, *Narrative of William Wells Brown, a Fugitive Slave* (Boston, 1848), 94–95 and *passim*; William Wells Brown to *National Anti-Slavery Standard*, April 21, 1855, reprinted in Carter G. Woodson, ed., *The Mind of the Negro as Reflected in Letters Written During the Crisis 1800–1860* (Washington, 1926), 369–70.

walked away from slavery. Usually alone, but sometimes in
pairs or even groups, escaping slaves traveled long distances
at night, hiding and sleeping during the daylight hours. Knowledge of the North Star was not uncommon and was sometimes
supplemented by directions given by persons who befriended
them. One group of thirteen escapees from Virginia traveled
only at night for three weeks before reaching Pennsylvania;[11]
two Maryland slaves journeyed nine days and nights without a
guide before reaching the same state.[12] Although for the most
part fugitives took only the clothes on their backs and a little
food, some took other things, especially horses belonging to
their masters.[13] With a horse a runaway could travel much
faster and more easily, though of course it also added to the
danger of detection. All escapes were dangerous, and in many
the dangers were long lasting. It took one fugitive from Tennessee five weeks to reach Michigan.[14] Another young runaway
from the same state traveled forty nights before reaching the
Ohio River.[15] Three fugitives from Virginia walked from
Hedgeville to Greenville, Pennsylvania, and there they took the
train.[16] Such use of railroads was not unique, and it sometimes
led to capture. In 1855 an escaping slave was caught in Richmond hidden under a freight car. Two Louisville fugitives
who traveled by train in 1859 were apprehended by police
who met the train at another town.[17]

When they were away from home, slaves were required to
carry passes from their masters, and free Negroes had to have
papers which described them clearly and stated that they were
not slaves. The use of stolen, borrowed, rented, or forged

[11] Robert C. Smedley, *History of the Underground Railroad in Chester and the
Neighboring Counties of Pennsylvania* (Lancaster, Pa., 1883) , 228.
[12] Still, *Underground Rail Road*, 51–52.
[13] *National Anti-Slavery Standard*, June 28, 1856; *Liberator*, September 8, 1848;
Burch, Kirkland and Co. to Ziba B. Oakes, November 20, 1856, Ziba B. Oakes
Papers, Boston Public Library.
[14] Laura (Smith) Haviland, *A Woman's Life-Work: Labors and Experiences of
Laura S. Haviland* (4th ed., Chicago, 1889) , 213.
[15] *American Anti-Slavery Almanac* (Boston, 1838) , 45.
[16] Still, *Underground Rail Road*, 229.
[17] *Louisville Daily Courier*, July 6, 1859; *Richmond Enquirer*, September 22,
1855.

passes or free papers was common with fugitives.[18] Owners who advertised for runaway slaves often indicated that the fugitive had or was believed to have such papers.[19] A few slaves wrote their own papers, but they usually obtained them from others.[20] Frederick Douglass borrowed a sailor's "protection" papers, which he used in effecting his escape, and later he returned them to their owner. In the postwar edition of his autobiography, Douglass referred to this technique as one which had been used by many slaves.[21] The possession of such papers gave courage to fugitives, but to be of any use when suspicions were aroused, it was necessary for the papers to describe a person resembling the fugitive. A flair for acting sometimes helped. A slave named Charles who escaped from Missouri in 1846 carried stolen free papers for identification. The original owner had a crippled hand, and Charles played the role so well that the owner of a riverboat did not question his identity or the validity of his status as described in the papers he carried.[22]

All such escapes took courage. Timid slaves were not inclined to take the risks involved, nor would they have had the fortitude to continue. When Henry Bibb escaped from Indian Territory, he traveled across Missouri, from St. Louis to Ohio by steamboat, and thence overland through Ohio and Michigan to Detroit. Traveling on a stolen horse, Bibb posed as a free Negro and "always presented a bold front and showed the best side out," staying in the best hotels along the route. With such courage and determination it was possible for slaves, by their own efforts, to escape from the lower South as well as from the border states. And some did. In 1844 a slave who had walked all the way from Louisiana arrived in New England. The fugitive was "very shy, and would not trust himself in any

18 Catterall, *Judicial Cases*, 2:151–52, 3:617.
19 William T. Maclin to William B. Wise, January 29, 1846, William B. Wise Papers, Duke University Library; Chicago *Democrat*, October 19, 1836.
20 Catterall, *Judicial Cases*, 2:370; Drew, *The Refugee*, 152–53.
21 Douglass, *Life and Times*, 245–46.
22 Catterall, *Judicial Cases*, 5:167.

kind of vehicle."[23]  For several months another fugitive, this one a woman, made her way alone from Mississippi to Canada. She was not aided on her way until she had reached Illinois.[24] One fugitive took a year to go from Alabama to Ohio, and another young fugitive from that state covered twelve hundred miles "travelling only in the night, feeding on roots and wild [berries]," before reaching Pennsylvania.[25]

For light mulatto slaves, passing as white was sometimes possible and greatly simplified escape.  Many traveled as southern gentlemen by day instead of skulking in the woods and swamps until nightfall.  Lighter slaves probably enjoyed the additional advantage of being less valuable property than dark Negroes, and hence less likely to be pursued, since their owners were well aware of the difficulty of securing or recapturing them. It was more difficult to spot such a fugitive on trains and stages, and they seldom ran into difficulty on their journeys.  Theirs was the simplest escape, though to make the break from slavery required just as much courage for a mulatto as for one of his darker neighbors.[26]

Disguise, of course, was a common device of runaways. Women sometimes dressed as men, and men as women.  One ingenious mulatto even disguised himself by blacking his face and having his hair curled.[27]  One of the cleverest disguises was worked out by William and Ellen Craft, who had carefully

[23] *Narrative of the Life and Adventures of Henry Bibb, an American Slave, Written by Himself* (New York, 1849), 165; *National Anti-Slavery Standard,* February 29, 1844.
[24] Levi Coffin, *Reminiscences of Levi Coffin, the Reputed President of the Underground Railroad* (2d ed., Cincinnati, 1880), 254–56.
[25] James Freeman Clarke, *Anti-Slavery Days* (New York, 1883), 93; Theodore D. Weld to Sarah and Angelina Grimké, January 5, 1838, in Gilbert H. Barnes and Dwight L. Dumond, eds., *Letters of Theodore Dwight Weld, Angelina Grimké Weld and Sarah Grimké, 1822–1844* (2 vols., New York, 1934), 2:512–13.
[26] Still, *Underground Rail Road,* 107, 301, 381, 514–15; Drew, *The Refugee,* 123–32; Olmsted, *Journey in the Seaboard Slave States,* 2:295–96; Catterall, *Judicial Cases,* 1:360.
[27] Coffin, *Reminiscences,* 341–42; *The Annual Report of the American and Foreign Anti-Slavery Society, Presented at New York, May 6, 1851* (New York, 1851), 27; *Liberator,* January 12, 1849; *Richmond Enquirer,* September 22, 1855; J. Winston Coleman, Jr., *Slavery Times in Kentucky* (Chapel Hill, N.C., 1940), 129–30.

planned their escape from slavery in Georgia before setting out for the free states. With money William had saved they purchased male attire for Ellen, who was nearly white. She posed as an ailing planter going north for medical treatment, accompanied by his faithful servant. The planter was hard of hearing and obviously in such a decrepit physical condition as to be wholly dependent upon the slave. They played their parts well, traveling first class in the trains and steamboats and stopping at good hotels. Except for near-disaster in Baltimore, where the railroad agent tried to exact the required bond for slaves going north, the couple had no trouble.[28] Commenting on William Craft's description of the journey north, the *Liberator* said that the "ingenuity of the fugitives in laying their plans for escape, and their steadiness of nerve in their execution, would enable them amply 'to take care of themselves' under any circumstances."[29]

The self-help escape plan of the Crafts was given widespread publicity in the abolitionist press. But several years later, two men who tried the same method were apprehended. Their acting was not as good as the original team's and their conduct led to suspicion and discovery. Another difficult feat was accomplished by a slave who feigned an attack of epilepsy on the auction block. He was taken to jail and examined by a doctor who was also fooled. Left in his cell apparently asleep, the slave made his escape in the night and was not heard from again until word came of his arrival in Canada.[30]

The plan used by Henry Brown to escape from Virginia was even more original and daring than that worked out by the Crafts. Brown, who worked in a Richmond tobacco factory, had long contemplated escape. One day as he prayed he heard a voice say: "Go get a box, and put yourself in it." According

---

[28] Still, *Underground Rail Road*, 368–77; *Running a Thousand Miles for Freedom; or the Escape of William and Ellen Craft from Slavery* (London, 1860).

[29] *Liberator*, April 6, 1849.

[30] Coleman, *Slavery Times in Kentucky*, 129–30; Raymond A. Bauer and Alice H. Bauer, "Day to Day Resistance to Slavery," *Journal of Negro History*, 27:412–13 (October, 1942).

to Brown's own testimony, he "was not disobedient unto the
heavenly vision." He observed the largest shipping boxes at
the Richmond depot and then ordered a carpenter to build one
for him, revealing its intended purpose. Despite warnings from
the carpenter that he could not live for any time in the con-
tainer, Brown had a friend ship him to Philadelphia. In the
box he had some water and biscuits. Careful marking of the
crate did not prevent careless railway employees from putting
the box wrong side up and making Brown's trip nearly fatal
by placing him on his head. However, after a twenty-six-hour
trip the fugitive arrived in Philadelphia and the box was delivered to the office of the Philadelphia Anti-Slavery Society,
where it was opened and Brown walked out.[31] As Henry "Box"
Brown, the fugitive gained immediate fame. He wrote and
lectured, reaching many American audiences with his story of
slave life and his daring escape.[32] Brown was neither the first
nor the last slave to attempt escape by being crated and shipped
north.[33] Such a plan was discovered in New Orleans in 1825
when the slave was nearly suffocated, and both the slave and
his free Negro accomplice were arrested.[34] A number of others
escaped successfully in boxes, although the man who shipped
Henry "Box" Brown from Richmond was later arrested and
convicted when he attempted to use the same device with two
other fugitives.[35]

But of the slaves who fled to the North, probably the greatest
number used water transportation. Some stole skiffs and ca-
noes to cross the Ohio River, and some were taken across by
ferry operators.[36] Steamships running from southern ports pro-

[31] Charles Stearns, *Narrative of Henry Box Brown, Who Escaped from Slavery
Enclosed in a Box 3 Feet Long and 2 Wide* (Boston, 1849), 59–62; *Liberator*,
April 20, 1849; Lucretia Mott to Joseph and Ruth Dugdale, March 28, 1849, Lucretia Mott Papers, Friends Historical Library of Swarthmore College; Still,
*Underground Rail Road*, 81–86.
[32] *Liberator*, May 31, 1850.
[33] Still, *Underground Rail Road*, 46–48, 608–10; *Liberator*, October 31, 1856,
May 11, 1860.
[34] Phillips, ed., *Plantation and Frontier*, 80.
[35] Still, *Underground Rail Road*, 84–86.
[36] Marion J. Russell, "American Slave Discontent in the Records of the High
Courts," *Journal of Negro History*, 31:428–29 (October, 1946).

vided excellent opportunities for escaping slaves.[37] Light-colored slaves frequently could "pass" on steamboats as passengers. Others stowed away in the numerous holes and crannies in the steamships; one fugitive spent forty-eight hours outside a ship, under the guard, before he was caught.[38] Many stowaways were caught, but others escaped detection, sometimes with the aid of sympathetic ship officers or sailors. The famous fugitive Anthony Burns used this escape method in his flight from Richmond.[39] Legislation holding ship companies responsible for runaways in their vessels did not stop such escapes. Ships from such southern ports as Baltimore, New Orleans, and Norfolk sometimes carried runaways to northern ports, occasionally to Europe.[40] Slaves hired to work on ships were known to abscond when the ships put in at northern cities. Slaves would sometimes hide out in port cities and await a favorable chance to escape by ship. Usually such plans were made by the fugitives themselves, though in some instances the ship captain or crew members encouraged the escape.[41] In 1850 a Norfolk newspaper lamented that so many losses of slaves came from escapes by ship from that city. The editor was convinced that nearly all the coasting trade was "in the hands of Northern abolitionists" and that the free Negro crews of such ships indoctrinated the slaves "with the notions of freedom, and afterwards afford[ed] them the means of transportation to free soil." Some of the craft in southern waters, the editorial charged, "actually [made] the abduction of slaves a matter of trade and a source of profit."[42]

Whatever the motive of the Norfolk editor, at least some of his facts were substantially correct. There were ship captains who made a business of running off slaves whenever they

[37] *Life of William Grimes, the Runaway Slave, Brought down to the Present Time. Written by Himself* (Boston, 1848), 34–35.

[38] *The Friend*, 27:226 (April 1, 1854).

[39] Charles E. Stevens, *Anthony Burns, a History* (Boston, 1856), 178–79.

[40] Catterall, *Judicial Cases*, 4:169, 391, 492; *Liberator*, March 31, April 7, 1854; Salem, Ohio, *Anti-Slavery Bugle*, August 31, 1850.

[41] Catterall, *Judicial Cases*, 2:531; *Liberator*, November 10, 1848; *Louisville Daily Courier*, January 7, 1849.

[42] *Richmond Enquirer*, November 15, 1850, quoting *Norfolk Argus*.

could. The risks were great but the possibilities of profit were even greater. The people involved were not necessarily abolitionists, but for a good fee they were willing to help slaves escape. Some captains, of course, were motivated by benevolent feelings toward the fugitives. The majority, however, as William Still said of one of them, "would bring any kind of freight that would pay the most." One of these captains required at least three passengers paying a hundred dollars each before he would make a trip from Richmond to Philadelphia. The famous case of the *Pearl*, in which seventy-seven slaves attempted to escape from Washington, D.C., involved such a profit-making scheme. Captain Sayres of the *Pearl* agreed to transport the slaves because business was poor and he was offered a hundred dollars for the trip from Washington to Philadelphia—considerably more than the vessel could otherwise make in a trip of like duration. But in that trip there was no profit. The small craft was apprehended, and both Daniel Drayton, who had made the arrangements, and Captain Sayres spent nearly four and a half years in prison before they were pardoned by President Millard Fillmore.[43]

Ship captains were not the only ones to profiteer by helping fugitive slaves. Literate slaves, free Negroes, and whites wrote out passes, legal papers, and free papers for fugitives. Fees for such services varied up to twenty-five dollars. The English traveler Joseph Sturge believed that some white Southerners lived by the manufacture of forged free papers. If so, the majority of such papers were probably passes for temporary use.[44] Slaves and free Negroes would sometimes earn money by piloting fugitives across rivers, especially the Ohio. For more extensive trips, free Negro guides occasionally collected large fees. Anthony Bingey paid four hundred dollars to a guide for tak-

[43] Still, *Underground Rail Road*, 74–75, 166, 263; Daniel Drayton, *Personal Memoir of Daniel Drayton, for Four Years and Four Months a Prisoner (for Charity's Sake) in Washington Jail. Including a Narrative of the Voyage and Capture of the Schooner Pearl* (Boston, 1855), 24–25, 119.
[44] St. Louis *Republican*, August 22, 1855; Wilmington *Delaware Gazette*, December 29, 1856; Augusta, Ga., *Chronicle and Sentinel*, January 9, 1857; Sturge, *Visit to the United States*, 71–72.

ing a group of slaves part way through Ohio. An enterprising South Carolinian induced three slaves to steal money from their masters, and in return for the stolen cash he offered to help them run away.[45] Successful fugitives complained of extortion by certain of their abetters, and in 1854 Henry Bibb's Canadian *Voice of the Fugitive* published a warning against such procedures. "If any professed friend refuses to aid you or your friends in making their escape from Slavery," Bibb advised, "unless they are paid an extravagant price for it, they are not to be trusted: no matter whether they are white or black." Although he declined to mention names, Bibb referred to "a certain free coloured person" who had been extorting from fifty to three hundred dollars for about three or four days' use of his time in helping fugitives on their escapes. Such persons, said Bibb, were unsafe to be trusted as conductors on the underground railroad. He feared that if the slave hunters should offer a higher price, "the poor fugitive would be betrayed and dragged back into a living death."[46]

On occasion the fugitives were not only overcharged but cheated as well.[47] Reports reached Canada in 1857 of a white man who took money from slaves for helping them escape and then left them to their fate. Another scheme involved a white Kentuckian and his free Negro accomplice in an attempt to induce a slave to run to Indiana, then return him when a reward was offered for his capture.[48] When Isaac Mason's escape plans led to action, he and two others found that the guide they had hired was dead drunk, and so they left without his help.[49] After a slave in Norfolk had paid a ship captain a hundred

[45] Cleveland *Daily True Democrat*, September 21, 1849; Wilbur H. Siebert's interview with the Rev. Anthony Bingey in scrapbook "The Underground Railroad in Ohio, vol. 6," Siebert Papers, Ohio Historical Society; Catterall, *Judicial Cases*, 2:411–12.

[46] Brown, *The Black Man*, 212; *National Anti-Slavery Standard*, April 15, 1854, quoting *Voice of the Fugitive*.

[47] Jeffrey R. Brackett, *The Negro in Maryland, a Study of the Institution of Slavery (Johns Hopkins University Studies in Historical and Political Science*, ed. by Herbert B. Adams, extra vol. 6, Baltimore, 1889) , 90.

[48] *National Anti-Slavery Standard*, September 12, 1857; *Louisville Daily Courier*, January 21, 1859.

[49] *Life of Isaac Mason as a Slave* (Worcester, Mass., 1893) , 39–43.

dollars to carry him north, the captain betrayed the slave and turned the money over to his owner, receiving twenty-five dollars as a reward.[50] Another captain circulated exaggerated stories of northern freedom which led one slave to believe that in New England any slave was immune from capture or return. The captain demanded and received a hundred dollars to take the fugitive to Boston, but "the moment the vessel touched the wharf, the scoundrel bade the poor fellow be off in a moment; and [the fugitive] then discovered his liability to be pursued and taken."[51]

While some pretended friends of the fugitives took advantage of their plight for personal gain, there were groups who usually could be trusted by the bondsmen on the run. It was taken for granted by many runaways that people of their own race would befriend them, and many did. Free Negroes wrote passes, gave instructions and directions, and housed fugitives in their homes, in spite of heavy penalties which befell some of them for such activity. In 1837 a Federal court in Washington, D.C., convicted a free Negro of forging a certificate of freedom for one slave and a pass for another. The judge sentenced him to seven years in prison. Such severity was not uncommon.[52]

Most of the fugitives who wrote or dictated their autobiographies referred to help they got from bondsmen. A Tennessee slave who was sixteen years old at the time of the Civil War said many years later that he had seen many a runaway slave and that "darkies would help 'em round."[53] One such fugitive recalled: "We did not dare ask [for food], except when we found a slave's or free colored person's house remote from any

[50] Parker Pillsbury, *Acts of the Anti-Slavery Apostles* (Concord, N.H., 1883), 353–54.

[51] Theodore Parker, *The Boston Kidnapping: A Discourse to Commemorate the Rendition of Thomas Simms, Delivered on the First Anniversary Thereof, April 12, 1852, Before the Committee of Vigilance, at the Melodeon in Boston* (Boston, 1852), 59.

[52] Catterall, *Judicial Cases,* 2:320, 4:200; St. Louis *Daily Union,* November 2, 1846.

[53] *Unwritten History of Slavery: Autobiographical Accounts of Negro Ex-Slaves* (Fisk University, *Social Science Source Documents* no. 1, Nashville, 1945), 256.

other, and then we were never refused, if they had food to give."[54] Like free Negroes, slaves would give refuge to their more adventuresome comrades until it was believed safe to send them on their way.[55] Fugitives could mingle with large groups of cooperating slaves with little danger. A Louisiana planter captured such a runaway only after the clever fellow had lived in the neighborhood for more than a year.[56] Slaves caught harboring runaways seldom got off lightly, and in 1819 a South Carolina bondsman was sentenced to death for inducing a slave woman to leave her master.[57] When James W. Armstrong recaptured his slave Sam and learned that five slaves on a neighboring plantation had harbored him, he wrote the person in charge of the guilty slaves asking that they be delivered up for punishment. Armstrong intended to give each of them fifty stripes, as he had all the others who had befriended Sam.[58]

It was unusual but not unknown for free Negroes or slaves to betray a fugitive. It was a Negro hackman, hired by Daniel Drayton to transport two of the fugitives to the *Pearl,* who revealed the scheme to the authorities. For a hundred-dollar reward, a free Negro in Illinois arrested instead of assisting two slaves who came to him for help. On occasion, trusted slaves were used to capture fugitives. In 1846 a Georgia planter suggested a compensation of twenty-five dollars for the assistance of a slave in apprehending a runaway. A Louisiana planter recorded in his diary that his slave Dennis was pretending to be a runaway in order to hunt for a neighbor's absconded slave.[59]

Southern whites were not always interested in capturing fugitive slaves, nor did they consistently refuse to aid them. A

[54] Chace, "My Anti-Slavery Reminiscences," 159–60.

[55] *National Anti-Slavery Standard,* September 1, 1842.

[56] Edwin Adams Davis, ed., *Plantation Life in the Florida Parishes of Louisiana, 1836–1846, As Reflected in the Diary of Bennet H. Barrow* (New York, 1943), 226–27.

[57] Catterall, *Judicial Cases,* 2:313.

[58] James W. Armstrong to Irby H. Scott, November 26, 1851, Irby H. Scott Papers, Duke University Library.

[59] Drayton, *Memoir,* 33; St. Louis *Daily Union,* September 7, 1846; James H. R. Washington to George P. Harrison, March 18, 1846, James H. R. Washington Papers, Duke University Library; Davis, ed., *Barrow Diary,* 227.

fugitive was an object of pity both in the North and in the
South, and the impulse to assist a fugitive was not always at-
tributable to the individual's political or social views. Abolitionist writers sometimes admitted that there were people in
the South who would help fugitives, but they accused such people of ulterior motives. "South of the line money, in most cases,
was the motive; north, we generally worked on principle," said
Levi Coffin. But in both South and North there were some
who, though opposed to the abolitionists, would take pity on
a fugitive and render aid if possible.[60]

A former slave claimed that "there were a good many
white people in the South in those days who helped the runaway." Though such folk were often not slaveholders themselves, some were. Moses Roper was befriended and fed by a
white family and, when he pretended to have lost his papers,
one of the young sons in the family wrote some out for him
and sent him on his way. James L. Smith in desperation
begged food from a white family in Maryland. They were
friendly, did not betray him, and gave him a good breakfast
for twenty-five cents. Another slave, Linda, was concealed and
boarded while pursuers were hunting her. Linda's abetter, a
slaveowner, asked her to promise that her name should never
be mentioned in connection with the escape. A South Carolina
slave named Nelly, who had been subject to abuse, was given
refuge by a group of people who took pity on her plight and
wrote her master that they had her. They did not intend that
he should ever again have possession of Nelly, they said, though
they did not propose to impair any other rights which he might
be able to establish in respect to her as a slave.[61]

[60] Coffin, *Reminiscences*, 170–71; Clarke, *Anti-Slavery Days*, 81; Walter Kerr to
Wilbur H. Siebert, November 21, 1895, in scrapbook "The Underground Railroad in Indiana, vol. 1," Siebert Papers, Ohio Historical Society.

[61] Frank Hayward Severance, *Old Trails on the Niagara Frontier* (Buffalo,
1899), 241–42; Moses Roper, *A Narrative of the Adventures and Escape of
Moses Roper from American Slavery* (London, 1843), 93; *Autobiography of
James L. Smith, Including, Also, Reminiscences of Slave Life, Recollections of
the War, Education of Freedmen, Causes of the Exodus, Etc.* (Norwich, 1881),
47; Harriet (Brent) Jacobs, *Incidents in the Life of a Slave Girl. Written by herself*, ed. by Lydia Maria Child (Boston, 1861), 152; Catterall, *Judicial Cases*,
2:411.

Many people were reluctant or indifferent about returning runaway slaves. When a Maryland railroad agent was involved in court action for selling tickets to a number of fugitive slaves heading for Pennsylvania, he said it was not his business to inquire whether the customers of the road were slave or free. Certainly he was not the only white person living in the slave states who felt that way. Frederick Law Olmsted described a Southerner who was opposed to slavery but thought that the abolitionists had done their cause much harm. Olmsted described him as a person who "would not think it right to return a fugitive slave; but he would never assist one to escape." The same individual had from time to time purchased slaves who would otherwise have been taken farther south, in order to save them from such a fate.[62]

Court records show that fugitives sometimes hid out at certain plantations with the owner's knowledge and tacit consent. In North Carolina a planter was acquitted of harboring a runaway because the slave had not been concealed on the plantation but apparently was there without any attempt at concealment. Another planter from the same state pleaded that he had not turned a runaway slave in because the slave trusted him. Fugitives worked on the plantations or farms where they were staying, but it is doubtful whether this additional labor was the sole motivation of those who harbored them, for sympathy for fugitives was common. The large number of fugitives who escaped from jails in which they were confined suggests that local officials may have winked at such escapes. The practice of incarcerating fugitives was a nuisance for jailers, who on occasion were sued for carelessness by the owners of runaway slaves. The owner of a slave who let himself out of the jail window with blankets contended that the jailer should have chained the prisoner, but the judge ruled against him. It would have been too expensive to put a guard around the jail and too cruel to put the slave in irons, he said.[63]

---

[62] Catterall, *Judicial Cases,* 4:140–41; Olmsted, *Journey in the Seaboard Slave States,* 1:107–108.
[63] Catterall, *Judicial Cases,* 2:27, 78, 81, 130, 192, 3:193, 295.

Though slaveowners generally abhorred the idea of slave escapes, there are cases of such escapes having been instigated, in part at least, by slaveholders or members of their families. While he was awaiting sale to Georgia traders, one New Orleans slave was freed from the handcuffs by his young mistress, whose pity he had aroused. After releasing him, she made him swear not to betray her and told him which way to go and to follow the North Star. When a Maryland plantation was upset because of the death of a beloved master and it looked as though the slaves would have to be sold for debts, the master's granddaughter visited the slave quarters and told the slaves to escape. They were ignorant of places to go or how to get there, and so she told them to get passes and leave for the free states, which they did.[64] In Mississippi one slave found that he could trust neither the Negroes nor the whites, though he was hidden by his old master when he escaped to him. The master's wife, however, revealed that her husband was waiting for the reward to go higher and that he would then turn him in. She urged him to run to Canada and provided some money and directions. When William Ruth was about to be cheated out of the free papers promised him in the will of a former master, he "was assisted off by a man who was a slaveholder himself."[65] Perhaps a very aged former slave put his finger on the matter when he reminisced: "They was all kinds of white folks, just like they is now. . . . Devils and good people walking in the road at the same time, and nobody could tell one from t'other."[66]

Whatever aid the fugitives received was sporadic and sometimes came from unlikely sources. If any organized network of aid was available, most of the runaways did not know of it. Even Negroes who had lived in the northern states were un-

---

[64] *The Life of John Thompson, a Fugitive Slave; Containing His History of Twenty-Five Years in Bondage, and His Providential Escape. Written by Himself* (Worcester, Mass., 1856), 66; *An Autobiography: The Story of the Lord's Dealings with Mrs. Amanda Smith, the Colored Evangelist* (Chicago, 1893), 37.

[65] Drew, *The Refugee*, 282–84, 375–77.

[66] B. A. Botkin, *Lay My Burden Down: A Folk History of Slavery* (Chicago, 1945), 253.

aware of whatever underground railroad may have existed. Solomon Northrup, who had been born free in New York, was helpless when kidnappers sold him as a runaway slave in Washington, D.C. Northrup was finally befriended by a Canadian neighbor who was not an abolitionist but was aroused to indignation by his plight. The Canadian wrote letters to some friends in New York, obtained the aid of influential politicians, and finally helped him return to his home. But Northrup served as a slave for twelve years before he was able to return to the North. Another fugitive lived in Cleveland several years before returning to Kentucky to rescue his wife and children from slavery. His task was difficult. The family and three other fugitives traveled through the woods and suffered greatly from "fear, cold and hunger." After crossing the Ohio River into Indiana, they met some Quakers who fed them, gave them some money, "and placed them on the U.G.R.R." But the most dangerous part of the trip was over before the fugitives contacted the Quakers. When Lewis Clarke returned to Kentucky to rescue his three brothers, the four made their way unaided to Ripley, Ohio. From there they were "sent on by friends, from place to place," until they reached Oberlin. But Clarke had known nothing of such activity when he had escaped earlier. Leaving Lexington, Kentucky, Clarke, who was nearly white, had passed as free. He had first heard of abolitionists in Oberlin.[67]

An Illinois abolitionist said that assistance was more often than not a matter of a fugitive's inquiring for "certain persons to whom he had been directed by someone on the way." After giving the fugitives "something to eat, perhaps to wear, occasionally a shilling or two bits," he would send him along the way, instructed to follow the North Star until he reached the residence of another friend. In truth, the fugitive had to help himself. A Georgia slave family of father, mother, and four children got information about the way to Canada and trans-

[67] *Twelve Years a Slave: Narrative of Solomon Northrup* (New York, 1855), 271–90; *Liberator*, May 9, 1856; *Narrative of the Sufferings of Lewis Clarke, . . . Dictated by Himself* (Boston, 1845), 58.

portation aid from a friendly Quaker at the start of their flight.
He took them fifty miles in a wagon at night, hid them out for
a day, and then carried them an additional fifty miles. Unable
to help them further, he told them to wend their way following the North Star. The family went all the way to Buffalo,
New York, before they again received any help, this time from
a free Negro in that city. They had traveled through Pennsylvania without being aware of any organized assistance that
might be available to them. Josiah Henson left Kentucky
slavery with his family in 1830. They traveled by night and
rested by day. They were "thrown absolutely upon [their] own
poor and small resources," said Henson, "and were to rely
on [their] own strength alone." They "dared look to no one
for help." The Hensons traveled two weeks before reaching
Cincinnati, where they were kindly received and entertained
for several days. Then they were carried thirty miles in a wagon,
only to be again on their own resources until they met a friendly
boat captain who took them from Sandusky to Buffalo and then
paid their passage to Canada.[68]

J. W. Loguen, who, with another slave, ran away from Tennessee around 1835, found an abolitionist after reaching Ohio.
The two fugitives were discouraged when they realized that before they could attain freedom they would have to "track their
way from point to point, and from abolitionist to abolitionist,
by aid of the Star, through the dreary wilderness to Canada."
Actually they got very little aid and were cheated badly when
they sold their horse to a Quaker. For the rest of the trip they
thought it prudent not to make inquiries; so they trusted to
the North Star and eventually reached their goal. John Anderson's escape was also mostly a self-help affair. He left Missouri
with a stolen mule, traveled at night, and availed himself of the
boats tied along the rivers he had to cross. Suffering from ex-

[68] W. H. Lyford to Wilbur H. Siebert, March 21, 1896, in scrapbook "The
Underground Railroad in Illinois, vol. 3," Siebert Papers, Houghton Library;
Salem, Ohio, *Anti-Slavery Bugle*, October 2, 1846; *The Life of Josiah Henson,
Formerly a Slave, Now an Inhabitant of Canada, as Narrated by Himself* (Boston,
1849) , 50–58.

treme hunger, he was sometimes compelled "to levy contributions upon the eatable property of those whose dwellings lay
in his way." It was only after he arrived at Rock Island, Illinois, that Anderson contacted an abolition society. Their assistance consisted of paying his railroad fare from that city to
Chicago. Still another fugitive, Charles Garlick who escaped
from Virginia, wrote in his memoirs that the "underground
railroad was brought into use wherever practicable, there being occasional stations where I was assisted to elude my pursuers and sent ahead when safety was assured."[69]

The kind of aid these former slaves and others wrote about
was certainly not the well-organized and mysterious institution
of the legend, and it was often available only after the most difficult part of the journey was accomplished. It took one fugitive three months to make his way from the lower South to St.
Louis. From there he continued his journey with a forged pass,
traveling after sundown until he came to Indianapolis, where
he learned about the underground railroad. Abolitionists
helped him across Indiana to Michigan, where he settled for
about a year before going on to England. Jacob Cummings
fled from Tennessee and found an abolitionist only when he
arrived at New Albany, Indiana. One fugitive from Virginia
"fell in with the managers of the 'Underground Railroad' "
in Ohio, after getting that far by himself. William A. Hall was
successful in his fourth escape attempt. He left Nashville, Tennessee, alone, getting occasional help from Negroes, and finally
found an abolitionist at Ottawa, Illinois, who helped him get
to Chicago. A fugitive who stowed away on a boat reached New
Bedford in 1859 "ill clad, cold, weary, hungry, dispirited, without money and without friends, and not fully knowing the
route which he should take." The abolitionists, who said he

---

[69] *The Rev. J. W. Loguen, as a Slave and as a Freeman. A Narrative of Real
Life* (Syracuse, 1859) , 306, 333; Harper Twelvetrees, ed., *The Story of the Life of
John Anderson, the Fugitive Slave* (London, 1863) , 13–20; Charles A. Garlick,
*Life Including His Escape and Struggle for Liberty of Charles A. Garlick, Born a
Slave in Old Virginia, Who Secured His Freedom by Running Away from His
Master's Farm in 1843* (Jefferson, Ohio, 1902) , 6.

"presented rather a pitiful sight," cared for him and "furnished him with a little change, and a through ticket to Boston, on the underground railroad." Still another runaway bondsman reached New York after three weeks of "sleeping in woods and caves by day and traveling at night." There abolitionists gave him new clothes, provisions, some money, and a ticket for Canada. He too was a passenger on the underground railroad, according to the abolitionist press.[70]

Such underground railroad activity was clearly of value to the fugitives who received it, but it would be unwarranted to assume that they could not have succeeded without it. For in fact some did. In many cases those who did receive abolitionist aid had already made long trips on their own. Clearly, the fact that some slaves did succeed in running away from slavery is no proof of the existence of any highly organized or widespread scheme for running them from depot to depot until they found freedom in Canada.

Fugitive slaves who succeeded in making their way to the free states quickly learned that they were not yet in the Promised Land. Work was hard to come by. In 1846 an abolitionist in New London, Connecticut, found it impossible to get employment for a fugitive couple, though the husband was of "good natural endowment" and anxious for regular work and his wife was qualified to do washing, cooking, or housework. Wages were "unusually low and uncertain," and inquiries were made about the possibility of finding employment for the couple in a larger city. A free Negro in Louisiana said that Negroes could associate with whites more comfortably in the South than in the North. He felt that Northerners kept a greater distance from the Negroes and insulted them more about their color than was the case in his state. Certainly prejudice against Negroes was common throughout the nation, and

[70] L. A. Chamerovzow, ed., *Slave Life in Georgia: A Narrative of the Life, Sufferings, and Escape of John Brown, a Fugitive Slave, Now in England* (2d ed., London, 1855), 144–54; Wilbur H. Siebert interview with Jacob Cummings, n.d., in scrapbook "The Underground Railroad in Indiana, vol. 1," Siebert Papers, Ohio Historical Society; Drew, *The Refugee*, 314–20; *National Anti-Slavery Standard*, February 3, 1853; *Liberator*, April 16, 1858, December 2, 1859.

there is no reason to believe that at that time such prejudice was stronger in the South than in the North.[71]

Many northern communities favored the exclusion of Negroes from their limits, and at one time or another, Illinois, Indiana, Oregon, and Iowa all had constitutional clauses preventing free Negroes from settling within their boundaries. Only a few northern states considered Negroes citizens, and fewer still permitted them to vote. Politicians often catered to the prejudice which produced such discriminatory legislation. In 1850 Senator Jacob W. Miller of New Jersey undoubtedly echoed the sentiments of certain of his constituents when he answered the charge of southern senators that New Jersey had harbored fugitives: "The difficulty in New Jersey has been, not about surrendering fugitive slaves to their legal masters, but rather how to get rid of those worthless slaves which you suffer to escape into our territory, and to remain there to the annoyance of our people." Republican Congressman Cadwallader C. Washburn of Wisconsin agreed with his Democratic colleague that the Negro was out of place when in contact with the white man. "Because he is so out of place," commented Washburn, "we propose keeping him out of the free Territories, and not allowing him, with his unpaid labor, to come in contact with white men and white labor." Free Soiler Salmon P. Chase of Ohio held the opinion that when both races were free they would naturally separate. The state of public opinion in 1850, he thought, was such as to preclude the idea that the Negroes in Ohio could expect equality with the whites, and he felt that those free Negroes whose circumstances would permit it "would do well to emigrate to Jamaica, Hayti, Liberia and other countries, where the population is prepared to welcome them."[72]

---

[71] M. Hempstead to Mrs. Maria W. Chapman, April 1, 1846, Weston Papers, Boston Public Library; Olmsted, *Journey in the Seaboard Slave States*, 2:289. See also Leon F. Litwack, *North of Slavery* (Chicago, 1961).

[72] Henry Harrison Simms, *A Decade of Sectional Controversy, 1851–1861* (Chapel Hill, N.C., 1942), 127–29; *Congressional Globe*, 31 Cong., 1 sess. (1850), App., pt. 1, 311–12; *Congressional Globe*, 36 Cong., 1 sess. (1860), App., 265; Salmon P. Chase to C. H. and J. M. Langston, November 11, 1850, Salmon P. Chase Papers, Library of Congress.

Some who considered themselves abolitionists were as prejudiced as the colonizationists. Theodore Parker had no doubt that the African race was "greatly inferior to the Caucasian in general intellectual power, and also in that instinct for Liberty which is so strong in the Teutonic family." Commenting on the rapid growth of the American slave population, Parker said, "An Anglo-Saxon with common sense does not like this Africanization of America; he wishes the superior race to multiply rather than the inferior." In reporting cases of injustice toward slaves, the abolitionists usually put special emphasis on those involving mulattoes, implying that it was much worse to enslave a near-white person than a black.[73] Mrs. Elizabeth Buffum Chace, a New England abolitionist, found that some persons who were opposed to slavery and were willing to work for its abolition objected strongly to any association with Negroes in their antislavery labors. When a number of "very respectable young colored women" began attending abolitionist meetings in the Rhode Island town where she lived, and when her sister invited them to join, it "raised such a storm among some of the leading members, that for a time, it threatened the dissolution of the Society." Eventually the women were admitted, even though the other members were reluctant to accept them as equals.[74]

Negroes in the North, of course, were painfully conscious of this kind of prejudice. "We are not treated as freemen, in any part of the United States," complained a Philadelphia Negro in 1851. Negroes visiting England and Europe commented on the cordial reception they received and the "absence of that prejudice which is so disgraceful to America." How different it was in England, thought young Josephine Brown, who was able to attend school there with the others. In Buffalo there was

[73] Theodore Parker to Francis Jackson, November 24, 1859, quoted in John Weiss, *Life and Correspondence of Theodore Parker* (2 vols., New York, 1864), 2:174–76; Chicago *Western Citizen*, September 14, 1843; Milwaukee *Daily Free Democrat*, November 27, 1850.

[74] Chace, "My Anti-Slavery Reminiscences," 118–20.

a segregated school, and even in Massachusetts, Negro children had to "occupy a seat set apart" and "therefore often suffered much annoyance from the other children, owing to prejudice." Frederick Douglass found that one of the most pleasing features of his visit to Ireland was a "total absence of all manifestations of prejudice" against him on account of his color. He could, to his amazement, "go on stagecoaches, omnibuses, steamboats, into the first cabins, and in the first public houses, without seeing the slightest manifestation of that hateful and vulgar feeling." It reminded him of the times he had been barred from visiting a menagerie in Boston Common and from a revival meeting in New Bedford, from a warm cabin on a steamer going from New York to Boston and from New England omnibuses, as well as of the signs in Boston eating houses, "We don't allow niggers in here."[75]

Many Negroes who had freedom by escape, by manumission, or by birth, left the northern states for Canada. One of them, Nelson Moss, testified that during his three-year stay in Pennsylvania he had suffered more from prejudice than he had in Virginia. Some who had lived as free Negroes in the South were especially disappointed with conditions in the North. Oppressive laws, no work opportunities, lack of respect, inability to get ahead, and ill treatment were all cited by refugees who had left the free states for Canada. One woman who had lived ten years as a free Negro in Ohio said, "I would as lief live in the slave States as in Ohio. In the slave States I had protection sometimes, from people what knew me—none in Ohio."[76]

But in Canada, too, former slaves encountered racial preju-

[75] Letter to the editor from "A Colored Philadelphian" in *Liberator*, February 12, 1851, cited in Woodson, ed., *Mind of the Negro*, 224; William Lloyd Garrison to Elizabeth Pease, September 1, 1840, Garrison Papers, Boston Public Library; Josephine Brown to Mrs. May, printed in the *Liberator*, October 20, 1854, and quoted in Woodson, *Mind of the Negro*, 364; Frederick Douglass to Garrison, printed in the *Liberator*, October 10, 1845, and quoted in Woodson, *Mind of the Negro*, 396.
[76] Drew, *The Refugee*, 151–54, 174, 191, 305–307, 330–33, 358, 372–73, 374–75.

dice. The Canadian government did not officially sanction discrimination against the newcomers, but Negroes on occasion were "treated differently from the white in churches, in steamboats, and in hotels." A Toronto newspaper editorial in 1851 indicated that some Canadians wanted restrictive immigration measures to check the influx of Negroes into the country following the scare caused by the American Fugitive Slave Law of the previous year. "Already we have a far greater number of negroes in the province than the good of the country requires," ran the editorial, "and we would suggest the propriety of levying a poll tax on all who may come to us for the future. . . . We abhor slavery, but patriotism induces us to exclaim against having our country overrun by blacks, many of whom are woefully depraved by their previous mode of life."[77]

Descriptions of the lot of Canadian Negro refugees vary. Henry Bibb, the fugitive who became a newspaper publisher and promoter of Canadian colonization, painted a very attractive picture. He urged Negroes to run away from slavery, saying: "Bring along your axes with which to make low at your feet the tall forest on this, the Queen's free soil, which awaits your coming." On the other hand, alleged agents of the Canadian refugees who solicited money and clothing from the abolitionists pictured the former slaves as helpless and destitute. When abolitionist George Thompson visited Canada in 1852, he reported that he found two classes of fugitives there. One class, he said, was "too lazy to work and desirous of getting a name for benevolence"; the other opposed begging and was determined to be self-supporting. Another observer confided to William Lloyd Garrison that nine-tenths of the Negroes in Canada objected to begging for clothes, money, and other benevolences. The Cincinnati abolitionist Levi Coffin visited Canada and found many of the former slaves more comfortably situated than he had expected, but he later commented

    [77] John Hope Franklin, *From Slavery to Freedom: A History of American Negroes* (New York, 1952), 366; St. Louis *Republican*, January 7, 1853; St. Louis *Western Watchman*, September 18, 1851, quoting *Toronto Colonist*.

that the climate was unfavorable and that "there was much destitution and suffering among those who had recently come in."[78]

The fugitives themselves had mixed reactions. Thomas Rightso wrote to his former master asking him to tell Rightso's kinsmen that he was "pleased and happy" in his escape until he thought about his wife. Another, who profusely thanked his mistress for nursing him when he was sick, claimed that he had "enjoyed more pleasure in one month" in Canada than in all his life "in the land of bondage." A refugee who had lived for twenty years in the free states found that in Canada he met with prejudice only from the "low class of people," who did not have the power to carry it out there as in the United States. He believed that the law there was "stronger than the mob," which was not so in the United States. But after six years in Canada one fugitive wrote his master that he would return if money were sent him, and a few did go back when their passage was sent. The vast majority of the former slaves, however, were not inclined to return to bondage.[79]

The courage and ingenuity of those who successfully escaped from southern bondage should not obscure the fact that their numbers were small. Relatively few of the enslaved Negroes escaped. Considering how little they knew about any territory away from their own small world, and how slight the chances of success must have seemed, it is little wonder that this was true.

Dependent for the most part on their own resources, the fugitives asked for and received only a minimum of help in their flights from bondage. The records of those who told their stories and the ingenious escape methods and self-help plans that

[78] Milwaukee *Daily Free Democrat*, December 2, 1851, quoting *Voice of the Fugitive; Oberlin Evangelist*, July 21, 1852; Mary A. Shadd to Garrison, October 5, 1852, Garrison Papers; Levi Coffin, *Reminiscences*, 253.

[79] Thomas Rightso to John Walker, December 5, 1850, Richard B. Riddick Papers, Duke University Library; Joseph Taper to Joseph Long, November 11, 1840, Joseph Long Papers, Duke University Library; Drew, *The Refugee*, 174; Davis, ed., *Barrow Diary*, 231; Mineral Point, Wis., *Home Intelligencer*, May 10, 1860.

they devised prove that courageous slaves could escape even from the deep South without very much assistance. Furthermore, the aid they got came from various sources, the abolitionists being only one group of people who helped them escape. Such aid was usually temporary and seldom could be counted on to assure the success of escape attempts. For the greater part of their trip from the South the fugitives had to help themselves, and when anything like the traditional underground railroad provided transportation service, it was in many instances after the slaves had completed the most difficult part of their flights. Nor were the fugitive's difficulties at an end when he reached free territory. The Promised Land of the legend was in reality a harsh and difficult environment for the free Negro, however his freedom had been obtained.

## Chapter Four

# A DEEP-LAID SCHEME

LOOKING BACK across the years, a veteran of the underground railroad described it as a "deep-laid scheme, having in view the restoration of God-given rights to helpless, hunted fugitives, . . . resulting in gradual emancipation, and finally in total abolition with the consent of the slaveholders themselves."[1] The concept of a "deep-laid scheme" is an important part of the underground railroad legend, for the road is assumed to have had a highly organized network of regular stations dotting the North and even penetrating into the South. Occasionally passengers were even enticed aboard the freedom train by its zealous conductors.

However, there is little evidence to support the idea of a well-developed conspiracy. Certainly the abolition movement produced no such institution. Writing in 1892, Frederick Douglass referred to seven different antislavery groups.[2] There was a basic division between the moral suasionists, who rejected all political action, and those who favored it. Out of each of these groups developed a number of distinct splinter factions. The abolitionists differed among themselves on nearly every matter connected with their antislavery labors, and the underground railroad was no exception. Many who were active in the cause had only a limited interest in assisting fugitive slaves. Very few of them approved of luring slaves from the South, and those who did operated on their own, without the benefit of any intricate organization, as did the slave stealers who abducted slaves for profit.

In the early nineteenth century, abolitionists gave little attention to underground railroad activity. Instead, they confined their efforts almost exclusively to legal measures. They emphasized persuasion and refrained from violating even those laws which seemed to them to support slavery. Their publications and resolutions seldom alluded to proposals which, even by a liberal stretch of the imagination, could have been considered underground railroad work. Abolitionists who attended the second annual convention of the Vermont Anti-Slavery Society in 1836 supported a resolution "that the only eligible and sure means of overthrowing the system of slavery is by enlightening the public mind, by free discussion, and the operation of a correct public sentiment upon the consciences and hearts of the whole nation." As with many similar meetings of that period, this convention's thirteen resolutions did not mention fugitive slaves. An earlier publication of the New York Anti-Slavery Society attempted to quiet the fears of some that abolitionists were appealing to the slaves to rebel or run away. The abolitionists emphasized: *"We do not address ourselves to the oppressed;* but with hearts of benevolence to both master and slave, we beseech the master to grant to his slave, what humanity, justice, interest, conscience and God demand."[3]

Pioneer abolitionists like the Quaker Isaac Hopper gave aid to fugitives when there was no other way for them to obtain freedom, but they preferred legal means. Hopper advised a slave coachman who came to him for help in Philadelphia to stay six months in Pennsylvania with his master's consent, and thus take advantage of a state law which freed such persons. "It is desirable to obtain thy liberty in a legal way, if possible,"

[1] Eber M. Pettit, *Sketches in the History of the Underground Railroad Comprising Many Thrilling Incidents of the Escape of Fugitives from Slavery, and the Perils of Those Who Aided Them* (Fredonia, N.Y., 1879) , xv.

[2] Frederick Douglass to Marshall Pierce, February 18, 1892, Nathaniel P. Rodgers Collection, Haverford College Library.

[3] *Second Annual Report of the Vermont Anti-Slavery Society; with an Account of the Annual Meeting, Holden in Middlebury, February 16 & 17, 1836* (Middlebury, 1836) , 5–6; *Address of the New York City Anti-Slavery Society, to the People of the City of New York* (New York, 1833) , 5.

said Hopper, "for otherwise thou wilt be constantly liable to be arrested, and may never again have such a good opportunity to escape from bondage."[4]

The abolitionists did much to protect the rights of Negroes and to prevent the kidnapping of free Negroes into slavery. A Delaware abolition society active in the years 1801 to 1804 tried to insure the enforcement of Delaware laws which prohibited the removal of slaves out of the state for resale. This society took the position that nothing could be done if the owner in question could prove his legal right to hold a particular slave. The Pennsylvania Abolition Society, operating in the same period, helped a number of slaves whose freedom had been provided for in their masters' wills but who were nevertheless sold by the heirs. Early abolition societies concentrated on this kind of legal activity.[5]

Isaac Hopper and other early abolitionists also purchased or helped to purchase slaves in order to free them. In the early nineteenth century the prices for such slaves were often as low as seventy to a hundred dollars. Sometimes slaves who had run away were purchased in order to make their freedom legal. Abolitionists also gave assistance to fugitives who were attempting to raise money to purchase other members of their families.[6]

Purchases of fugitive slaves continued into the 1850's, when some of the abolitionists had dropped their earlier scruples

[4] Lydia Maria Child, *Isaac T. Hopper: A True Life* (Boston, 1853) , 48–49, 201.
[5] "Minutes of the Proceedings of the Acting Committee of the Society for the Abolition of Slavery, March 13, 1801 to July 23, 1804," in Thomas Garrett Scrapbook, Delaware Historical Society; Mary Stoughton Locke, *Anti-Slavery in America from the Introduction of African Slaves to the Prohibition of the Slave Trade (1619–1808)* (*Radcliffe College Monographs*, no. 11, Boston, 1901) , 99–100; William Allinson Diary, 1804–1805, in Allinson Collection, Haverford College Library; W. J. Buck, undated 3-vol. ms. history of the Pennsylvania Abolition Society, 2:252, Historical Society of Pennsylvania; Report of Committee on Fugitives, undated ms., Papers of the Pennsylvania Society for Promoting the Abolition of Slavery, Historical Society of Pennsylvania.
[6] Clipping from West Chester, Pa., *American Republican*, n.d., 1833, Chester County (Pa.) Historical Society; Christopher Prince to Mrs. M. W. Chapman, December, 1845, Weston Papers, Boston Public Library. There are several folders of material concerning the purchase and manumission of slaves by the Abolition Society of Pennsylvania in the society's papers in the Historical Society of Pennsylvania.

about illegal underground railroad service. The famous slave Anthony Burns, who was returned from Boston to slavery in Virginia and North Carolina, was later purchased and freed— largely through the efforts of Leonard Grimes, a free Negro— for the sum of $1,325. Frederick Douglass was also granted legal freedom by his former master after his friends raised the necessary money. Such activity was noted in the South. In 1850 a Kentucky newspaper commented approvingly of the purchase and manumission of slaves, a practice which was "much more consonant with law and justice . . . than the practice of harboring and secreting slaves that too commonly prevails in the free States."[7]

Some of the abolitionists, however, had scruples against purchasing slaves, for such a procedure tacitly recognized the institution of slavery. One of Lucretia Mott's friends admitted to the Quaker humanitarian: "The feelings of some among us, who scrupulously maintain that no combination of circumstances can justify the purchase of a slave, have been closely tried when called upon to save their fellow human beings from a return to slavery." She referred to a woman who had been taken from her home and returned to slavery, leaving her husband and baby in the North. The owner expressed a willingness to sell her to her friends, supposing "there is humanity enough in the neighborhood, to advance 900 dollars." But the abolitionist was indecisive as to what might be done. Theodore Parker, however, was adamant. When asked to help purchase a fugitive slave, he confided to his journal: "I could not give money to feed the hunters of human flesh." The Boston abolitionist Samuel May, Jr., was "taken quite aback" when he learned that Frederick Douglass had consented to his purchase for seven hundred and fifty dollars. Although the former slave "felt as if a mountain had been taken off from his soul," May was astounded that Douglass would "acknowledge, or consent

[7] Lewis Tappan to Mrs. Lydia E. Sturge, August 3, 1857, Lewis Tappan Letter Book, Library of Congress; Levi Coffin, *Reminiscences of Levi Coffin, the Reputed President of the Underground Railroad* (2d ed., Cincinnati, 1880) , 577; Lexington, Ky., *Observer and Reporter*, December 4, 1850.

that others (his friends) should acknowledge, that any man had
the right of ownership in him." May later said that the manumission of Douglass was "exceedingly unpopular" among the
Boston abolitionists and that no paper except William Lloyd
Garrison's *Liberator* had defended it. A Philadelphia abolitionist, Sarah Pugh, shared May's views. When the question of
purchasing William Wells Brown arose, she asked if Brown
had given his consent. "I hope he has not," she said, "for he
would lose half his manhood. Douglass has never been a free
man since." The Chicago *Western Citizen* maintained that
the supporters of the Compromise of 1850 were buying up slaves
in the North who were claimed by their owners in order to
avoid a collision of the Fugitive Slave Law with the moral sense
of the public. They noted that the market price was thereby
raised and that there seemed to be "some value attached to this
property on foot." The slaveholders, they charged, came "forward with a draft on the pockets of the Northern supporters
of the law, instead of the legal papers for the arrest."[8]

Contentiousness was quite common in antislavery circles,
and it is hardly probable that abolitionist groups which were
so often in disagreement with each other were at the same time
joined in a secret and nationally organized conspiracy to aid
fleeing slaves. For they were by no means unanimous on the
value of such activity. The abolitionists' aim was to end slavery, not to help a few former slaves, and even those most interested in fugitive aid usually made a clear distinction between
the two activities. Aid to fugitives did not necessarily contribute to the greater cause, and in some cases might be injuri-
ous to it. After the passage of the Fugitive Slave Law of 1850,
a Chicago abolition newspaper suggested that it might "be

[8] Alice Elisa Hambleton to Lucretia Mott, October 28, 1839, Papers of the
Pennsylvania Society for Promoting the Abolition of Slavery, vol. 11, p. 13, His-
torical Society of Pennsylvania; Theodore Parker Journal, entry for Septem-
ber 13, 1851, Parker Scrapbook, Boston Public Library; Samuel May, Jr., to Dr.
John Bishop Estlin, December 1, 1846, February 25, 1847, May Papers, Boston
Public Library; Sarah Pugh to Richard Webb, May 22, 1854, William Lloyd
Garrison Papers, Boston Public Library; Chicago *Western Citizen*, December 17,
1850.

expedient for some fugitives to suffer martyrdom . . . and consent to return awhile to slavery as propagandists of liberty, and as a standing appeal to the humanity of the North." A. T. Foss of Manchester, New Hampshire, regretted that a fugitive slave had chosen to flee to Canada rather than face the possibility of a return to slavery. The abolitionists sent him north reluctantly. "We should much have preferred to have had him remain, and tested the strength of the Fugitive Slave Bill (accursed Bill!) in Manchester," lamented Foss.[9]

In their annual report for 1844 the Boston Female Anti-Slavery Society asked the question, "Who is an Abolitionist?" Not necessarily he who frees his slaves, they answered, nor he who gives aid to fugitives or money to purchase their children. Aiding fugitives was a humane and benevolent pursuit, they said, "though in its nature, owing to the necessary secrecy of its performance, and its tendency to relieve the glutted market, not often beneficial even indirectly to the cause." Abby K. Foster lamented to Garrison that, while there was much antislavery sentiment in New York, it had often been exploited and fooled by "various schemes, professedly to accomplish the same object —such, for instance, as the running off of slaves, for which large amounts of money were collected and for which nobody was made responsible."[10]

An abolitionist writer in 1840 was concerned that contributions of money for antislavery work should not go to foreign places. He was thinking specifically of Canada. "Moneys contributed to aid the escape of fugitive slaves—or to buy slaves out of bondage—or to provide schools for those who have escaped into Canada, or the like, do not seem to come within the scope of our Society policy. We are for abolishing slavery itself," he continued, "not by aiding it to run away, but so that slaves need not run away to get their liberty." The Garrisonian

[9] Chicago *Western Citizen*, November 5, 1850; A. T. Foss to Theodore Parker, n.d., cited in John Weiss, *Life and Correspondence of Theodore Parker* (2 vols., New York, 1864), 2:123.
[10] *National Anti-Slavery Standard*, November 21, 1844; Abby K. Foster to Garrison, August 22, 1851, Garrison Papers.

abolitionists consistently regarded agitation against slavery as their most significant activity. In 1858 when a New York antislavery worker questioned the value of using the proceeds of antislavery fairs for fugitive aid as well as antislavery propaganda, Samuel May, Jr., urged her to stick to the single cause. He was sure that it was "ultimately wisest and best" for the abolitionists "to have but a single aim in such fairs and to ask for money for the single object of direct aggression upon Slavery in its Strongholds. The stronger and more perseveringly this is urged," he assured her, "the surer will it be that a class will arise to sustain all lesser and subsidiary movements. Thousands will be thereby *shamed* into helping Fugitives, or will do it as a *salve* to their consciences, which can only be reached by having their whole and highest duty fully, and faithfully, and uncompromisingly set before them." When May consulted Garrison, he found they were in agreement. Garrison believed that a committee on fugitives was needed in New York but that the proceeds from the Anti-Slavery Fair should all go to the American Anti-Slavery Society for the greater cause.[11]

This was not the first time the Garrisonians had faced a possible loss of funds as a result of the controversy over fugitive aid work. In 1850 the Female Anti-Slavery Society of Glasgow, Scotland, had withdrawn cooperation from the Garrisonian abolitionists because they were "hostile to Christianity." The Scottish society, on the other hand, commended the work of the Vigilance Committee of New York, which "invoked no sectarian bias" and directed its efforts to protecting fugitive slaves, giving relief to the needy fugitives and forwarding them to Canada when they appeared to be in danger. About twenty-five hundred fugitives a year went through New York from the South, said the report. "To consult the interests of these," said the society, "is a most humane and Christian duty, in which all may co-operate, without imperilling any sacred principle." Garrison's followers were furious, and Maria W. Chapman

[11] *Liberator*, November 27, 1840; Samuel May, Jr., to Mrs. Abigail Hopper Gibbons, May 30, June 11, 1858, May Papers.

wrote an answer to the Scottish women. She denied that any money given the American Anti-Slavery Society went for anything other than the abolition of slavery, and admitted that the objects of the vigilance committee were "humane and good ones." Most abolitionists, she argued, were "engaged in the work of secreting, forwarding, feeding, clothing and placing fugitive slaves," but that when such work was proposed as a substitute for the American Anti-Slavery Society's job of "propagating those principles and inculcating that course of conduct whose universality will shake down slavery itself, . . . *then* the idea of a Vigilance Committee becomes a mere hypocritical pretence." This was to "shelter two-and-a-half thousand, instead of freeing two-and-a-half millions! the greater all the while including the less! You would shelter the few fugitives," she said. "You leave unblamed both the multitude of bloodhounds engaged in hunting them, and the nation that is cheering on the chase."[12]

In another tract Mrs. Chapman continued her opposition to overemphasizing fugitive aid work. To "organize vigilance committees, and establish underground railroads" was to "hide from tyranny, instead of defying it," she argued. She did not wish to discourage "mercy or compassion in an individual case, but a disgraceful mistake in the economy of well doing; . . . preferring the less, which *ex*cludes the greater, to the greater, which *in*cludes the less." She believed that slavery could only be abolished "by raising the character of the people who compose the nation; and *that* can only be done by showing them a higher one."[13]

From time to time certain abolitionists also deplored the emphasis which underground railroad activity placed upon getting slaves out of the country. Their objective, they said, was to make it safe for fugitives to stay. Marius Robinson con-

---

[12] *Anti-Slavery Cause* (a four-page pamphlet published by Glasgow Female Anti-Slavery Society in 1850) , Weston Papers; Maria W. Chapman to the nine signers of the above pamphlet, June 8, 1850, Weston Papers.
[13] Maria W. Chapman, *How Can I Help to Abolish Slavery?* (*Anti-Slavery Tract* no. 14, New York, 1853) .

gratulated another abolitionist when he heard that some citizens of his town had prevented the recapture of a fugitive. Robinson was glad that some fugitives would "assert their right to select their own residence." Abolitionists should be ashamed, he said, if all they could do was to help them along stealthily, "and with all a smuggler's fear and watchfulness, thrust the human commodity upon our British neighbors." In the spring of 1857 Thomas Wentworth Higginson made two speeches to antislavery audiences in which he also deplored the sending off of fugitives. He said, "The Underground Railroad makes cowards of us all. It makes us think and hesitate and look over our shoulders, and listen, and wonder, and not dare to tell the truth to the man who stands by our side. It may be a necessary evil," he asserted, "but an evil it is." It was degrading to let any man leave a city because he had entered it "upon the Southern track." It was "degrading, dishonourable, demoralizing," he thundered. In his second address Higginson insisted that there was no real need for sending slaves away. Speaking in Boston he said, "once resolve that Boston is the terminus of the Underground Railroad henceforth, and Boston is Canada —these streets, though a part of a Republic, are as free as if they were ruled by a Queen."[14]

Even the abolitionists most active in underground railroad work were sometimes on the defensive about placing so much emphasis on that phase of their service. Few of them spent more time and energy helping fugitive slaves than J. Miller McKim of the Philadelphia Vigilance Committee, yet when he granted permission to reprint a letter on fugitive slaves in the *Liberty Bell*, he said that he would have preferred to write on some other subject. He feared it might give some of the friends abroad the impression that he was "a man of one idea, literally, and that idea a very narrow one."[15]

When Mrs. Andrew H. Ernst moved to Cincinnati in 1841,

[14] *National Anti-Slavery Standard,* May 16, June 20, 1857.
[15] J. Miller McKim to Mrs. Maria W. Chapman, December 11, 1857, Weston Papers.

she decided to organize some kind of woman's activity as *"near to Abolition"* as she might then go. As a Garrisonian, she hoped eventually to draw together a group of women who would agitate against slavery itself. But the best she could do was to organize a sewing circle which aided fugitives who passed through Cincinnati. "Poor creatures!" she declared, "We are glad to help them tho' from the beginning I have never felt that by it we advance real Freedom one step." It only brought together the antislavery folk who, when the right time came, would not confine themselves "to the physical enfranchisement of these oppressed ones but by such means as might be then present," would try to "awaken a purer public opinion." Sarah Pugh of Philadelphia was more excited about her fugitive aid service. She found the escapes "perfectly marvellous" and rejoiced in them; nevertheless, interesting and exciting as they were, she felt that they were "only an incidental part of the great work" before them, which was "to implant principles to render it possible for the slave to stand on 'his own his native soil!' Redeemed, regenerated and disenthralled by the irresistible gains of Universal Emancipation."[16]

Universal emancipation was indeed the abolitionists' goal, and those who kept the goal in view were too busy agitating against slavery to organize a nationwide system for running off fugitives. Such well-known figures as William Lloyd Garrison and Wendell Phillips gave primary attention to antislavery agitation; their contacts with underground railroad work were mainly in connection with cases where the fugitive issue served propaganda purposes. Even Theodore Weld, who worked extensively in the western antislavery movement, seems to have had very limited contact with fugitives from the South. Weld served as a member of the New York Vigilance Committee, but there is no evidence that he sheltered runaway slaves either at Lane Institute or in any of his later residences.[17]

[16] Mrs. Andrew H. Ernst to Miss Weston, July 28, 1850, Weston Papers; [Sarah Pugh] to [Mrs. M. W. Chapman] November 4, 1857, Weston Papers.
[17] Benjamin P. Thomas, *Theodore Weld: Crusader for Freedom* (New Brunswick, 1950) , 78, 177–78.

There was no unanimity on such matters in the Society of Friends, either, though the Quaker conductor is a familiar part of the legendary picture of the underground railroad. Some Quakers rejected all association with abolitionists, shunning their seeming hatred of the slaveholders and fearing the possibility of a civil war. Levi Coffin recalled in later years that most American Friends "had fallen into the popular current and denounced abolitionism," though all the yearly meetings had some "noble exceptions, . . . who stood firm in the face of opposition and battled for the right."[18]

In 1837 the Reverend Theodore S. Wright commented in a speech before the New York State Anti-Slavery Society that although the Quakers had done more for the cause of emancipation than any other sect, but for a few exceptions they only went halfway. Their race prejudice, he said, prevented them from treating individual Negroes "according to their moral worth." In 1849 a western antislavery advocate charged that "Friends considered themselves far more holy than the abolitionists, and therefore bade them to 'stand by themselves.' " Levi Coffin found a similar attitude in the Indiana Yearly Meeting where, according to his testimony, "many were led to believe that there was some disgrace about abolitionism."[19]

While it is true that some of the best known abolitionists were Quakers, there were also Friends who were opposed to slavery yet rejected the methods and violent language of the abolition movement. Feelings ran high in the Society of Friends. One abolitionist critic of the Philadelphia Quakers found "about as much of the spirit of Woolman, Penn and Benezet . . . in them, as there is in an empty Quaker bonnet."[20] Abolitionists were more than once "read out of Meeting," and abolitionist assemblies were prohibited in many of the meeting houses. In 1843, Indiana abolitionist Quakers split from the main group

---

[18] Coffin, *Reminiscences*, 236.
[19] Herbert Aptheker, ed., *A Documentary History of the Negro People in the United States* (New York, 1951), 171–73; Salem, Ohio, *Anti-Slavery Bugle*, July 6, 1849; Coffin, *Reminiscences*, 230.
[20] *Liberator*, July 4, 1851.

and founded the Yearly Meeting of Anti-Slavery Friends. A decade later, Pennsylvania dissenters founded a Society of Progressive Friends, and several other Friends' groups also split over the antislavery issue.[21]

Late in the nineteenth century a Quaker abolitionist recalled that members of the Society of Friends "were generally Abolitionists, but many of them would not do to trust."[22] He was speaking of underground railroad work, and there was some basis for his statement. In 1843, the North Carolina Yearly Meeting passed a resolution condemning "those Friends who had given shelter improperly 'to slaves.' " Members of the Rich Square Monthly Meeting in the same state announced that they wished to make known their "utter disapproval of such interference in any way whatever," though they did not in the least degree relinquish their "testimony to the injustice of slavery."[23] A New Jersey Friend in 1849 accused the antislavery Quakers of inducing weak minds to go south to run off slaves to the North "whilst they themselves remain in safety at home to attend at the gates of the 'underground railroad,' for the purpose of running the Slaves off to Canada." This, he continued, irritated the slaveowner and shut his ears against the abolitionists' arguments, and even prevented Southerners from discussing it among themselves except in order to devise better ways to secure the slaves.[24]

Of course, most Quakers—like many other people—would have been moved by the sight of a helpless refugee from slavery and probably would have helped him on his way whether or not they approved abstractly of such aid. But the Quaker reputation for underground railroad service rests largely on the repu-

[21] Robert C. Smedley, *History of the Underground Railroad in Chester and the Neighboring Counties of Pennsylvania* (Lancaster, 1883) , 254–55; Coffin, *Reminiscences*, 230; Thomas E. Drake, *Quakers and Slavery in America* (New Haven, 1950) , 174–75.
[22] James H. Arnett to Wilbur H. Siebert, April 30, 1896, in scrapbook "The Underground Railroad in Ohio, vol. 5," Siebert Papers, Ohio Historical Society.
[23] Stephen Weeks, *Southern Quakers and Slavery: A Study in Institutional History* (*Johns Hopkins University Studies in Historical and Political Science*, ed. by Herbert B. Adams, extra vol. 15, Baltimore, 1896) , 242 n.
[24] *National Anti-Slavery Standard*, January 11, 1849.

tation of certain Friends. Levi Coffin, who gained fame as the probable model for Harriet Beecher Stowe's Simeon Halliday, and who later wrote his own memoirs, Thomas Garrett, with his long and famous service in the underground railroad, and a few other prominent antislavery Friends have contributed to a reputation which many of their contemporaries would have deplored. Some other religious groups, including the Reformed Presbyterians (Covenanters) and the Wesleyan Methodists, were probably just as consistent in their record of giving help to fugitives.[25]

Even those antislavery workers who were especially active in the work of helping fugitives disapproved of enticing slaves from the South. Thomas Garrett would render assistance only to fugitives who came to him voluntarily. Addison Coffin, who was proud of his record as an underground railroad worker in North Carolina, recalled, "at no time or under no circumstances did we solicit or advise a slave to leave his master." Levi Coffin, his cousin, made frequent business trips into the South, and he had no trouble in that section. Although he made clear his opposition to slavery, he told his southern acquaintances that it was no part of his business in the South "to interfere with their laws or their slaves." Oberlin College's President James H. Fairchild recalled that the majority of abolitionists there did not regard it as "legitimate to go into the Slave States and entice the slaves from their masters." They had no "scruples in regard to the master's real ownership," but looked upon venturing into the South as a "reckless undertaking, involving too much risk, and probably doing more harm than good."[26] In 1844 an abolitionist writer urged his fellow reformers to refrain from any organized attempt to run off slaves. Such activity

[25] For material on the activities and traditions of the Covenanters in the underground railroad, see D. Ray Wilcox, "The Reformed Presbyterian Church and the Anti-Slavery Movement," thesis, Colorado State College of Education, Greeley, 1948.

[26] Thomas E. Drake, "Thomas Garrett, Quaker Abolitionist," in *Friends in Wilmington, 1738–1938* (Wilmington, Del., n.d.) , 79; Drake, *Quakers and Slavery in America*, 185; Coffin, *Reminiscences*, 279; James H. Fairchild, *Oberlin: The Colony and the College* (Oberlin, 1883) , 115.

would constitute civil war and would be "opposed to the spirit of the Anti-Slavery reform." "It behooves us that our zeal shall not outrun our discretion," he continued, "and that in our eagerness to relieve the few cases of individual suffering, which by these means we may reach, we should not overlook the consequences of our action upon the whole mass."[27]

In the years preceding the Civil War, antislavery politicians frequently denied that there was a conspiracy to lure slaves out of the South. In 1850 Congressman George W. Julian of Indiana maintained that very few slaves were enticed from their masters. "The great majority of escapes," he assured his colleagues, "are prompted by other causes than northern interference." Julian pointed out that the slave had "the power of locomotion, and the instinct to be free," and that the flight of the bondsman was the "necessary consequence of the oppression under which he groans." Congressman Owen Lovejoy of Illinois held similar views. "I tell you," he said on the eve of the Civil War, "that I have no more hesitation in helping a fugitive slave than I have in snatching a lamb from the jaws of a wolf, or disengaging an infant from the talons of an eagle. . . . It is simply a question whether it will pay to go down into the den where the wolf is."[28]

Some of the more conciliatory political leaders of both sections testified to the absence of any organization for running off slaves. In 1850 Congressman Moses Corwin of Ohio assured Southerners that "not one in ten thousand of our millions of people" in the Old Northwest "would place the smallest obstacle in the way of your receiving runaway slaves." He denied that his constituents were "properly chargeable with assisting" the Negroes to escape.

Congressman William H. Bissell of Illinois admitted that there were "vicious as well as deluded people" in the North who probably had helped slaves to elude the pursuit of their

---

[27] *National Anti-Slavery Standard*, December 26, 1844.
[28] *Congressional Globe*, 31 Cong., 1 sess. (1850), App., pt. 1, 574; *Congressional Globe*, 36 Cong., 1 sess. (1860), App., 206.

owners, but he was confident that their number was "very greatly overestimated by gentlemen from the South." The annoyance only required a few, who worked secretly, but their acts were "by no means countenanced by the mass of the people." Some southern spokesmen agreed. Senator George E. Badger of North Carolina believed that the extremist sentiments of such men as William Seward were the exception. "I have not the smallest idea in the world," he said, "that the Senator from New York speaks the opinion of the northern people generally, or the people of any one State in the Union." He was confident that most Northerners would obey a more stringent fugitive slave law if it were passed. This opinion reflected the North Carolinian's "fullest confidence in the patriotism, the intelligence, the sense of justice, and stern integrity of the great mass of people at the North."[29]

Although most of those who considered themselves abolitionists would have rejected the views of men like Bissell and Badger, they could agree that running slaves out of the South was unwise if not morally wrong. There were a few who ventured into the slave states to help fugitives escape, but those few met with stern disapproval from the majority of their co-workers in the movement. Levi Coffin urged John Fairfield, who was one such daring adventurer, to "quit his dangerous work." Coffin and the Cincinnati abolitionists "had no sympathy with his mode of operation," but Fairfield ignored them. He reportedly was killed while leading a slave insurrection in Tennessee.[30] A Boston editor tried in vain to dissuade Charles T. Torrey from his plan to invade the South and run out slaves. The friendly editor deplored his "singular mania" which made him "fearless of consequences, and apparently ready and willing to become a martyr to the cause."[31]

[29] Moses B. Corwin, *Speech of Hon. Moses B. Corwin, of Ohio, on the Proposition to Admit California as a State into the Union. Delivered in the House of Representatives, April 9, 1850* (Washington, 1850), 6–7; *Congressional Globe*, 31 Cong., 1 sess. (1850), App., pt. 1, 227, 387.
[30] Coffin, *Reminiscences*, 436, 446.
[31] Remarks of the editor of Boston *Daily Mail*, reported in St. Louis *Missouri Reporter*, June 2, 1846.

The Oberlin reformers, also, disapproved of those of their number who went into the South to entice and lead slaves to freedom.[32]

When three students of the Mission Institute of Quincy, Illinois, were jailed for taking slaves from Missouri, their friends published a pamphlet describing the incident but also making clear their own disapproval of the young men's action. According to the published account, the three slave abductors "erred *in judgment,*" and their course was "not *the way* to effect on a large scale the emancipation of the enslaved." The writers of the pamphlet denied the necessity of "forming secret plans" or of "doing anything in the dark." Antislavery advocates would have more success in reaching the consciences of slaveholders by pursuing an "openly honorable and manly course" rather than resorting to "expedients that have a contrary appearance."[33]

Those who actually entered the slave states in order to entice or abduct Negroes carried on their labor without the advantages of a smoothly operating underground railroad. When Richard Dillingham, an Ohio Quaker, was caught in Tennessee with three fugitive slaves, he confessed his guilt in court but insisted that he had undertaken the venture alone, without instigation from any source. Calvin Fairbank boasted that he had guided forty-seven Kentucky and Virginia slaves "toward the North Star," and that he "piloted them through the forests, mostly by night," without help.[34] Dr. Alexander M. Ross, a Canadian abolitionist, informed many slaves of the routes to the North and furnished weapons and food to some who decided to make the break from bondage, but his memoirs record the story of a reckless individual working alone and unaided in the southern states. When Seth Conklin made a trip south to rescue Peter Still's family, he found no underground railroad network

[32] Robert Samuel Fletcher, *A History of Oberlin College from Its Foundation through the Civil War* (2 vols., Oberlin, 1943) , 1:398.
[33] *Narrative of Facts, Respecting Alanson Work, Jas. E. Burr & Geo. Thompson, Prisoners in the Missouri Penitentiary, for the Alleged Crime of Negro Stealing. Prepared by a Committee* (Quincy, Ill., 1842) , 5–6.
[34] *Frankfort* (Ky.) *Commonwealth*, May 8, 1849; Calvin Fairbank, *Rev. Calvin Fairbank During Slavery Times* (Chicago, 1890) , 10.

prepared for him. He wrote that he searched the country opposite Paducah, Kentucky, and found the region for fifty miles around "inhabited by Christian wolves."[35]

Negroes who had successfully escaped from slavery occasionally returned to aid others. The legendary exploits of Harriet Tubman are undoubtedly exaggerated, but her adventures cannot all be discounted as fiction. She made a number of trips from Canada into the South to rescue members of her family and others from bondage. In August of 1857, Thomas Garrett reported from Wilmington that he had just given thirty dollars to Harriet Tubman's parents to pay their passage to Canada. Her father had sheltered eight slaves who broke out of a Dover jail, and in consequence his arrest was imminent. His master had "secretly advised him to leave." His wife, who belonged to another master, also absconded. "With such an experienced guide as Harriet," commented Garrett, "they passed safely on."[36] After making his own successful escape to Canada with his family, Josiah Henson returned to Kentucky to help a number of other slaves escape. Both Harriet Tubman and Josiah Henson worked with abolitionist friends when they could find them, but for the most part they relied on their own ingenuity in taking slaves north.[37]

Those few abolitionists and Negroes who abducted slaves took only a small number from the South. More, probably, were taken away by slave stealers who kidnapped them for profit. Southern newspapers carried frequent reports of slave stealing and occasionally suggested that gangs engaged in it were organized into a sort of underground railroad.[38] Slave

[35] Alexander Milton Ross, *Recollections and Experiences of an Abolitionist; From 1855 to 1865* (2d ed., Toronto, 1876) , *passim;* Kate E. R. Pickard, *The Kidnapped and the Ransomed. Being the Personal Recollections of Peter Still and his Wife "Vina," After Forty Years of Slavery* (Syracuse, 1856) , 285.

[36] Earl Conrad, *Harriet Tubman* (Washington, D.C., 1943) , *passim;* Sarah E. Bradford, *Scenes in the Life of Harriet Tubman* (Auburn, N.Y., 1869) , 21–25; Thomas Garrett to Eliza Wigham, December 27, 1856, to Mary Edmundson, August 11, 1857, Cope Collection, Haverford College Library.

[37] *Truth Stranger Than Fiction. Father Henson's Story of His Own Life* (Boston, 1858) , 149.

[38] Salem, Ohio, *Anti-Slavery Bugle,* July 28, 1849; *Richmond Daily Enquirer,* January 31, 1846.

stealers sometimes enticed slaves from their masters with stories of the underground railroad to freedom, but transported them instead to southern traders.[39] Early in 1861, in answer to a Kentuckian's charge that his state lost $200,000 annually in slaves, William Kellogg of Illinois disclosed that another congressman had told him that there were at that time in Maryland "men under indictment for stealing more negroes than there have been slaves taken from the South in the past year by any combination of northern men."[40] Slave stealers faced stiff penalties if they were apprehended; some were executed and others received heavy prison sentences.[41]

Not surprisingly, southern courts also invoked severe penalties on abolitionists caught helping slaves escape. Calvin Fairbank's fugitive slave adventures cost him seventeen years in prison, although an accomplice, Delia Webster, was pardoned by a Kentucky governor after she had served only six weeks of a two-year sentence.[42] Charles T. Torrey died in a Maryland prison where he was serving time for aiding slaves to escape. A Tennessee court sentenced Richard Dillingham to three years in the penitentiary, and Lewis W. Paine spent twice that time in a Georgia prison for trying to aid one slave to escape.[43] Jonathan Walker gained fame because of the unusual sentence he received. As a shipwright working off the Florida coast, Walker had agreed to use his small boat to transport some runaway slaves to the Bahamas. He was caught and sentenced to fifteen days in jail, to pay heavy fines, to spend an hour in the pillory, and to have burned on his right hand the letters "S.S." for slave stealer. Walker spent about seven months in jail before his abolitionist friends paid his fine and court costs.[44]

[39] *Anti-Slavery Standard*, October 1, 1853.

[40] *Congressional Globe*, 36 Cong., 2 sess. (1861) , App., 193.

[41] *Anti-Slavery Standard*, February 7, 1857; Frankfort, Ky., *Tri-Weekly Commonwealth*, August 31, 1857.

[42] Fairbank, *Rev. Calvin Fairbank During Slavery Times*, 11; J. Winston Coleman, Jr., "Delia Webster and Calvin Fairbank, Underground Railroad Agents," *Filson Club History Quarterly*, 17:137 (July, 1943) .

[43] *Frankfort* (Ky.) *Commonwealth*, May 8, 1849; Lewis W. Paine, *Six Years in a Georgia Prison* (New York, 1851) , *passim*.

[44] *Trial and Imprisonment of Jonathan Walker, at Pensacola, Florida, for Aiding Slaves to Escape from Bondage* (Boston, 1846) , *passim*.

Although the few abolitionists who operated in the South apparently worked without benefit of any highly organized system, local district attorneys did their best to find one, and newspapers, even when aid was clearly rendered by one person operating alone, talked about underground railroad operations. When there was no clear proof that suspected abolitionists had actually helped slaves to escape, they were sometimes dealt with outside the law. Several cases of this type occurred after the Harpers Ferry raid had aroused emotions to a white heat. An article in the *Wytheville* (Virginia) *Telegraph* told of "a philanthropic pilgrim from the land of wooden nutmegs, supposed to be an agent of some Abolition Aid Society or underground railroad," who was arrested and nearly killed by a group of local citizens who hung him up five times and let him down just in time, then released him and warned him to leave. "Our people," explained the editor gratuitously, "have no tolerance for the treasonable, thieving, murderous crew." In another Virginia community, an outsider who was seen talking to slaves and free Negroes and who was accused by a slave of asking him if he wished to be free was tarred and feathered and released only when he promised never to return.[45]

While Southerners were seeing in a few isolated cases evidence of a widespread plot to deprive them of their property, those few abolitionists who actually favored an aggressive conspiracy against slavery were generally opposed by antislavery people. It was precisely such a plan that John Brown had in mind and shared with some trusted acquaintances before the Harpers Ferry fiasco. Brown wanted to establish a series of fortified underground railroad stations which could be used to run off slaves and make such property untenable near the free frontier.[46] As late as 1859, Brown found little support for

[45] *Trial of Rev. John B. Mahan, for Felony, in the Mason Circuit Court of Kentucky, November 13–19, 1838. Reported by Joseph B. Reid and Henry R. Reeder, Esqs.* (Cincinnati, 1838); *Louisville Journal,* August 14, 20, 1858; St. Louis *Republican,* July 8, 1859; *Richmond Enquirer,* November 22, 1859, quoting *Wytheville* (Va.) *Telegraph; New York Herald,* January 1, 1860.
[46] Milwaukee *Daily Free Democrat,* October 27, 1859.

such a scheme. Gerrit Smith, a wealthy abolitionist in Syracuse, contributed a hundred dollars for Brown's assistance to fugitive slaves, but later he vigorously denied knowledge of any planned insurrection.[47] Wendell Phillips also disavowed knowledge of the plan, stating that he had always discouraged and discountenanced the idea of stampeding slaves.[48] The Milwaukee *Daily Free Democrat,* which usually expressed extremist abolition sentiments, saw in the Harpers Ferry incident "a crazy exaggeration of sound theories and principles," just as the Fugitive Slave Law was "a crazy exaggeration of unsound ones."[49]

Basically, John Brown's plan was an attempt to systematize the matter of running slaves out of the South. Abolitionist response to it indicates that they had no such scheme in operation prior to 1859, and even at that period of sectional hostility could not be persuaded to sanction or support it.

Despite their opposition to slave-stealing forays in the South, most northern antislavery men would willingly help such fugitives as came their way. But some of them found little opportunity to befriend the fugitives. Their underground railroad service was distinctly limited by a lack of any such nationwide organization as the slaveowners visualized. One aged abolitionist recalled that he had only managed to see one fugitive slave, and that "He turned out to be a liar and no fugitive and was so announced shortly after in the Anti-Slavery papers." Another who once helped a fugitive on his way to Canada admitted, "this was the first and only time I came in personal contact with the Underground Railroad." A resident of Bloomfield, Indiana, recalled: "The underground railroad was not in operation in this part of Indiana." A resident of Bond County, Illinois, said that fugitive slaves were not unknown there in ante bellum times, but that they were not very numerous and "there was no particular need of an underground R.R." An Ohio resident who considered himself an underground railroad

[47] Milwaukee *Daily Free Democrat,* October 31, 1859.
[48] *Richmond Enquirer,* December 30, 1859.
[49] Milwaukee *Daily Free Democrat,* October 20, 1859.

operator admitted that only about half a dozen persons had come under his care during his antislavery career. Still another Ohioan said: "As to the underground railroad operations I did not have much opportunity to aid runaways as but few passed through Warren," where he lived.[50]

New England abolitionists had similar comments. A veteran of the antislavery struggle recalled, "New England was rather out of the regular line of communication." In Maine, where he had lived prior to 1846, he said, "it was extremely rare for any fugitive slave to be seen." He later saw more in eastern Massachusetts but "still in comparatively small numbers." Another Massachusetts abolitionist said in later years that he "occasionally piloted a colored man" two and a half miles from his father's to his brother's house. There were a good number of people in Hanover County, Connecticut, who would have been glad to help fugitives, said another former antislavery worker, but they had little "opportunity to do personal work for this class." He could recall only two fugitives ever having stopped in the town. One was helped on to Canada, and the other remained in Connecticut and worked there for a number of years. In 1856 a Covenanter abolitionist in Vermont lamented to William Still that he heard nothing from the underground railroad. "You are probably not aware," he said, "that fugitives are never seen here. Indeed the one half of the people have never seen more than a half-dozen of colored people."[51]

[50] Richard Cordley, *Pioneer Days in Kansas* (Boston, 1903), 135; Edward L. Pierce to Wilbur H. Siebert, March 21, 1893, in scrapbook "The Underground Railroad in Massachusetts, vol. 1," E. H. C. Cavins to Siebert, December 5, 1895, in scrapbook "The Underground Railroad in Indiana, vol. 1," W. S. Gale to Siebert, January 21, 1896, in scrapbook "The Underground Railroad in Indiana, vol. 2," N. A. Hunt to Siebert, February 12, 1896, in scrapbook "The Underground Railroad in Indiana, vol. 1," N. D. Rose to Siebert, September 24, 1894, in scrapbook "The Underground Railroad in Ohio, vol. 5," B. F. Hoffman to Siebert, October 7, 1892, in scrapbook "The Underground Railroad in Ohio, vol. 10," Siebert Papers, Ohio Historical Society.

[51] Thomas T. Stone to Siebert, November 3, 1893, in scrapbook "The Underground Railroad in Massachusetts, vol. 2," Siebert Papers, Ohio Historical Society; Samuel H. Lee to Siebert, April 3, 1896, N. P. Bishop to Siebert, April 10, 1896, in scrapbook "The Underground Railroad in Connecticut," Siebert Papers, Houghton Library of Harvard University; the Rev. N. R. Johnston to William Still,

According to the testimony of an aged and ardent abolitionist who had lived in Lynn, Massachusetts, before the Civil
War, the organization he had belonged to found that its members had little opportunity for underground railroad service.
Some fugitives lived in the town, but there was little danger,
and life for the abolitionists was dull. To break the monotony,
the antislavery reformers would hold mock slave hunts with
some "burly member" impersonating the slave hunter, "and
others, each with his part assigned him met the hunter, and
notwithstanding his struggles the eight or ten stout fellows
who 'went for him' seized him and held him safely in charge."[52]
All of this was fun, but it lacked the excitement of a real slave
hunt. And, of course, such a lark was of little value to the
antislavery cause or to the fugitives.

The underground railroad activity described by these abolitionist veterans was of a haphazard nature, unlike the complex
organization brought to mind by the legendary institution. On
occasion, in the period before the Civil War, spokesmen for
the antislavery cause denied that such a conspiratorial network
existed. In 1842 a New York abolitionist editor ridiculed complaints published in southern papers that there was a "secret
combination, extending from the east bank of the Mississippi,
through Illinois to Michigan, by means of which slaves are
transported, clandestinely, to any place whither they desire to
go." The increase in escapes, said the reformer, probably reflected nothing more than "an experiment on the part of the
slaves, from curiosity, to *try* whether they *can* 'take care of
themselves.'" The next year a Chicagoan answered similar
charges that the abolitionists had a complete organization which
induced slaves to run away and then helped them on their way
to Canada. Though he admitted that the Illinois abolitionists
made it a matter of principle to aid any passing fugitives who
might need assistance, he denied any concerted action. "There

December 18, 1856, quoted in William Still, *The Underground Rail Road* (Philadelphia, 1872) , 587.
[52] George W. Putnam to Siebert, November 5, 1893, in scrapbook "The Underground Railroad in Massachusetts, vol. 1," Siebert Papers, Ohio Historical Society.

is no organization whose object is to induce slaves to escape," he insisted.[53]

Many years later, when any danger of revealing the underground's secrets was long past, some who had been prominent in the antislavery movement made similar statements. In 1896 Thomas Wentworth Higginson said: "There was *no* organization in Mass., answering properly to the usual description of the U.G.R.R." The aged abolitionist believed, however, that such an organization had existed in the West. But Oberlin College's President James H. Fairchild, a western abolitionist, said that the "work of helping fugitives, although quite effective, had no visible and little *real* organization." Fairchild was convinced that the most nearly organized systems were found at such points as Cincinnati, Philadelphia, and Wilmington, Delaware, where there were communities of free Negroes who would receive the fugitives and give them shelter for a time until arrangements could be made to send them on their way.[54]

The importance of free Negroes in such work is overlooked in legendary accounts. Yet it was known for the Negroes of some northern cities to arrange their own fugitive aid without consulting the antislavery people. In 1837 James G. Birney told Lewis Tappan about the escape of a man and wife from New Orleans to Cincinnati, and of their being put on the stage for Canada. He said, "Such matters are almost uniformly managed by the colored people. I know nothing of them generally till they are past."[55]

Certainly abolitionists frequently participated in such affairs, but they did not work with a large-scale, well-developed organization. Theirs was no "deep-laid scheme" to run away the

[53] *National Anti-Slavery Standard*, September 22, 1842; Chicago *Western Citizen*, December 28, 1843.

[54] Thomas Wentworth Higginson to Wilbur H. Siebert, July 24, 1896, February 5, 1893, in scrapbook "The Underground Railroad in Massachusetts, vol. 2," Siebert Papers, Houghton Library; James H. Fairchild, *The Underground Railroad* (Western Reserve Historical Society, *Tract* no. 87, vol. 4, Cleveland, 1895), 103–104.

[55] James G. Birney to Lewis Tappan, February 27, 1837, quoted in Dwight L. Dumond, ed., *Letters of James Gillespie Birney 1831–1857* (2 vols., New York, 1938), 1:376.

slaves. Rather it was a matter of a relatively small number of energetic individuals who organized vigilance committees and local underground railroad service. And, although they are forgotten in the legend, the free Negroes contributed much to the success of whatever organized aid was offered to fleeing slaves.

*Chapter Five*

# FRIENDS OF THE FUGITIVE

THE UNDERGROUND Railroad appears to be quite a flourishing institution," reported the *National Anti-Slavery Standard* in the fall of 1856. The occasion for the comment was the arrival of a notice from a Negro vigilance committee in Albany. The committee reported that in a period of ten months 287 fugitives had passed through the city on their way to Canada.[1] The story called attention to the contribution of free Negroes in the matter of assisting fugitive slaves. Significant, too, was its emphasis on a local vigilance committee, for the history of the underground railroad primarily concerns persons and events in local organizations. The existence of a number of locally systematized efforts to aid fugitive slaves has contributed to the legend of a national underground organization. Not all of the legend is false; some of it is well grounded in fact. At times and in some areas the underground railroad was indeed a flourishing institution.

Although the abolitionists could not agree about the relative importance to their cause of fugitive aid work, there were those among them who made a specialty of rendering assistance to fugitive slaves. Levi Coffin of Newport (Fountain City), Indiana, and later of Cincinnati, J. Miller McKim and William Still of the Philadelphia Vigilance Committee, and Thomas Garrett of Wilmington, Delaware, all enjoyed a well-deserved reputation for underground railroad service. Some others within the abolitionist ranks also gained special distinction for such activity. When Lydia Maria Child wanted to assure a warm welcome in Boston for Joseph Carpenter and his wife, she reminded William Lloyd Garrison of their record in helping fugitive slaves. "You know what a thorough abolitionist Joseph has been for thirty years," she said, "and what regiments of fugitives he has sheltered."[2]

For more than twenty years, Levi Coffin lived at Newport, Indiana, and while there he enlisted a number of antislavery workers in fugitive aid work. Later he helped organize a similar group in Cincinnati. Both communities had sheltered fugitives before Coffin's arrival, and in both places the work had been done largely by free Negroes. When he moved to Newport in 1826, Coffin learned that fugitives often went through the town and usually stopped with Negroes, who were not very skillful in hiding them and sending them on to Canada. Coffin organized the work and assisted those who had previously done it. In Cincinnati, too, the Quaker abolitionist found "that the fugitives generally took refuge among the colored people." There, too, he soon decided that there were only "a few wise and careful managers among the colored people." The majority were too careless and a few could not be trusted; once again Coffin systematized the local work which had been done on a haphazard basis.[3]

The organized efforts of Levi Coffin and some neighboring antislavery sympathizers constituted, on a limited basis, what southern partisans viewed as part of a nationwide system for assisting fugitive slaves. To a great extent, stories of such activity provide the basis for the popular legend. Friends of the fugitive soon learned of Coffin's work. While he lived at Newport, slaves were conducted to his home from Cincinnati and Madison and Jeffersonville, Indiana. The "depots" were usually twenty-five or thirty miles apart. Coffin and his friends

[1] *National Anti-Slavery Standard,* November 8, 1856.
[2] Lydia Maria Child to William Lloyd Garrison, May 13, 1858, Garrison Papers, Boston Public Library.
[3] Levi Coffin, *Reminiscences of Levi Coffin, the Reputed President of the Underground Railroad* (2d ed., Cincinnati, 1880), 107–108, 297–98.

transported fugitives in wagons from one town to another, and on occasion they had to elude persons who were hunting the slaves in their care. They provided some of the ex-slaves with clothing and other necessities, and boarded them occasionally until they could be sent further north.[4]

Levi Coffin carried on much of his work openly. His reputation was widely known, and his home a center of antislavery activity which he made no effort to hide. He once took a woman fugitive to a Quaker meeting at West Elkton and chided one of his neighbors for speaking cautiously. Coffin asked if there was anyone in the village who would capture a slave. "If there is," he said, "hunt him up. . . . I think we could make an abolitionist of him." As popular sentiment on the slave question intensified, Coffin and the others found even less reason to keep their fugitive aid work secret. Years later he recalled that public opinion in his neighborhood became so strongly antislavery that he often kept fugitives at his house "openly, while preparing them for their journey to the North, without any fear of being molested."[5]

Levi Coffin met little opposition, even though he made it known that he would shelter and help as many runaway slaves as came to his house. He threatened anyone who molested him with legal prosecution, and as a bank director, he used his influence to curb some of the proslavery men in his neighborhood. Slave hunters and hired accomplices often passed through his town; although they knew him well, and knew he harbored slaves and helped them to escape, they never searched his premises or molested him in any way. As far as Coffin knew, none of the fugitives he aided on their way was captured or returned to slavery.[6]

In his reminiscences Levi Coffin suggests that the number of fugitives he assisted was very large. During his two decades of underground railroad service at Newport, he recalled, the num-

[4] Coffin, *Reminiscences,* 110–14.
[5] Coffin, *Reminiscences,* 206, 228–30.
[6] Coffin, *Reminiscences,* 116–18, 120.

ber "varied considerably in different years, but the annual
average was more than a hundred." In Cincinnati he was also
busy in the work. Mrs. Andrew H. Ernst, who was an active
leader in the Cincinnati fugitive sewing circle, told a friend that
fugitives went through Ohio "by hundreds in a year." In 1850
she reported that "from 6 hundred to a thousand pass through
our city annually."[7] Certainly the underground railroad as
operated by Levi Coffin for more than thirty-five years was a
flourishing institution.

The area around Wilmington, Delaware, and Philadelphia
was another one that was relatively well organized for underground railroad work. Thomas Garrett of Wilmington, some
antislavery Quaker farmers of Chester County, Pennsylvania,
and the members of the Philadelphia Vigilance Committee
were key persons in the area.[8] It was the interest and persever-
ance of Garrett that provided essential leadership for the
cause. He spared neither time nor expense, and threw himself
into underground railroad work with enthusiasm. In a number
of instances he assisted Harriet Tubman in her rescue adventures. Garrett's service was mostly a matter of sheltering fugitives, making arrangements for their transportation, and paying
necessary expenses.[9]

When possible, Thomas Garrett favored sending fugitives to
Chester and neighboring counties, where a group of Quakers
were active in the underground railroad.[10] Sometimes they
carried fugitives in farm wagons to other friendly farmers
farther north, and at other times to Philadelphia. Numerous
fugitives passed this way in relative safety, though even in this
area the activity was not quite so highly organized as the legend

[7] Coffin, *Reminiscences*, 113; Mrs. Andrew H. Ernst to Miss A. W. Weston,
June 18 [n.d.], July 28, 1850, Weston Papers, Boston Public Library.

[8] For a combined traditional and factual account of the underground railroad
in the region, see Robert C. Smedley, *History of the Underground Railroad in
Chester and the Neighboring Counties of Pennsylvania* (Lancaster, 1883).

[9] Thomas E. Drake, "Thomas Garrett, Quaker Abolitionist," in *Friends in Wilmington, 1738–1938* (Wilmington, Del., n.d.), 75–86.

[10] Thomas Garrett to Eliza Wigham, December 27, 1856, Cope Collection, Haverford College Library; "Reminiscences of Thomas Garrett," Garrett Scrapbook,
Historical Society of Delaware.

suggests. One of the active stations was Nathan Evans' farm in Williston, Chester County. Yet in October, 1842, his son, David Evans, recorded in his journal that when two fugitives, a man and woman, arrived, he "made considerable exertion to get a horse and dearborn to take them on but did not succeed." Two days later a young Negro transported the couple to another place. In July, 1844, Evans started out with two fugitives "but lost them before [they] got to [their] destination." Presumably the two ran away from their conductor. Some of the fugitives stayed on to work on the neighboring farms rather than travel further north.[11] Lindley Coates of Lancaster County sometimes carried fugitives to other stations and sometimes took them "a considerable distance and then directed [them] how and where to go." Others merely obtained the names of friends, and then proceeded alone, "taking their own chances." It was not unusual for the abolitionists of this neighborhood to send fugitives as regular passengers on the train for Philadelphia, where a member of the vigilance committee would await their arrival at the station. In the fall of 1855, William Still of the vigilance committee informed a Chester County abolitionist that someone would be sent to meet any fugitives they might send by rail to the city. Later some of the fugitives traveled on the train to New York.[12]

If the Philadelphia Vigilance Committee sometimes operated without the secrecy associated with the legendary underground railroad, Thomas Garrett's behavior was even more open. Like Levi Coffin, Garrett proudly proclaimed his antislavery views and made no attempt to hide his light under a bushel. In 1856 he informed an English friend that Delaware was an exception to the lack of freedom of speech and the press in the slave states. "There is almost as much anti-slavery feeling here as in Bos-

11 "Journal of David Evans, vol. 4, 1841–1844," entries for October, 1842, July, 1844, Chester County (Pa.) Historical Society.
12 Smedley, *History of the Underground Railroad*, 85; J. Miller McKim to R. D. Webb, May 23, 1856, Garrison Papers; William Still to E. F. Pennypacker, November 24, 1855, Pennypacker Papers, Friends Historical Library of Swarthmore College.

ton," he commented, "and quite as freely expressed." He also
claimed that, in one newspaper at least, he could publish anything he wished on the subject of slavery so long as he always
put his name on what he wrote.[13]

Garrett described his fugitive aid work in a number of letters
and usually mentioned the number of slaves he had assisted.
In November, 1856, for example, he boasted, "My slave list is
now 2038, still they go."[14] From time to time he openly announced in abolition meetings the large number of fugitives he
had helped to safety and to freedom.[15] So well known was Garrett's activity that the owners of several fugitives won verdicts
against him totaling nearly eight thousand dollars.[16]

By the time of the Civil War, Garrett claimed that his regis-
ter of fugitives totaled more than twenty-seven hundred, but
he did not say exactly how he arrived at the figure or how
much aid he had to extend to a runaway before he included him
in his statistics. Certainly he assisted many, and most of his fugitives would also have been included in any similar lists kept by
others in the area. Most estimates of the numbers of escaping
slaves who used the facilities of the underground railroad are
postwar guesses, but even contemporary records are difficult
to interpret. Daniel Gibbons of Lancaster County maintained
a record of his underground railroad contribution, yet even
with such a document as a basis for their statements, two authors differed on his total. William Still said that Gibbons
aided nine hundred fugitives, and Robert C. Smedley placed
the number at a thousand.[17] The discrepancy in this case is relatively slight, yet it indicates how difficult it is to be exact in the

[13] Garrett to Eliza Wigham, October 27, 1856, Cope Collection, Haverford College Library.
[14] Garrett to Joseph A. Dugdale, November 29, 1856, Dugdale Papers, Friends
Historical Library of Swarthmore College.
[15] *Liberator*, May 22, 1857; Marion L. Bjornson Reed, "The Underground Railroad in Delaware," thesis, University of Pennsylvania, 1928, 12–13.
[16] *Congressional Globe*, 33 Cong., 1 sess. (1854), 1789. The lawsuits were settled
by a compromise payment of only two thousand dollars, but in writing to an abolitionist friend about the case, Garrett gave no hint of the actual settlement.
Reed, "Underground Railroad in Delaware," 24–25.
[17] Drake, "Thomas Garrett," 83; William Still, *The Underground Rail Road*
(Philadelphia, 1872), 647; Smedley, *History of the Underground Railroad*, 56.

matter of the actual number of passengers on the underground railroad.

In Philadelphia, fugitives were received and aided by a vigilance committee, organized in 1838 by Robert Purvis, a free Negro, and other abolitionists. Apparently the committee even had the use of a secret room with a trapdoor, similar to the devices so often described in traditional accounts.[18] At times the Philadelphia line was also a flourishing institution. In 1839 a committee member wrote another abolitionist that the committee was doing more than the colonization society to send away slaves. Within about a month's time he had "sent ten or twelve 1000 dollars worth of that kind of goods to Victoria's domains," and he expected to send another twenty thousand dollars' worth in about a month. The optimistic reformer was convinced that if the South did not emancipate the slaves, they would all run out of Maryland and Virginia within three or four years.[19] Yet by 1850 the Philadelphia Vigilance Committee had virtually ceased to exist, and a new committee was not organized until 1852.

Some other communities pointed with pride to their reputations for offering a haven to fugitive slaves. When a pair of New England abolitionists visited Ohio in 1855, they reported to Garrison and his wife: "Here, we find ourselves in a thoroughly anti-slavery atmosphere. Salem, we are told, has the honor to be a place especially feared and hated by the South, as one from which it is useless to attempt the recovery of a fugitive slave."[20] Oberlin, with its large abolitionist population, had an even more distinctive reputation. Many stories of Oberlin adventures and thrilling escapes from slave hunters have been told, though only two open attempts to recapture fugitives were made between 1835 and 1860, and both of them failed.[21] There

[18] Smedley, *History of the Underground Railroad*, 356.
[19] Edward H. Coates to Mrs. M. W. Chapman, December 15, 1839, Weston Papers.
[20] Margaret Burleigh and Mary Grew to Mr. and Mrs. Garrison, August 5, 1855, Garrison Papers.
[21] James H. Fairchild, *The Underground Railroad* (Western Reserve Historical Society, *Tract* no. 87, vol. 4, Cleveland, 1895), 111–12.

is no question that many fugitives were assisted by Oberlinites to find their way to Canada and also that a number of fleeing bondsmen settled down to live in the Ohio town. The town's reputation in that respect was well known, and the abolitionists in Oberlin made no attempt to cover up their work. On New Year's Day, 1859, they announced in a meeting in the Oberlin College chapel that of the 340 Negroes living in Oberlin, 28 were fugitives from slavery. Such fugitives were often openly cared for in the homes of the Oberlin College faculty, and the arrival of former slaves in the town provided the students with an opportunity for a little diversion from their classes.[22]

Secrecy in aiding fugitives became even less important as the rift between the North and South deepened and more people became willing to assist runaways. Even before passage of the unpopular Fugitive Slave Act of 1850, fugitives were given aid freely and often with little or no real danger to them or their abetters. The bogus fugitives who rode the underground line illustrate this point. Impostors were not uncommon, and the abolitionists were frequently warned of their existence. In 1848 the *Liberator* exposed a girl who was traveling through New England, pretending to be a fugitive. The abolitionists thought it "high time to put a stop to her career." Several years later a New York abolition paper commented, "We hear very frequently of cases of imposture under pretence of having run away from slavery. Sympathy with fugitives is now so general that dishonest coloured persons often succeed in getting pretty liberal supplies of clothes and money without running any serious hazard of detection and exposure." In Rhode Island a Negro had "taken up the fugitive slave business" and was "driving it with considerable success." In 1857, readers of Garrison's paper were again cautioned "to be less credulous, and more searching, in every case where any one presents himself as a fugitive slave." They were urged to take special care "not to

---

[22] *Oberlin Students' Monthly*, February, 1859; Robert Samuel Fletcher, *A History of Oberlin College from Its Foundation through the Civil War* (2 vols., Oberlin, 1943), 1:397.

bestow liberal pecuniary aid, unless the case is fully authenticated."[23]

Some impostors asked for money to purchase themselves or to buy members of their families whom they pictured as victims of slavery. Just as actual fugitives often carried false credentials, so did their bogus counterparts frequently display forged letters and documents from well-known antislavery leaders. They also told vivid escape stories. One New England abolitionist gave refuge to a pretended fugitive who was actually an escapee from the New York State Prison. The man "made himself very interesting and agreeable . . . by his stories of southern life, by his elegant manners, and especially by his great desire to learn [the New Englander's] ideas about right and wrong, and for improvement of himself in all directions."[24]

Beginning in the 1830's, a number of Negro organizations offered aid to fugitive slaves, though with much less publicity than attended the activities of abolitionist groups. A New York Committee of Vigilance, organized by free Negroes in 1835, had no connection with any antislavery society but extended help to "persons arriving from the South" and worked to prevent the kidnapping of free persons into slavery. In 1837 the committee reported that it had protected a total of 335 persons from slavery. David Ruggles, its secretary, was an unusually competent person. Samuel J. May, a Syracuse abolitionist, later credited Ruggles with assisting in the escapes of more than six hundred slaves.[25]

Late in 1845 a group of New England Negroes formed a freedom association and announced its purpose in the columns of the *Liberator*. The association's object was "to extend a helping hand to all who may bid adieu to whips and chains, and

---

[23] *Liberator*, October 13, 1848, June 25, 1852, December 25, 1857; *National Anti-Slavery Standard*, July 14, 1855.

[24] Elizabeth Buffum Chace, "My Anti-Slavery Reminiscences," in *Two Quaker Sisters* (New York, 1937), 164.

[25] "The First Annual Report of the New York Committee of Vigilance, for the year 1837," reprinted in Herbert Aptheker, ed., *A Documentary History of the Negro People in the United States* (New York, 1951), 162–63; Charles H. Wesley, "The Negroes of New York in the Emancipation Movement," *Journal of Negro History*, 24:86–87 (January, 1939).

by the welcome light of the North Star, reach a haven where they can be protected from the grasp of the manstealer." The Negro friends of the fugitives opposed paying "one farthing to any slaveholder for the property they may claim in a human being." Their mission was rather "to succor those who claim property in themselves, and thereby acknowledge an independence of slavery." The notice also pointed out that a lack of means sometimes handicapped their work, and requested donations of money or clothing and information of places where fugitives might remain temporarily or permanently as the case might demand.[26]

Negro leaders also assisted fugitives by working with the white abolitionists on the vigilance committees they established. Frederick Douglass in Rochester, the Reverend J. W. Loguen and Samuel Ringgold Ward at Syracuse, Robert Purvis and William Still in Philadelphia, and Lewis Hayden in Boston were among the most active of the Negro underground railroad operators. Although much of their activity was of a less glamorous nature than the legendary institution brings to mind, all contributed labor and thought to the cause of helping the fleeing bondsmen.

The Fugitive Slave Law of 1850 stimulated some new activity on the part of northern Negroes. In Chicago they organized a police organization to protect themselves against "being brought back to bondage." The organization of seven divisions of six men each was to patrol the city in turns and "keep an eye out for interlopers."[27] A New York meeting of Negroes, mostly women, passed resolutions condemning the Fugitive Slave Law and counseled armed resistance to it. The chairman appointed a secret committee to assist any fugitives whose liberty might be endangered.[28]

The new Fugitive Slave Law seemed to pose a serious threat to the freedom of Negroes in the North, and some were panic

---

[26] Aptheker, ed., *Documentary History*, 253–54.
[27] Milwaukee *Daily Free Democrat*, October 12, 1850.
[28] *National Anti-Slavery Standard*, October 10, 1850.

stricken. Rumors of slave hunters spread, and Negroes were advised to carry arms. The first rendition under the law—that of James Hamlet in New York in the fall of 1850—seemed to confirm already existing fears, and the scare resulted in a mass migration to Canada. Rather large groups of Negroes left Pittsburgh, Cleveland, Boston, and other northern cities. Many of them had lived in the North for years, and some had been born free in the South or in the cities where they were residing. By the end of May, 1851, about four hundred Negroes had left Massachusetts for Canada.[29] Some of the underground railroad traditions probably derive from this migration of Negroes from the northern states to Canada, when opposition to the unpopular 1850 law found expression in aid to the refugees. But the Negroes involved had been living for a time in the North, and those who were fugitive slaves had probably received no such assistance in their original escapes.

Abolitionists viewed the exodus to Canada with mixed feelings. The antislavery politician Joshua Giddings said in Cleveland that if the fugitives reached British soil, they could not be returned to slavery, and that the United States courts recognized this. Sherman M. Booth, the Milwaukee abolitionist, commented in his newspaper, "If this is good *law,* we trust our various Railroads pointing toward Canada, will arrange special trains for taking all the fugitives to the lines, and having them washed free in the waters of the St. Lawrence—north side." Some antislavery people deplored the excessive excitement and tried to quiet the Negroes' fears. A Pennsylvania Quaker told his coworkers in abolitionism that he did not think the Negroes' danger "was much increased by this law and advised Friends to counsel them to quietness and forbearance." The Cleveland *True Democrat* believed the Negroes were "unnecessarily alarmed," and the Salem, Ohio, *Anti-Slavery Bugle*

[29] *Liberator,* October 4, 1850, February 14, 1851; Cleveland *Daily True Democrat,* October 1, 5, 1850; Milwaukee *Daily Free Democrat,* October 1, 22, 1850; Fred Landon, "The Negro Migration to Canada after 1850," *Journal of Negro History,* 5:26–27 (January, 1920) ; Theodore Parker Scrapbook, 64, Boston Public Library.

hoped no fugitive would leave that part of the country. They should rather arm themselves "and associate together for mutual protection." The Pennsylvania Abolition Society pointed out that public feeling was such that those who were legally free needed to be under little apprehension. The veteran abolitionist Thomas Garrett shared these views. He told Garrison, "I very much doubt, whether on the whole there will be more arrested under the new Law, than the Law, as it stood for years past, there are so many more, who feel an interest in affording them Shelter, and Protection."[30]

To guarantee that the fugitives would receive shelter and protection, antislavery sympathizers organized new vigilance committees. In some communities the earlier committees, organized by free Negroes or abolitionists, were defunct by 1850. Some had come into existence because of one or more cases of fugitive rendition and had died out after the excitement abated. In the wave of apprehension which followed passage of the Fugitive Slave Act, the new committees appeared in a number of northern cities. These committees and their activity doubtless contributed to the underground railroad legend, but much of their work was not carried on in secret and was of such a routine nature as would scarcely come to mind in connection with the mysterious route.

The Philadelphia committee was an important one, since it functioned in a section where there was some semblance of organized fugitive aid or underground railroad activity. By 1850 the original Philadelphia Vigilance Committee "had become disorganized and scattered," with its work falling on a few individuals whose irregular methods had caused "much dissatisfaction and complaint" among the abolitionists.[31] The new committee, organized in 1852, was more active than its

[30] Milwaukee *Daily Free Democrat*, October 17, 1850; David Evans Journal, entry for December 1, 1850, Chester County (Pa.) Historical Society; Salem, Ohio, *Anti-Slavery Bugle*, October 12, 1850, quoting Cleveland *Daily True Democrat*, and October 26, 1850; Washington *National Era*, November 21, 1850; Thomas Garrett to William Lloyd Garrison, December 5, 1850, Garrison Papers.
[31] Still, *Underground Rail Road*, 611.

predecessor. One of its agents, J. Miller McKim, wrote a New England friend of the cause that as a member of the committee he had "occasion to observe some of the finest specimens of native talent the country produces." The day before he wrote, said McKim, he had helped "20 able-bodied refugees who came away from a far Southern City in a body on the *Underground*." A few weeks earlier the committee had had sixteen at one time, four different groups from four different Quakers.[32] Providing financial aid to fugitives on the run appears to have been the main activity of the committee, which furnished funds to board fugitives with free Negro families, sometimes for as long as thirteen days but usually for shorter periods. It purchased shoes, clothing, medicine, and other necessary items for the former slaves. Occasionally the Philadelphia committee advertised antislavery meetings in the press, and once it spent twenty dollars for handbills and other expenses connected with a meeting. In nearly all instances the committee spent money in small amounts rather than large; very few of the items in the financial records were for more than five dollars. The committee's journal from December, 1852, to February, 1857, contains a record of approximately 495 fugitives it assisted. William Still's published account, covering eight years, lists approximately eight hundred fugitives, including about sixty children.[33]

The Philadelphia Vigilance Committee questioned each of the fugitives it assisted. William Still, an employee of the Pennsylvania Anti-Slavery Society and chairman of the Acting Vigilance Committee, carefully recorded the essential facts, kept notes on all the more interesting cases, and preserved the organization's financial records and some of its correspondence. He later incorporated much of this material in his book, *The Underground Rail Road*. Still thought of the vigilance committee and the underground railroad as synonymous. In 1893 he said that his "doubtless were the only records that were kept

[32] J. Miller McKim to David Lee Child, November 22 [n.d.—probably 1855], David Lee Child Papers, Boston Public Library.
[33] Philadelphia Vigilance Committee Journal, 1852–1857, Pennsylvania Historical Society; Still, *Underground Rail Road*, *passim*.

of the U.G.R.R.," though when he preserved them, he never dreamed that they could be published in his lifetime.[34]

The Boston Vigilance Committee, organized in 1850 with a membership list of more than two hundred, was another of the more widely publicized organizations. Its activity provided the main ground for assuming that an underground railroad ran into the city. But much less of its work was directly related to traditional underground railroad activity than that of the Philadelphia committee. By June of 1854, Francis Jackson, the treasurer, reported that his records showed the names of 230 fugitives who had been assisted by the vigilance committee since the passage of the Fugitive Slave Law. Most of them had gone on to Canada. The Boston committee engaged in more propaganda work than did its Philadelphia counterpart. In April, 1851, it printed a warning to the Negroes of Boston to "Keep a Sharp Look Out for KIDNAPPERS, and have TOP EYE open." When Thomas Sims was returned to slavery from Boston, the committee asked clergymen throughout the state to pray for him during their services. They also circulated a petition requesting the removal of Joseph Eveleth, the sheriff of Suffolk County, for helping to send the bondsman back. Still another vigilance committee circular, directed to clergymen to be read in churches, asked for donations for the committee's work. The circular carefully pointed out that the vigilance committee did not countenance or counsel "a forcible resistance to the execution of the law."[35]

The Boston committee spent money to hire Faneuil Hall for an antislavery meeting, to place notices in the public press, and to pay expenses of abolitionist speakers. For some of the fugitives it provided transportation costs, fuel, medical attention, and even an artificial leg for a man who had had his foot

---

[34] William Still to Wilbur H. Siebert, November 18, 1893, in scrapbook "The Underground Railroad in Pennsylvania, vol. 3," Siebert Papers, Ohio Historical Society.

[35] Francis Jackson to Theodore Parker, June 11, 1854, printed notice entitled "Caution!!" April 24, 1851, Garrison Papers; unidentified newspaper clipping, "The Fugitive Requests Prayers," April 5, 1851, petition and covering letter, 1851, Finance Committee Circular, Theodore Parker Scrapbook, Boston Public Library.

crushed by railroad cars while he was fleeing north. Money also went from the committee treasury to pay for legal service. The Crafts were given two hundred and fifty dollars for passage to England in order to escape men who were hunting them in New England. Austin Bearse, a ship captain, was often paid for doing work for the committee, mostly transporting slaves from Boston harbor. But the committee did not sanction his plan to go to Virginia to resist the pilot boat which was searching vessels for fugitive slaves off the capes. In addition, the committee occasionally asked for volunteers to offer protection to fugitives or employment for those who were willing to stay. And there were many who remained in Boston. The names of a number of fugitives appear repeatedly in the committee's records over a period of months, indicating that they were not in any real danger of being pursued.[36]

After the passage of the Fugitive Slave Law of 1850, only two fugitives were actually returned to slavery from Boston, but those two cases and a few attempted renditions gave the committee plenty of opportunity for exciting action. The first fugitive arrested in Boston under the law was Fred Wilkins, known as Shadrach, who was seized in February, 1851. But Shadrach was rescued by an armed mob and sent on to Canada. The whole affair was carried out by sympathetic Negroes led by one who had no connection with the abolitionists. Although the vigilance committee had not participated in the rescue, its members found it an exciting diversion. According to Wendell Phillips, the abolitionists held meetings every night for some time after the rescue. In the long evening sessions they made plans to evade if they could not resist, watched the doors to see that no spies entered the room, and planned to protect their property in case they were convicted and fined. The whole affair reminded Phillips "of those foreign scenes which have

[36] Wilbur H. Siebert's copy of Record Book of Boston Vigilance Committee is in scrapbook "The Underground Railroad in Massachusetts, vol. 2," Siebert Papers, Ohio Historical Society; *National Anti-Slavery Standard*, February 26, 1859; Austin Bearse, *Reminiscences of Fugitive-Slave Law Days in Boston* (Boston, 1880), 34–39.

hitherto been known to us, transatlantic republicans, only in books." Yet, he said, "We enjoy ourselves richly and I doubt whether more laughing is done anywhere than in Anti-slavery parlours." After President Fillmore issued a special proclamation directing that those responsible for the rescue should be prosecuted, a number of people were arrested, but none of the Boston trials resulted in conviction.[37]

Several months later, Thomas Sims was returned to Georgia from Boston. In this case the committee refused to act on a plan to rescue the fugitive by force. The lack of a clearcut underground organization in the area is shown by the record of the Sims affair. Even the vigilance committee was indecisive and vacillating. The meetings, according to Thomas Wentworth Higginson, were "a disorderly convention, each man having his own plan or theory, perhaps stopping even for anecdote or disquisition, when the occasion required the utmost promptness of decision and the most unflinching unity in action." Higginson attributed the failure to act, in part, to the non-resistance beliefs of some of the members. Even Theodore Parker, thought one abolitionist, had "shrunk in the *wetting*," for his sermon on the Sims case was considerably milder than earlier ones.[38]

In May, 1854, Anthony Burns was arrested in Boston as a fugitive slave and placed in the courthouse. This time the vigilance committee decided to attempt a rescue, but because of conflicting plans and hasty organization, the rescue failed, and in the scuffle one of the United States marshal's special guards was killed. Theodore Parker, Thomas W. Higginson, and others were arrested, and for a few weeks there was great excitement in Boston. Higginson prepared himself stoically for "months and years in jail" as a protest against slavery, but the

[37] Thomas Wentworth Higginson, *Cheerful Yesterdays* (Boston, 1898), 135–36; Wendell Phillips to Elizabeth Pease, March 9, 1851, Garrison Papers; St. Louis *Daily Union*, March 8, 1851.
[38] Harold Schwartz, "Fugitive Slave Days in Boston," *New England Quarterly*, 27:197–201; Higginson, *Cheerful Yesterdays*, 145; [D. Weston] to A. W. Weston, April 15, 1851, Weston Papers.

charges against the abolitionists were dropped. Burns, on the other hand, was taken from Boston under heavy guard, amid the tolling of church bells. The whole affair had cost the United States, Massachusetts, and the slave's owner more than twenty thousand dollars.[39]

Abolitionists throughout the country followed the Burns case with great interest, and the proceedings helped publicize the Boston Vigilance Committee far and wide. An Albany anti-slavery worker wrote Garrison: "Gloriously goes on the work! See to it that you let not a *fact* or a *comment* escape you." If it took two months, he should publish the whole Burns story. The abolitionist continued: "Excuse me for being so stupid as to believe it furnishes far more important materials for History, than it would have furnished, had the man been rescued on Friday night. *Everything seems to work together for good to the Anti Slavery Cause.*" Garrison agreed that the affair prom-ised great good to the cause. The vigilance committee made the most of it and among other things printed and distributed a thousand copies of Theodore Parker's sermon on the rendition of Burns.[40] This, however, was the last rendition in the city and the last serious attempt at any.

Most of the excitement in Boston, then, was over three fugi-tives. Shadrach escaped to Canada with the assistance of local Negroes; Sims was returned to slavery after abolitionist groups failed to agree on rescue plans; and Burns was returned, despite popular opposition, after the failure of a poorly organized res-cue.[41]

In various other northern cities, groups of free Negroes, sometimes assisted by abolitionists, rescued alleged fugitives. In 1846 a mob of Negroes and abolitionists in Chicago rescued

[39] Thomas W. Higginson to Louisa Higginson, May 31, 1854, Thomas W. Hig-ginson Papers, Boston Public Library; Schwartz, "Fugitive Slave Days in Boston," 204–11.

[40] W. L. Crandall to Garrison, May 31, 1854, Mary Grew to Mrs. Garrison, June 10, 1854, Garrison Papers.

[41] Burns was purchased and freed a year after his rendition, and Sims after nearly a decade in slavery. Louis Filler, *The Crusade Against Slavery, 1830–1860* (New York, 1960) , 205.

a couple of runaways who had been apprehended by slave hunters from Missouri. In 1847 a mob of Negroes in Pittsburgh knocked down a slave hunter and two Virginia constables and scurried away with the slave they had arrested. They carried the fugitive to Ohio, and a Baltimore newspaper reported that the three slave hunters were arrested and charged with a "tumultous and riotous arrest of a slave." In 1849 a crowd of free Negroes in Cincinnati thwarted a master's attempt to recover a young fugitive slave who had been his daughter's servant.[42]

After 1850 the abolitionists took more initiative in such rescues, though sometimes they were planned and carried out mainly by free Negroes. In November, 1850, two fugitives in Ypsilanti, Michigan, were pursued by officers, but by the time the officers reached the house where the fugitives had been hiding, "the game had vamoosed, and the nicely concocted plans and labor was entirely lost." The following year a Kentuckian attempted to arrest a fugitive in Cincinnati. There was a scuffle on the street, and when things quieted down, the fugitive was not in sight. In 1852 a group of Negroes and whites in Sandusky, Ohio, prevented two slave hunters from taking fugitives off a boat heading for Canada. Another rescue occurred in New York after the United States commissioner there surrendered a fugitive slave to his master. "After the decision," reported a Richmond paper, "a scene of confusion ensued between the counsel on both sides, some saying the proceedings were right, and others the reverse. In the meantime the slave was hurried off."[43]

In a number of instances there were attempts at rescues when there was really no one to rescue. In the summer of 1855, for example, an abolitionist-led group persuaded a party of recently freed Negroes to leave a Virginian who was actually taking them to Ohio to buy them land and help them settle on

[42] Chicago *Western Citizen*, November 10, 1846; *Daily Richmond Enquirer*, April 21, 1847; *Frankfort* (Ky.) *Commonwealth*, December 11, 1849.
[43] Milwaukee *Daily Free Democrat*, November 26, 1850; *National Anti-Slavery Standard*, June 19, 1851, October 28, 1852; Richmond *Daily Enquirer*, April 6, 1852.

it. The antislavery people did not believe that the Negroes
were free. "They enticed them away from their friend; that is,
stole them away from themselves," reported a Louisville newspaper. In 1854 abolitionists in Syracuse received word that a
fugitive slave in the custody of a United States marshal on his
way to the South would arrive on the six-thirty train. The bells
were rung and two thousand people turned out to attack the
cars, only to find a Negro resident of their own city on the train,
but no fugitive. An excited Pittsburgh vigilance committee
rushed to the hotel room of a supposed slave hunter in that
city, but learned that their information was false and that the
occupant was none other than the man who had rescued Solomon Northrup from Louisiana. The *Pittsburgh Journal* commented, "It was rather mortifying that, after the years he had
spent in the anti-slavery cause, he should so suddenly find himself classed with so dishonourable a set."[44] A similar false alarm
excited the abolitionists in Syracuse, who organized a rescue
only to find that the "slave hunters" were merely two men from
Kentucky in town on other business. A Negro barber in Manchester, New Hampshire, was able on at least two occasions to
raise money to get to Canada on the pretext that his master
was hot on his heels. It was, said the local paper, "a humbug"
and a "desperate attempt . . . to get up a fugitive slave case"
in that city. The pretended fugitive got to Canada "with a
respectable surplus in his pocket." "This running away from
'supposed to be Southern gentlemen,' is likely to become a lu-
crative business," commented the editor.[45]

One of the most widely publicized rescues was the "Jerry Rescue" of Syracuse. In October, 1851, while the first antislavery
convention to be held in Syracuse was in session, William
Henry, or "Jerry," was arrested there as a fugitive slave. By

[44] *Louisville Journal,* June 26, 1855; Milwaukee *Daily Free Democrat,* June 1,
1854; *National Anti-Slavery Standard,* August 4, 1855, quoting *Pittsburgh Journal,*
and May 9, 1857.

[45] Items copied from Manchester, New Hampshire, *Union Democrat,* June 14,
21, 1854, in scrapbook "The Underground Railroad in New Hampshire," Wilbur H. Siebert Papers, Houghton Library of Harvard University.

that time popular sentiment against the Fugitive Slave Law was so strong that abolitionists were confident a rescue would be supported by public opinion. The vigilance committee decided to attempt to rescue Jerry, even though some members thought that the United States commissioner would probably free him rather than return him to slavery. While the fugitive's legal hearing was in progress, he was forcibly removed from the courtroom in a well-planned maneuver and then hidden in the city for several days until it was safe to send him on to Canada.[46]

A number of abolitionists and free Negroes were indicted in Federal court for their part in the Jerry rescue. The subsequent trials gave the antislavery workers plenty of opportunity for agitation. They held meetings supporting the rescue and denouncing the Fugitive Slave Law. Samuel J. May was jubilant. "The sentiment of our City and County is nobly right on the question which the rescue has raised," he said. "Men that I supposed cared not at all for the enslavement of our colored countrymen, have taken pains to express to me their detestation of the attempt to rob Jerry of his liberty." He regretted, however, that some who were indicted would dodge the issue and plead innocent. May favored open conflict. He told Garrison: "I have seen that it was necessary to bring people into direct conflict with the Government—that the Government may be made to understand that it has transcended its limits— and must recede." The first trial ended in acquittal, and the government dropped the other indictments, probably because of the success of the abolitionist propaganda campaign.[47]

There were a number of other well-publicized rescue cases in various parts of the North. Although the attention given these rescues helped popularize the idea that a conspiratorial underground organization networked the North, most of them were actually the result of impromptu action rather than any

[46] Cleveland *Daily True Democrat*, October 6, 1851; Samuel J. May, *Some Recollections of our Antislavery Conflict* (Boston, 1869) , 374–79.
[47] Samuel J. May to Charlotte G. Coffin, October 15, 1851, May to Garrison, November 23, 1851, Garrison Papers; May, *Recollections*, 380–82.

long-range planning. In 1851 a group of free Negroes in Christiana, Pennsylvania, sheltered a fugitive who was pursued by his master. In the ensuing scuffle, which came to be known as the Christiana Riot, some shots were fired and the master was fatally injured and his nephew seriously wounded. The fugitive escaped and went on to Canada. In 1854 a mob in Milwaukee rescued Joshua Glover, a runaway slave, from the jail where he was detained. Sherman M. Booth, the antislavery editor, headed the emergency vigilance committee which had been organized to prevent Glover's return to slavery. The subsequent arrest of Booth and others led to a series of involved legal disputes. In the fall of 1858 a group of several hundred, led mostly by Oberlin abolitionists including some Negroes, rescued a fugitive slave from the hands of a United States marshal in the nearby town of Wellington. Several months later the Federal government indicted thirty-seven of the alleged rescuers; the Oberlin-Wellington rescue cases became one of the most celebrated legal fights growing out of the Fugitive Slave Law.[48]

Though in some localities energetic organizers systematized the efforts to aid fugitive slaves, their organizations were local in character and their activities were often open, rather than secret. Abolitionists frequently took the initiative in these matters, especially after 1850, but they sometimes built on the groundwork laid by free Negroes, who played a more significant part in assisting fugitives than that with which legend credits them.

The rescues or attempted rescues of persons arrested as alleged slaves under the Fugitive Slave Law were few, though highly publicized. They probably seemed to the public at the time to support the current rumors of abolitionist conspiracy to transport slaves. Yet the actual records of these incidents

---

[48] *A History of the Trial of Castner Hanway and Others, for Treason, at Philadelphia in November, 1851* (Philadelphia, 1852), 33–38; Vroman Mason, "The Fugitive Slave Law in Wisconsin, with Reference to Nullification Sentiment," in *Proceedings of the State Historical Society of Wisconsin at its Forty-third Annual Meeting Held December 12, 1895* (Madison, 1896), 122–25; Jacob R. Shipherd, ed., *History of the Oberlin-Wellington Rescue* (Boston, 1859), 91.

give no evidence that they were connected with a general conspiracy, and some, like the Boston cases, betray a lack of the organization, discipline, and planning which would characterize a successful underground.

For the abolitionists, however, underground railroad activity —reputed or real—had a value apart from its practical value to the fugitive. The fugitive issue, especially after the passage of the controversial Fugitive Slave Act of 1850, fired the public imagination and gave the abolitionists a larger and more receptive audience than they had ever before enjoyed.

## Chapter Six

# THE FUGITIVE ISSUE

I F OHIO IS ever abolitionized," wrote Samuel May, Jr., "it will be by the fugitive slaves from Kentucky; their flight through the State, is the best lecture,—the pattering of their feet, that's the *talk*."[1] Despite differences within the movement on the value of fugitive aid work, many antislavery leaders came to recognize the dramatic potential of the fugitive as a means of reaching new converts and keeping the morale of the movement high. "There are only a few, unfortunately, who can understand an abstract idea or comprehend a general principle," wrote one of them. "To make our antislavery idea fully understood we must put legs on it."[2] Levi Coffin sometimes got contributions of money from known proslavery men after showing them the fugitive who was to be aided. Once when he sheltered a well-dressed fugitive woman and her handsome son, Coffin invited several prominent people who were not abolitionists to his house to see a "curiosity from the South." The ruse worked. The visitors were greatly surprised and could hardly believe it possible that such people were slaves, liable to be bought and sold. Coffin later introduced the two fugitives to a number of persons whom he wished "to interest in behalf of the poor slaves in bondage, as well as the fugitives who escaped."[3]

In 1846, when a fugitive who had escaped to Boston was retaken and returned to slavery, Samuel May, Jr., reported that some of the best men in Boston, "many of them not acting as

Abolitionists usually, being *exceedingly stirred,* indignant at the outrage, and scorning the base servility of a Boston merchant to the Southern Moloch, determined to call a public meeting." John Quincy Adams presided at the gathering, and strong demands were made on the Boston owners of the brig in which the slave had escaped to purchase his freedom. When slave hunters appeared in an Ohio town, the neighboring abolitionists reported that they were "glad to see indications of sympathy for the fugitives." Even those who had never been known as antislavery men appeared greatly concerned for the safety of the endangered ones.[4]

As the antislavery movement gained in popularity, fugitive slaves became a focal point for a number of abolitionist activities. The reformers constantly faced the problem of lagging interest and lukewarm followers. To overcome this kind of apathy, the leaders of the movement promoted antislavery meetings, petitions to Congress, the circulation of papers, tracts, and pamphlets, and activities in behalf of various related causes.[5] But the movement was generally lagging in the midforties, and local groups increasingly turned to the aid of fugitives as a more tangible and satisfying expression of their antislavery convictions.

"We are having glorious times here," wrote a Chicago abolitionist in 1846, "or have had for the last ten days, from the attempt to return two Fugitive Slaves." The mayor had called a meeting but the abolitionists took it over, passed resolutions, and sang stirring antislavery songs. "Everything we disliked was

[1] Undated note, May Papers, Boston Public Library.

[2] J. Miller McKim to Mrs. Maria W. Chapman, December 11, 1857, Weston Papers, Boston Public Library.

[3] Levi Coffin, *Reminiscences of Levi Coffin, the Reputed President of the Underground Railroad* (2d ed., Cincinnati, 1880), 323, 325–27, 411–12.

[4] Samuel May, Jr., to Dr. John Bishop Estlin, September 26, 1846, May Papers; Salem, Ohio, *Anti-Slavery Bugle,* December 25, 1846.

[5] "Why Do Abolitionists Grow Cold in Their Work?" in Salem, Ohio, *Anti-Slavery Bugle,* February 5, 1847; Henry Wilson, *History of the Rise and Fall of the Slave Power in America* (3 vols., Boston, 1872–1877), 2:566; Theodore Weld to Lewis Tappan, February 22, 1836, in Gilbert H. Barnes and Dwight L. Dumond, eds., *Letters of Theodore Dwight Weld, Angelina Grimké Weld and Sarah Grimké; 1822–1833* (2 vols., New York, 1934), 1:263.

voted down and everything we liked was voted up," he reported jubilantly. They had recently sent off "thirteen chattels," and they were confident that hundreds more were on their way and that there was a "fair prospect of plenty of business for the 'Underground Railway' for the winter."[6] Obviously that kind of activity was good for group morale, but the resolutions and songs were more characteristic of the activity of these local societies than was organized underground work. They held countless meetings, gathered contributions for fugitives and for the former slaves in Canada, recruited teachers for schools among the Canadian refugees, and sent money, food, and clothing to the northern Canaan. Some localities held bazaars and antislavery fairs for the benefit of fugitive slaves. In Cincinnati, women met weekly to sew and make coarse clothing for the fugitives who passed through that city.[7] And local abolition societies thrived on resolutions.[8] In 1842 the Illinois State Society resolved to entreat their fellow citizens "to extend the hand of kindness and hospitality in *all things necessary for his escape,* to every panting fugitive from the Southern Prison House, who may come within the reach of their benevolence." The same group resolved to refuse to testify if called to court to witness against anyone accused of aiding fugitives. The next year the group resolved that "to aid the slave catcher in the free States, is no better than to aid the kidnapper on the coast of Africa." The Putnam County, Illinois, society resolved in the summer of 1843 that their Negro brethren who were escap-

[6] James H. Collins to George W. Clark, November 7, 1846, in scrapbook "The Underground Railroad in Illinois, vol. 1," Wilbur H. Siebert Papers, Ohio Historical Society.

[7] *Liberator,* January 16, 1846; "Minutes of Committee for the Relief of Fugitives in Canada," November 11, December 7, 1850, Zebina Eastman Papers, Chicago Historical Society; Mrs. Andrew H. Ernst to Miss Weston, November 14, 1852, Weston Papers.

[8] Eli Thayer, whose colonization scheme for Kansas met with disapproval from some of the abolitionists, said that the Garrisonian abolitionists passed resolutions as a substitute for action. He called them "resolution builders," comparing them to the moundbuilders of prehistoric times. "In this industry they excelled, by far, all other people whether secular or religious," he said. "They never came any nearer to the attainment of an object than to pass a resolution about it." Eli Thayer, *A History of the Kansas Crusade: Its Friends and Its Foes* (New York, 1889), 88.

ing from bondage were "peculiarly entitled to the sympathy, advice, assistance and comfort of the abolitionists; the penal laws of the State of Illinois to the contrary notwithstanding." Meeting in the summer of 1849, the Western Anti-Slavery Society resolved that there was "cause for joy and exultation in the escape of so many slaves from their prison house, and in the change in public opinion" which rendered the "fugitive bondman comparatively safe from his blood thirsty pursuers." They were encouraged to persevere in their labors "until there shall be no spot in the Free States where the flying captive may not find relief and succor, and until our whole land shall be purified from its foulest curse, its most crying abomination."[9]

The dramatic value of the fugitive was of course greater when the bondsman himself could be exhibited, and this was done frequently at antislavery gatherings. On one occasion Garrison pointed out a whole row of escaped fugitives on the platform of an antislavery convention and "defied the whole South to reclaim them." Parker Pillsbury made good propaganda use in England of a young slave girl who had escaped to Liverpool stowed away among a cargo of cotton. After his lecture, Pillsbury introduced the girl and the Negro boatswain who had helped her. The incident, reported Pillsbury, "produced quite a thrilling sensation." William and Ellen Craft appeared at the Great London Exhibition of 1851. Before going to England, the Crafts had attended American antislavery meetings. They, too, produced a startling effect, partly because of Ellen's very light complexion. Samuel May, Jr., commented that "she was a living proof that Slavery has no prejudice against colour, and is as ready to enslave the whitest and the fairest as any other."[10]

[9] Minute Book of the Illinois Anti-Slavery Society, entries for May 26, 1842, June 7, 1843, Chicago Historical Society; typewritten copy of Putnam County, Illinois, Anti-Slavery Society minutes, July 4, 1843, in scrapbook "The Underground Railroad in Illinois, vol. 3," Siebert Papers, Ohio Historical Society; Minute Book of the Western Anti-Slavery Society, entry for June 20, 1849, Library of Congress.

[10] Thomas Wentworth Higginson, *Cheerful Yesterdays* (Boston, 1898), 135; *Liberator*, April 11, 1856; *National Anti-Slavery Standard*, July 24, 1851; Samuel May, Jr., to Dr. John Bishop Estlin, February 2, 1849, May Papers.

In the summer of 1848 an abolitionist from Pittsburgh attended the annual meeting of the Western Anti-Slavery Society in Salem, Ohio, with a very light former slave who was then his adopted daughter. She stood on the platform next to the daughter of Joshua R. Giddings, and it was impossible for the audience to distinguish between the two girls. Henry C. Wright took the opportunity to make an appeal to the audience which was to be long remembered. Several years later a fugitive who had recently served as a slave in Virginia was introduced to the same antislavery group. A vote was taken to determine how many in the large tent would help return him to slavery, and only one person had the temerity to answer in the affirmative. Marius Robinson then made an impassioned appeal to the assembly to do for the three million slaves who could not escape what they had indicated they were willing to do for the one before them. At another Ohio meeting a clergyman hid a fugitive slave family of father, mother, and four children behind a screen. At an appropriate moment he drew back the curtain saying: "There is a specimen of the fruits of the infernal system of slavery." The dramatic technique had the desired effect. "The audience were surprised and horror-stricken. Many eyes were filled with tears." The crowd then contributed generously, enough to send them "on their way rejoicing."[11]

Some few former slaves became professional fugitives, working as speakers and organizers for the antislavery cause. Abolitionist leaders recognized the special value of such people. In 1839 Theodore Weld commented, "the attention of abolitionists should be turned far more to the great importance of getting into the field intelligent colored men." Besides helping to combat prejudice, an eloquent Negro would "in all parts of the North draw larger audiences than if white, in most cases far larger." A Negro who was a fugitive was an even more effective drawing card. It was an unforgettable experience to hear of the horrors of slavery from one of its victims. The

[11] Western Anti-Slavery Society Minute Book, entries for August 17, 1848, August 27, 1854, Library of Congress; *National Anti-Slavery Standard*, August 25, 1855.

fugitive stories "produced a great effect on all who heard them," said one abolitionist. At a meeting where a number of fugitive slaves were speakers and afterward answered questions from the audience, an abolitionist reported, "Old friends of the slave were confirmed, and new converts made to the anti-slavery faith." A Wisconsin abolitionist attended a meeting in 1853 where a fugitive spoke to a house crowded with attentive listeners. He later commented in his diary, "I have no doubt but what good, much good will be done by this injured son of Africa and that he will be a means in God's hands, of assisting in the overthrow of the diabolical sin of American Slavery."[12]

Some of the fugitives were outstanding agitators. Henry Bibb gave a series of talks in Milwaukee in 1851, at one of which the large audience "cheered, clapped, stamped, laughed and wept, by turns." He vividly portrayed terrible scenes, telling, for example, how his own wife was tied up, stripped, and whipped by her drunken master while he himself begged vainly to be punished in her stead. After two evenings, Bibb had covered about half his personal narrative, and closed his second lecture "in the middle of a hen-coop, . . . fleeing from a slave trader, in the city of St. Louis." William Wells Brown also used a combination of wit and pathos when he lectured or gave a reading of one of his own antislavery dramas. One of Brown's plays ended with a fugitive's seeking aid to escape to Canada, and usually after this scene there was "scarcely a dry eye in the house."[13]

Lewis Clarke, another professional fugitive, "generally found large audiences, and a great desire to hear about slaves," as he traveled throughout New England. Henry Box Brown, who had been shipped to Philadelphia from Richmond, was also a

[12] Theodore Dwight Weld to Gerrit Smith, October 23, 1839, in Barnes and Dumond, eds., *Weld-Grimké Letters*, 2:811; James Freeman Clarke, *Anti-Slavery Days* (New York, 1883) , 92; *Liberator*, March 2, 1849; Dustin G. Cheever diary, entry for October 9, 1853, Dustin G. Cheever Papers, State Historical Society of Wisconsin.

[13] Milwaukee *Daily Free Democrat*, July 10, 1851; *National Anti-Slavery Standard*, October 20, 1855, April 19, 1856, May 9, 1857; *Liberator*, August 1, 1856.

useful addition to the fugitive speakers' bureau. One abolitionist reported soon after Brown reached the North that everyone who saw him was astonished. "They all glory in it," he said, "and I think it will have a strong tendency to cement the Anti Slavery feeling here." Brown traveled in the North and in Europe with an exhibit which included pictures of life in the South and the box in which he had made his daring escape. In England he had himself confined in the box and traveled in it from Bradford to Leeds, where he was taken out in the presence of spectators.[14]

Probably the best known of the fugitive speakers was the proud and aristocratic Frederick Douglass. He was talented both as a speaker and as an organizer. "The very look and bearing of Douglass are an irresistible logic against the oppression of his race," said James Russell Lowell. Like the other fugitives who became agitators, Douglass played on the emotions of his listeners, reminding them that he had been merely "a piece of property—a marketable commodity." He told them: "My back is scarred by the lash—that I could show you. I would I could make visible the wounds of this system upon my soul."[15]

The value to the antislavery movement of such talented fugitives, however, was sometimes offset by conflicts and misunderstandings in which some of them were involved. They were individualists who had been unable to tolerate slavery. For some of the same reasons, perhaps, they at times had difficulty in working with the abolitionist leaders, who were themselves strongminded and sometimes eccentric. Frederick Douglass was one of a number of Negro antislavery workers whose independent ways led to disagreements with some of his white coworkers

[14] *Narrative of the Sufferings of Lewis Clarke, . . . Dictated by Himself* (Boston, 1845), 60; Joseph Rickeston to Debora Weston, April 29, 1849, Weston Papers; *Liberator*, May 31, 1850; *National Anti-Slavery Standard*, June 19, 1851.

[15] Benjamin Quarles, *Frederick Douglass* (Washington, 1948), 19; *American Slavery, Report of a Public Meeting Held at Finsbury Chapel, Moorfields, to Receive Frederick Douglass, the American Slave, on Friday, May 22, 1846* (London, 1846), 8; *Tenth Annual Report of the Board of Managers of the Massachusetts Anti-Slavery Society, Presented January 26, 1842* (Boston, 1842), 18.

in the movement. Although he had been one of their most valuable organizers, Douglass broke completely with the Garrisonians in 1851 over the issue of political action. Personality clashes also played a part in the split. Abby K. Foster attended an antislavery meeting in the spring of 1852 specifically "to keep an eye on Douglass." "He is playing a double part in order to get aid from all parties," she confided to Garrison, "and our good honest friends have been induced to pour their money and sympathy without stint into his lap."[16] William Wells Brown appeared to his abolitionist friends to have too much personal ambition. According to Samuel May, Jr., Brown was a "very good fellow, of fair abilities," but he liked to make "popular and taking speeches," and kept a "careful eye upon his own benefit."[17] Henry Box Brown quarreled with his abolitionist associate while they were touring England. His partner reported that Brown had defrauded him of his share of the proceeds and had fallen into bad habits.[18]

Despite these problems, however, the abolition crusade made good use of the fugitives and their stories. Written accounts were almost as valuable as the appearance of a living fugitive. From time to time the *Liberator* published letters from former slaves to their masters.[19] Escape stories were used by antislavery speakers and published in annual reports and abolitionist newspapers. By 1836 twelve antislavery papers were publishing fugitive narratives.[20] The abolitionists emphasized the propaganda appeal of the fugitives and deplored the necessity, in some instances, for secrecy. A New Bedford abolitionist commented on the arrival of a fugitive in that town from Boston: "I should not think it at all safe though to publish his story,

---

[16] Charles H. Nichols, Jr., "A Study of the Slave Narrative," thesis, Brown University, 1949, 227–28; Benjamin Quarles, "The Breach Between Douglass and Garrison," *Journal of Negro History*, 23:150 (April, 1938); Abby K. Foster to William Lloyd Garrison, March 30, 1852, Garrison Papers, Boston Public Library.

[17] Samuel May, Jr., to Dr. John Bishop Estlin, May 21, 1849, May Papers.

[18] J. C. A. Smith to William Lloyd Garrison, August 6, 1851, Garrison Papers.

[19] Letters to the *Liberator* from fugitives are reprinted in Carter G. Woodson, ed., *The Mind of the Negro as Reflected in Letters Written during the Crisis 1800–1860* (Washington, 1926), 202–209, 213–19.

[20] Nichols, "Slave Narrative," 235.

which is a great pity, for there never was a prettier one." Angelina Grimké rejoiced to hear of another fugitive's escape, "tho' some of the pleasure was abridged by the caution to keep these things close." She suggested that when the man was safely on his way, his story should be published. "Such narratives are greatly needed," she said; "let it come burning from his own lips in England and publish it here; it must do good. Names, dates and facts will give additional credibility to it. Many a tale of romantic horror can the slaves tell."[21]

The first book-length slave narrative was Charles Ball's, published in 1836. Although it was supposed to have been prepared from the former bondsman's verbal narrative, it was highly fictionalized and a hoax.[22] James Williams' story, which had been dictated to John Greenleaf Whittier, was published two years later, but it was also questioned because of discrepancies in facts and finally was withdrawn.[23] Though there were some other counterfeit escape tales, most of the narratives were genuine. A steady stream of slave reminiscences followed the first few, and many of them reached large numbers of people. By 1849, eight thousand copies of William Wells Brown's narrative had been sold; by 1852, Josiah Henson's book had sold six thousand copies. Moses Roper's story ran into ten editions within nine years, and two years after publication, Solomon Northrup's book had sold twenty-seven thousand copies.[24] Frederick Douglass wrote three book-length autobiographies which went into numerous editions.[25]

The biographies of fugitive slaves were often edited and dis-

21 Debora Weston to Mrs. Maria W. Chapman, March 4, 1840, Weston Papers; Angelina Grimké to Theodore Weld, January 21, 1838, in Barnes and Dumond, eds., *Weld-Grimké Letters*, 2:525.

22 Nichols, "Slave Narrative," 26.

23 Lydia Maria Child and D. L. Child to Angelina and Theodore Weld, December 26, 1838, in Barnes and Dumond, eds., *Weld-Grimké Letters*, 2:732; Nichols, "Slave Narrative," 7.

24 Nichols, "Slave Narrative," 9, 235; Marion Wilson Starling, *The Slave Narrative: Its Place in American Literary History* (New York University, thesis abstract, New York, 1949), 5.

25 *Narrative of Frederick Douglass* (Boston, 1845); *My Bondage and My Freedom* (New York, 1855); *The Life and Times of Frederick Douglass* (Hartford, 1882).

tributed by antislavery workers. One reviewer of several of the narratives pointed out that they were "calculated to exert a very wide influence on public opinion." They contained "the *victim's* account of the workings of this great institution." The books were scattered over the whole North, and their accounts of what men had personally endured were effective. "Not only curiosity," the reviewer continued, "but a sense of justice, predisposes men to hear the testimony given by those who have suffered, and who have had few among their number to describe their suffering." Another writer was confident that the fugitive slave literature was "destined to be a powerful lever" which would abolitionize the free states. "Argument provokes argument, reason is met by sophistry; but narratives of slaves go right to the hearts of men," he said.[26]

Abolitionist groups who emphasized aid to fugitives found that, besides its value in reaching new converts, actual or alleged underground railroad activity was an excellent device for raising funds. Those who specialized in fugitive aid service frequently called upon sympathizers for funds to operate the underground line. In 1842 Joshua Coffin of the Philadelphia Vigilance Committee sent word to Boston of their rush business with fugitives. They had more fugitives than they could take care of, their funds were nearly exhausted, only a few actually knew the great expense of their operations, and couldn't the Boston group help? Five Bostonian antislavery workers answered the appeal, but their contributions totaled only twenty dollars. Other local groups periodically appealed for money on the basis of the large numbers of unfortunate fugitives they were helping to reach Canada. Some who contributed to the antislavery cause specifically asked that the money be used for such purposes.[27]

[26] Ephraim Peabody, "Narratives of Fugitive Slaves," in *Christian Examiner,* 47:64 (July, 1849); Nichols, "Slave Narrative," 241–42.

[27] Joshua Coffin to Mrs. Maria W. Chapman, September 26, 1842, Weston Papers; Levi Coffin to Francis Jackson, September 11, 1842, Stephen Myers to Jackson, May 22, 1858, Garrison Papers; "Circular to the Friends of Freedom," issued by the Albany Anti-Slavery Office, April–May, 1848, Garrison Papers; Lewis Tappan to Richard Littleboy, March 3, 1857, Lewis Tappan Letter Book, Library of Congress.

Many local groups made the most of fugitive aid to appeal for money, but none were as systematic in such appeals as the Kansas abolitionists. A regular series of letters from Kansas reached the East. In each of them the great work of the Kansas abolitionists was detailed. There a "certain Rail Road" was "in full blast," but the funds had nearly run out. The road was always active. One operator reached home after an eight-day trip during which he suffered more than he could describe. "My hands and feet are froze," he said, "my ears are about an inch thick and my cheek bones are distitute of skin, and what is worse I have only a fiew hours for rest to day, as I must start on the road again at night fall, to seek a place of safety for two of my black brethren that I have brought thus far from the land of bondage." In Kansas they had "many hair-bredth escapes, considerable fighting, and some interesting conversation."[28] Always there was the appeal for cash. The desired money, of course, would be spent "economically in carrying forward the irrepressible conflict." The Kansas letters all followed this pattern, even though written by different persons.[29]

Though some attacked fugitive aid as irrelevant to the issue of abolition, others—even J. Miller McKim, who cautioned against overemphasizing work with fugitives—argued that it would contribute to the ultimate emancipation of all the slaves. "I rejoice in their multiplying escapes," McKim wrote, "not simply or mainly because of the individual victims who are thereby rescued from bondage,—though this is no small gain to humanity—but because of the moral influence they exert upon the whole slave system, and the evidence they afford of a change going on in public sentiment."

McKim believed that slave escapes greatly weakened the "tenure by which slave property" was held. Chattels, "even when but partially enlightened," were "a very uncertain sort of

[28] J. E. Stewart to Thaddeus Hyatt, December 20, 1859, Stewart Papers, Hyatt Collection, Kansas Historical Society.
[29] Samuel F. Tappan to Thomas W. Higginson, January 24, 1858, April 17, 1859, Thomas W. Higginson Papers, Kansas Historical Society; E. Mite to "My Dear Friend," December 28, 1858, Weston Papers; John Doy to Samuel May, Jr., January, 1859, May Papers.

possession." The public opinion of the North did not hinder their flight, and even in the South, white men gave aid to fugitives. All these symptoms promised that the country was moving toward emancipation "with accelerated speed." Border slaves were uncertain property, and the "border" itself was every year reaching farther into the South. The process would continue until it made things "absolutely unbearable" for the slaveholder and literally forced states into emancipation. McKim was convinced that former slaves were in communication with others still in slavery, and that when those who had such information in Virginia, Maryland, and North Carolina were sold south, they became "missionaries—apostles of Freedom—preachers of treason and agents for the Underground railroad."[30]

Other abolitionists attributed the reputed increase in successful escapes to the influence of antislavery agitation. Gerrit Smith, speaking to a New York State abolition convention in 1842, said: "We rejoice, with all our hearts, in the rapid multiplication of escapes from the house of bondage. There are now a thousand a year, a rate more than five times as great as that before the anti slavery effort." In 1850 the Massachusetts Anti-Slavery Society reported that the tide of fugitives had "continued to pour in a swelling flood, in spite of the masters." They felt that they could "point with pride to one of the triumphs of the Abolitionists." Where one slave had made a successful escape twenty years earlier, fifty were then making good their flight, they claimed. Recapture attempts were unheard of in New England. This state of things was produced, said the report, by the "Abolitionists and the Abolitionists only."[31]

Abolitionist emphasis on fugitive aid and the antislavery

[30] *The Liberty Bell. By Friends of Freedom* (Boston, 1858) , 325, 327; J. Miller McKim to Richard D. Webb, April 4, 1856, Garrison Papers.
[31] Gerrit Smith, "Address from the abolitionists to the slaves," delivered in January, 1842, and reprinted in *Gerrit Smith and the Vigilant Association of the City of New-York* (New York, 1860) , 24; typewritten copy of the Eighteenth Annual Report of the Massachusetts Anti-Slavery Society, January 23, 1850, in scrapbook "The Underground Railroad in Massachusetts, vol. 1," Siebert Papers, Ohio Historical Society.

propaganda which centered around fugitive slaves were not lost upon southern congressmen, and in the sectional struggle which raged in Congress the assertion of slaveholders' property rights eventually submerged the issue of states' rights itself; the more stringent Fugitive Slave Law was enacted as part of the compromise of 1850, and though it had little effect as a means of recovering fugitives, it soon became the focus of a national controversy of incalculable value to the abolition cause. The new law placed the South in the peculiar position of supporting a piece of legislation which actually enlarged the powers of the Federal government. The Charleston *Mercury* recognized the inconsistency. "In the urgency of our contest with an aggressive adversary," commented the *Mercury* editorially, "we lose the landmarks of principle—to obtain an illusive triumph, we press the Government to assume a power not conferred by the instrument of its creation."[32]

Many Northerners objected to the Fugitive Slave Law for similar reasons. They did not favor extending the power of the Federal government, especially for the purpose of protecting the slave property of the South. Furthermore, the law seemed a threat to civil liberties. It denied jury trials to the fugitives and provided for a fine and imprisonment for any person who refused to assist in the arrest of a slave. Fugitive Slave Law incidents and the uses abolitionists made of them contributed immensely to the growing antislavery sentiment in the North.[33]

Actually, the Fugitive Slave Law had little to do with the problem of recovering fugitive slaves. The act had no meaning except as a factor in the sectional struggle for power. It was, as the *Richmond Whig* stated, "a HARSH MEASURE—better calculated to inflame and exasperate sectional feeling, and endanger the security of slave property, than to produce any salutary results."[34] But many Southerners came to look upon

[32] *National Anti-Slavery Standard*, October 6, 1855, quoting Charleston *Mercury*.
[33] Russel B. Nye, *Fettered Freedom: Civil Liberties and the Slavery Controversy 1830–1860* (East Lansing, Michigan, 1949), 197–216.
[34] *Daily Richmond Enquirer*, October 9, 1852, quoting *Richmond Whig*.

the acceptance of the Fugitive Slave Law as a test of the compromise, and those north and south who defended the compromise itself pointed out that the significance of the law was not a matter of its practical results, but of the principle implied in its enactment. A contributor to *Brownson's Boston Quarterly Review* contended that Southerners did not insist on the law and its enforcement "for the sake of a few dozen runaway slaves" which generally cost more to recover than they were worth. Feeling was often strongest, he pointed out, in the states where slaves seldom made their escape. They insisted on the law because "in executing it we give them assurance that we are willing and able to abide by our constitutional engagements, and are not disposed to abuse the power of the federal government, now passing, once for all, into our hands." Southern comments show that he was right. An editorial in a Wilmington newspaper asserted that the Fugitive Slave Law was as much designed to recognize the right of slaveowners to reclaim their runaway slaves as to enforce that right. "The number of slaves escaping from the South is inconsiderable," the writer continued, "and that the number of fugitives remaining at the North has been greatly exaggerated, may be inferred from the fact that so few arrests have been made." It was not the great value of property annually lost through runaways that made the South demand the law, "but it was for the purpose of declaring and establishing its constitutional rights."[35]

The abolitionists, too, recognized that the real issue of the Fugitive Slave Law was not the rendition of runaway slaves. In 1856 Charles Francis Adams sent a letter to be read at the Syracuse celebration of the Jerry Rescue in which he asserted that the law "was not contrived simply for the mere recovery of escaping slaves. Its purpose was wider and deeper. It was to gauge the depth to which the people of the United States would consent to pledge themselves to uphold a system which they abhorred." In 1855 another antislavery speaker asserted that

---

[35] *National Anti-Slavery Standard*, August 28, 1851, quoting *Brownson's Quarterly Review;* Wilmington *Delaware State Journal*, April 1, 1851.

with the passage of the Fugitive Slave Law, slavery "commenced showing itself out on the surface" and that the law helped tens of thousands to see that "freedom and slavery can no more exist together than truth and falsehood." Political abolitionists in a convention the same year stated: "The infamous Fugitive Slave Bill is a reproduction, on the soil of Massachussets, New York, and Ohio, of the most diabolical features of the slave code, and that, too, under the Federal authority."[36]

If the Fugitive Slave Law was ineffective as a device for recovering fugitives, its failure was even more conspicuous as a compromise measure expected to moderate sectional strife and revive southern confidence in the government. In 1854 South Carolina's Senator Andrew P. Butler said he had never had any great confidence in the enactment, but that there would have been no need for such a law had the states performed their constitutional duty in relation to returning fugitives. Congressman W. O. Goode of Virginia said the Fugitive Slave Law only gave the North an opportunity to display an "insulting violation of plighted faith, and to outrage the rights of the South by an utter disregard of all social, moral, religious, legal, and constitutional obligation." John A. Quitman insisted that the Fugitive Slave Law had been "permitted to become a law as a blind to hide the vast sacrifices demanded of the South."[37]

Despite the outcries from North and South, however, all the clamor over fugitive slaves and their abetters actually concerned very few persons.[38] In 1852 the Salem, Ohio, *Anti-Slavery Bugle* commented on the failure of the Federal government to prosecute under the act in two cases in Massachusetts

[36] *National Anti-Slavery Standard*, June 16, 1855, November 15, 1856; "Address of the Convention of Radical Political Abolitionists," in *Proceedings of the Convention . . . Held at Syracuse, New York, June 26th, 27th, and 28th, 1855* (New York, 1856), 31–32.

[37] *Congressional Globe*, 33 Cong., 1 sess. (1854), pt. 2, 1516, and 35 Cong., 1 sess. (1858), App., 509; John A. Quitman to C. S. Tarpley and others, July 17, 1852, in John F. H. Claiborne, *Life and Correspondence of John A. Quitman* (2 vols., New York, 1860), 2:170.

[38] Henry Harrison Simms, *A Decade of Sectional Controversy, 1851–1861* (Chapel Hill, N.C., 1942), 118.

and New York. "Frequent repetition of this farce," thought
the *Bugle's* editor, would be "about the best means to make the
law and the institution it was designed to support, abhorred
as it should be." Several months later the same paper alleged
that "not even one of the thousands who have refused obedience to this law, has yet been condemned."[39] Actually, there
were probably not more than a dozen cases prosecuted under
the act during its fourteen-year existence, although in some of
those cases there were a number of defendants.

By the spring of 1853 about fifty Negroes had been reported
arrested as fugitives throughout the northern states. The number was so small that the Massachusetts Anti-Slavery Society was
more than ever convinced that the act, like the other compromise measures, "was but an electioneering trick, not designed
nor expected to be of material advantage to the Slaveholders."
It was passed so that the politicians would get the South's support and was meant "rather as a homage to the Slave Power
than as a Remedy from which intelligent Slaveholders hoped
for much relief from the flight to which this form of riches was
peculiarly exposed."[40]

In 1856, Samuel May, Jr., published an impressively documented pamphlet entitled *The Fugitive Slave Law and Its
Victims*. A revised and enlarged edition appeared in 1861.
Drawing material from both northern and southern newspapers, May listed all the atrocities and crimes which he could
directly or indirectly relate to the law and its working. Although padded with much irrelevant material, the pamphlet
reveals the sparse use which was made of the law in the decade
between its passage and May's 1861 edition. Altogether, slightly
more than two hundred people were remanded to slavery in that
time, not all of whom were technically arrested under the act.
Of those arrested, about thirty were freed by the courts, mostly

[39] Salem, Ohio, *Anti-Slavery Bugle*, November 6, 1852, March 19, 1853.
[40] Salem, Ohio, *Anti-Slavery Bugle*, March 19, 1853; *Twenty-first Annual Report
Presented to the Massachusetts Anti-Slavery Society, by Its Board of Managers,
January 26, 1853* (Boston, 1853) , 43.

because of mistaken identity, and about fifteen were rescued or escaped without assistance. May also listed about sixty cases of kidnapping of free Negroes, of whom about a third escaped or were later freed. It is impossible to discover what disposition was made of some of the cases mentioned by May, and others are difficult to classify. Nevertheless, the booklet reveals in striking fashion that for practical purposes the Fugitive Slave Law had very little value. The small number of fugitive rescues also points up the lack of any centralized, aggressive underground railroad system.[41]

But the small number of fugitives returned under the law and the even smaller number of prosecutions did not make the issue less effective. Nothing served the abolition agitators better than the "infamous law," and they recognized its value. "The Fug. Slave Bill is awakening the country to the horrors of slavery & creating widespread sympathy for the slaves," said Lewis Tappan in 1851. Horace Greeley's *New York Tribune* was convinced that the act was "a very bad investment for slaveholders," for it "produced a wide and powerful feeling among all classes averse to the institution itself." Frederick Douglass said, "The Fugitive Slave Bill has especially been of positive service to the anti-slavery movement." It illustrated the "horrible character of slavery toward the slave, . . . revealed the arrogant and overbearing spirit of the slave States towards the free States," and produced a "spirit of manly resistance" among the Negroes. The American Anti-Slavery Society, in its annual report for 1856, commented: "If the Fugitive Slave Act of 1850 has been a successful assertion of arbitrary power in almost every instance in which it has been exerted, so has it also served to bring the system of Slavery, in its undisguised de-

---

[41] Samuel May, Jr., *The Fugitive Slave Law and Its Victims* (*Anti-Slavery Tracts*, n.s., no. 15, rev. and enl. ed., New York, 1861). Theodore Parker's biographer says that more than two hundred arrests of alleged fugitive slaves were made from the passage of the 1850 law until the middle of 1856. A dozen of those proved their freedom in court and an additional half dozen were rescued. He gives no documentation for his statistics. John Weiss, *Life and Correspondence of Theodore Parker* (2 vols., New York, 1864), 2:93.

formity, with all its sorrows and cruelties, home to the people of the North, as it had never been brought home before."[42]

The various slave rescues helped to keep this dramatic issue alive. For several years the commemoration of the Jerry Rescue was an annual event with the Syracuse abolitionists. When planning the first such celebration, Samuel J. May asked Garrison and Wendell Phillips to attend and to speak if at all possible. "We are determined to make a great occasion of that anniversary," he said, "and we want to have here all the great guns of the Anti-Slavery battery." He wanted Garrison to help them "to give a suitable expression of the sentiments of liberty, hatred of oppression, and determination to withstand the fugitive Slave law, as it is called." The leaflet announcing the celebration said that the rescue "was the trumpet peal to the Sons of Liberty throughout the world. . . . It was the heroism of the Right. It stirred the hearts, and quickened the pulse, of the Friends of Freedom throughout America; and it is fitting that it should be commemorated, in congratulations, in rejoicings, in exultation, in argument and eloquence and song." The anniversary meeting was held in the newly completed rotunda of the New York Central Railroad. Gerrit Smith and Garrison were there, and other notables of the antislavery cause sent greetings. Theodore Parker wrote: "In a time of trial, your townsmen stood the rack." He congratulated the rescuers and said: "Do it continually, till the American Government shall understand that though they make wicked statutes in the name of 'Union,' " the people "will violate any such wicked device, and bring it to nought."[43]

[42] Lewis Tappan to (illegible), September 4, 1851, Lewis Tappan Letter Book, Library of Congress; *National Anti-Slavery Standard*, July 2, 1853, quoting New York *Tribune;* Frederick Douglass, *The Anti-Slavery Movement. A Lecture by Frederick Douglass, Before the Rochester Ladies' Anti-Slavery Society* (Rochester, 1855) , 42–43; *Annual Report Presented to the American Anti-Slavery Society, by the Executive Committee, at the Annual Meeting, Held in New York, May 7, 1856* (New York, 1856) , 44.

[43] Samuel J. May to Garrison, August 5, September 21, 1852, Garrison Papers; *National Anti-Slavery Standard*, September 16, 1852; Samuel J. May, *Some Recollections of Our Antislavery Conflict* (Boston, 1869) , 384; Theodore Parker to Samuel J. May, September 25, 1852, reprinted in *National Anti-Slavery Standard*, October 28, 1852.

While such gatherings as the Jerry Rescue celebrations certainly had a profound influence on public opinion, the most significant propaganda item to be inspired by the Fugitive Slave Law of 1850 was a work of fiction, *Uncle Tom's Cabin.* Mrs. Stowe's novel was first published in the antislavery newspaper *National Era,* in installments running from June 5, 1851, to April 1, 1852. It appeared in book form in March, 1852, and its effect was immediate and unanticipated. Twenty thousand copies of the two-volume edition were printed within three weeks after publication. On the first three months' sales, the author realized more than ten thousand dollars, believed to be the largest royalty paid up to that time.[44] Three hundred thousand copies were printed the first year, and the book was soon translated into nearly every European language. Millions of copies eventually were printed, and the book's impact in molding opinion was indisputable. At least fourteen different proslavery novels answered its indictment of the institution.[45] Many more people were reached by the various dramatizations of the novel, and there was even a special version for southern audiences.[46]

The *Oberlin Evangelist,* which previously had crusaded against novel reading, assured its readers that there was no danger in reading *Uncle Tom's Cabin.* It gave only the truth about slavery without exaggeration, and it honored religion. The editor of the *Evangelist* was sure that it would have widespread influence because it was directed to the "heart and conscience of the nation." He put his finger on the secret of the novel's success. Although in many ways Mrs. Stowe did give a balanced picture of slavery, the book's appeal was directly to the emotions, and readers throughout the world were moved by it. Henry Wilson said its "pictures had been burned into the popular mind and heart by the very fervor of the genius that inspired and wrought them." Another abolitionist writer

[44] *Liberator,* April 9, July 16, 1852.
[45] Merle E. Curti, *The Growth of American Thought* (2d ed., New York, 1951), 446.
[46] Nichols, "Slave Narrative," 276; *Liberator,* March 3, 1854.

rejoiced that while legislators were opposing agitation, Mrs. Stowe "was preparing a firebrand which was to make it blaze with a new fury."[47] *Uncle Tom's Cabin* undoubtedly had its effect in popularizing the antislavery cause, and its dramatic escape episode has certainly become part of the legend of the underground railroad.

But the abolitionists also had valuable assets in the underground railroad martyrs among their own ranks. Even before the passage of the law of 1850, there were a few persons who had faced trial and imprisonment for giving aid to fugitives. Most of these had been prosecuted under various state laws in the South. Like the fugitives themselves, the freed martyrs could inject personal drama into public issues. They published their narratives, and were sought after as speakers and guests at antislavery meetings. After Jonathan Walker was released from a Florida jail, he published his narrative and toured several states as an antislavery speaker, producing a thrilling effect at the dramatic moment when he held up his branded hand for all to see. Whittier wrote a poem entitled *The Branded Hand*—"Its branded palm shall prophesy 'Salvation to the Slave!' "—and abolitionist papers published pictures of the brand with its history.[48]

After 1850, abolitionists gave still more publicity to the antislavery martyrs. In 1851 the government indicted thirty-eight abolitionists and free Negroes in Pennsylvania for their alleged participation in the Christiana rescue and riot. The charge was treason. When the first defendant was acquitted, the other cases were dropped, but the prosecution helped to excite public sympathy for the abolitionists. J. Miller McKim told Garrison, "the cause is in a very promising position just now. . . . These Treason Trials have been a great windfall." Another

[47] *Oberlin Evangelist*, May 10, 1852; James C. Malin, *The Nebraska Question, 1852-1854* (Lawrence, Kans., 1953) , 119; Wilson, *History of the Rise and Fall of the Slave Power in America*, 2:519; *Twenty-first Annual Report of the Massachusetts Anti-Slavery Society*, 53.

[48] *Liberator*, December 6, 1844, August 15, 1845, April 9, 1847, February 9, 1849; *Trial and Imprisonment of Jonathan Walker, at Pensacola, Florida, for Aiding Slaves to Escape from Bondage* (Boston, 1846) .

antislavery worker reported to Joshua Giddings, "The treason trials are making a great deal of talk here now, and thousands are ready to listen who have long been indifferent."[49]

By their insistence on a Federal confirmation of the right to hold and recover slave property, southern leaders in Congress presumably had hoped to crush the growing abolition movement by opposing to it the powers, both legal and moral, of the Federal government. But in so doing, they ended the isolation in which the abolitionists had labored as nonpolitical reformers. Astute antislavery leaders now made common cause with the diverse forces arrayed against the government and the party in power. The Milwaukee abolitionist editor, Sherman M. Booth, became engaged in a drawn-out legal duel with the government over his prosecution under the Fugitive Slave Law, and he turned the case to the advantage of the cause in numerous editorials appealing to sectional pride and states' rights sentiment among his readers. The Federal government, he charged, sought "to establish the law of Slavery and kidnapping on the free soil of Wisconsin" and to make it a slave state.[50] At one point Booth was freed on a writ of habeas corpus by the Wisconsin Supreme Court, which declared the Fugitive Slave Law unconstitutional. Another time he was rescued from prison by an antislavery mob. A Federal trial resulted in a sentence of a month in jail and a thousand-dollar fine plus costs. But the case dragged on in the courts until 1860, when Booth finally submitted to judicial defeat. Refusing to pay his fine, he faced an indeterminate period of imprisonment, but he forbade his friends to pay it for him, telling them "it would be far more creditable . . . and better for the cause" to give the money to his wife. Furthermore, he refused to request a presidential pardon, saying: "I think I am doing more here than I could out." But despite Booth's reluctance, he was pardoned by Presi-

---

[49] J. Miller McKim to Garrison, December 31, 1852, Garrison Papers; Oliver Johnson to Joshua Giddings, December 8, 1851, Giddings Papers, Ohio Historical Society; *A History of the Trial of Castner Hanway and Others, for Treason, at Philadelphia in November, 1851* (Philadelphia, 1852).
[50] Milwaukee *Daily Free Democrat*, March 16, 1854.

dent James Buchanan the day before Lincoln's inauguration.[51]

The Booth case brought forth speeches, resolutions, and mass meetings throughout Wisconsin and in many other northern communities. In Philadelphia, Passmore Williamson's case also provided grist for the antislavery mill and proved a morale builder for the abolitionists as well. Williamson, a Philadelphia Quaker, was arrested and charged with contempt of court because he refused to reveal the whereabouts of a fugitive whom he had helped persuade to leave her master. Williamson was in jail several months before his petition to have the contempt charges removed was heard and acted upon favorably by the court. In his prison cell the young martyr received congratulations from his coworkers. "I am glad you are deprived of your liberty," wrote a New Jersey abolitionist, and that "slavery has laid its hateful paw on a free, white, male citizen of pure blood." One abolitionist told Williamson, "I have reason to believe that there are some who almost envy your position however uncomfortable it may be for a short time." Charles Sumner saw in Williamson's imprisonment another indication of the madness which would precede the fall of the Slave Oligarchy. "Verily the day is at hand," he assured him, "when returning Justice shall once more bear sway. Then, among the Triumphs of Freedom, will be a reckoning with unjust judges." Lewis Tappan informed Williamson that it rejoiced "the friends of freedom" to know that he would not falter, "painful as it must be to be separated from [his] family." Thomas Wentworth Higginson said: "I bless God for you. We need many such." Three thousand members of the Western Anti-Slavery Society drafted a letter to Williamson informing him that his incarceration had taught the American people "that there is no safety for their own freedom while the slave power rules."[52]

[51] Vroman Mason, "The Fugitive Slave Law in Wisconsin, with Reference to Nullification Sentiment," in *Proceedings of the State Historical Society of Wisconsin at Its Forty-third Annual Meeting Held December 12, 1895* (Madison, 1896), 134; Sherman M. Booth to John Fox Potter, March 16, 1860, John Fox Potter Papers, State Historical Society of Wisconsin.

[52] *National Anti-Slavery Standard*, August 4, 1855; letters to Passmore Williamson from Herbert F. Gard, October 20, 1855, Henry Ferguson, October 13, 1855, Charles Sumner, August 11, 1855, Lewis Tappan, August 8, 1855, and Thomas W.

Three years later, when William M. Connelly was tried in Cincinnati for harboring a fugitive slave, the *Daily Enquirer* reported a rumor that the prosecution would "make very curious revelations with regard to the Underground Railroad, which is supposed to have done a large business here during the last two years." No such revelations were forthcoming, but the Connelly trial did make for lots of excitement in the Queen City. After a long trial in a packed courtroom, Connelly was sentenced to twenty days in prison and fined ten dollars. It was a brief term, but Connelly and his friends made the most of it. The events began with a series of sympathy demonstrations. Women of the antislavery movement carried strawberries and homemade pastries to the imprisoned Connelly. Arrangements were made with the jailer to have comfortable furniture in his cell and also to have good fare sent in to him. A stream of visitors went to the jail, including representatives of Methodist and Unitarian conferences meeting in Cincinnati during his brief ordeal.

The climax of the affair was to be a gala procession and torchlight parade to celebrate Connelly's release from jail. Those who planned the event, however, mistakenly thought that his sentence was to expire in the evening. When they learned that he would be released at noon, an emergency committee consulted Connelly and the jailer, both of whom agreed that he should be kept under lock and key until the proper release demonstration could take place. Even a drenching rain failed to dampen the spirits of the jubilant crowd. The German Turner society was prominent in the Connelly parade, which included a uniformed band and some highly decorated carriages bearing prominent local Republicans. The crowd went to Turner Hall, where Connelly told of his experiences and effectively discredited Stanley Matthews, the Democratic district attorney who had prosecuted him.[53]

---

Higginson, August 10, 1855, Williamson Scrapbook, Chester County (Pa.), Historical Society; Western Anti-Slavery Society Minute Book, August 26, 1855.

[53] Levi Coffin, *Reminiscences*, 587–88; *Liberator*, June 18, July 2, 1858; Cincinnati *Daily Enquirer*, May 5, 23, June 12, 1858; Selden Gale Lowrie, "Stanley Matthews," in *Dictionary of American Biography*. Matthews, who had previously

The antislavery faction of the new Republican party, as well as the nonpolitical abolitionists, used the Connelly case and other incidents for their own purposes. An increasing number of political uses were made of such events as the election of 1860 approached. Political overtones characterized the trial which grew out of the Oberlin-Wellington affair. In December, 1858, the Federal government indicted thirty-seven who had been involved in the rescue a few months earlier.[54] Sympathetic onlookers crowded the courtroom and cheered the defendants. Each of the groups involved attempted to use the case for its own advantage. The defendants, all antislavery Republicans, tried to discredit the Buchanan administration, to force the Republican party to become more openly abolitionist, and to arouse antislavery sentiment in general. The administration hoped to enforce the law and to discredit the Oberlin abolitionists. The rescuers and their supporters claimed that Democrats controlled the court and handpicked the jury. Mass demonstrations accompanied every legal move.[55] Lorain County brought kidnapping charges against the Kentuckians who had first taken the fugitive, and so paved the way for a compromise settlement. The Federal government made its legal point with several convictions, but the continued agitation which would have accompanied additional legal proceedings would only have served to embarrass the administration. None of the abolitionists served more than eighty-five days in prison; cases against those not yet tried were dropped through an agreement with Lorain County, which in turn dropped the kidnapping charges.[56] Thus the Federal authorities were released from the dilemma which an unfavorable public opinion had created.

---

been a Whig, felt the effects of the Connelly case for many years. Political opponents used the incident against him to defeat him as a candidate for Congress in 1876 and later opposed his appointment to the Supreme Court on the same grounds. He was finally permitted to sit in the court after 1881 despite the continued pressure of former abolitionists.

[54] *Annual Report of the American Anti-Slavery Society by the Executive Committee for the Year Ending May 1, 1859* (New York, 1860), 91–92.

[55] Robert Samuel Fletcher, *A History of Oberlin College from Its Foundation through the Civil War* (2 vols., Oberlin, 1943), 1:406–10.

[56] Jacob R. Shipherd, ed., *History of the Oberlin-Wellington Rescue* (Boston, 1859), 263.

While the Oberlin martyrs paced their cells in Cleveland jail, abolitionists and Republicans made good use of their imprisonment. Meetings were held in various northern cities. Thousands attended one in Cleveland, held in the jailyard itself. Joshua Giddings and Salmon P. Chase spoke, and four of the prisoners made stirring speeches from their cell windows. The orators denounced the Democratic administration, the Fugitive Slave Law, and the Dred Scott Decision. The Democrats were branded as "opposed to civil and religious liberty," and ladies in the audience were advised by one speaker to influence their men to vote against the slave power. They should tell their husbands and lovers, he advised, "to go to the polls and do their duty, then come back and claim their reward." The prisoners added to such efforts with *The Rescuer,* a newspaper which they published from their prison cells. In it they urged the Republicans to reject the "temporizing policy of the eleventh hour men" who were endeavoring to degrade the Republican party and render it as ineffectual as its Whig predecessor.[57]

Impressive ceremonies marked the return of the Oberlin prisoners. More than two thousand sympathizers met them. Bells rang triumphantly and bonfires lined the route to the church where three hundred more greeted them. Several of the heroic rescuers made brief speeches, and the Cleveland sheriff who had become their friend was introduced, made a short talk, and paid them high compliments. Even the jailer was introduced at the friendly gathering, and told the throng he had been happy to act as the rescuers' postmaster during their incarceration. The meeting lasted into the night. A collection was taken for relief of the prisoners and the choir sang the Marseillaise "with thrilling effect." Finally at midnight the gala event closed with the singing of the Doxology. With minor changes the whole procedure was repeated several weeks later when the last of the rescuers was released and returned to

[57] Shipherd, *Oberlin-Wellington Rescue,* 251, 256; Fletcher, *History of Oberlin College,* 1:410; *The Rescuer,* July 4, 1859, Oberlin College Library.

Oberlin. "God be thanked for Oberlin!" wrote an Ohio abolitionist. "She has fought the fight, and won the victory! and
won it for the whole country. All honor then to Oberlin."[58]

The Oberlin-Wellington affair and similar cases growing out
of the Fugitive Slave Law enabled the abolitionists to reach untold thousands previously impervious to their message, and the
opportunity of discrediting the Democratic administration effectively cemented the political alliance of abolitionists and Republicans. And among other things, the whole controversy
helped to build the reputation of the underground railroad.

In the popular legend of the underground, much of the
drama is provided by the determined pursuit of the fugitives.
Actually, however, those who escaped into the northern states
were not likely to be pursued. This aspect of the legend, perhaps more than any other, seems to be a direct reflection of the
propaganda battles of the sectional controversy.

Senator Walker Brooke of Mississippi said in 1852 that few
slaves escaped from his state and when they did, their masters
considered "the time, and trouble, and expense of recapturing
them as being more than they are worth." A writer in the
*North American Review* maintained that of the slaves who had
escaped between 1845 and 1850, no attempt had been made "to
reclaim them in more than one case out of a thousand."[59] Professional slave catchers advertised their services, but most of
them operated within the southern states, for pursuing fugitives
into the North was expensive and the value of a recaptured runaway was slight. Such individuals were sold if possible, and
usually traders were instructed to sell them outside the state
from which they had absconded. But they were not easy to sell
and almost invariably brought prices well below the current
market, for the runaway's potential influence on other slaves, as

[58] *National Anti-Slavery Standard,* July 16, 1859, quoting *Cleveland Herald,* and
July 30, 1859, quoting letter in *Ashtabula Sentinel.*
[59] *Congressional Globe,* 32 Cong., 1 sess. (1852), pt. 3, 1951; "The Action of
Congress on the California and Territorial Question," *North American Review,*
71:260 (July, 1850).

well as his own discontent and proven daring, made him un-
welcome to slaveholders. A newspaper in Atlanta, noting that
a large number of runaways had been sent south, remarked that
it was certain "they are not calculated to add either to the security of our firesides or the value of our present negro property."
Slave vendors guaranteed some slaves not to be habitual runaways, and if such a guarantee proved false, the sale could be
rescinded.[60]

After 1850, the pursuit of fugitive slaves became, like the
Fugitive Slave Law itself, more a symbolic than a practical matter. The recovery of a slave under the new law often cost many
times the market value of the runaway, and each rendition was
potentially a source of public controversy which might well end
in violence. It was estimated that the return of Thomas Sims to
Georgia cost his owner three thousand dollars and the government more than five thousand.[61] A Virginia slaveowner reported in 1859 that it cost him more than six hundred dollars to
recover a fugitive slave from Ohio.[62] One master, Edward Gor-
such, lost his life in the mob violence at Christiana, Pennsylvania, where he had gone in an attempt to return some of his
slaves to Virginia.[63]

Despite the small number of slaves actually pursued into the
North, abolitionists found the fugitive issue—and in particular
the Fugitive Slave Law of 1850—of enormous value in win-
ning sympathy for a once unpopular movement. Those fugitive slaves who joined the abolitionist ranks proved unusually
effective as speakers. The slave narratives, with their emphasis
on the harsher aspects of the institution, reached thousands of
readers. *Uncle Tom's Cabin* touched the emotions of millions. Many Northerners who had no interest in the abolition

[60] Ralph Betts Flanders, *Plantation Slavery in Georgia* (Chapel Hill, N.C.,
1933), 149, 216; *Liberator*, February 14, 1851, quoting an Atlanta, Ga., newspaper;
Edward Epps to Ziba B. Oakes, October 25, 1856, Oakes Papers, Boston Public Library; Catterall, *Judicial Cases*, 2:316, 531–32, 3:47, 371, 519, 560, 603.

[61] Richmond *Daily Dispatch*, March 27, 1852.

[62] Louisville *Daily Courier*, April 9, 1859.

[63] *Richmond Enquirer*, September 26, 1851.

movement joined the abolitionists in opposition to the Fugitive Slave Law, and the fugitive slave issue itself became not the practical but the psychological focus of the sectional controversy. Abolitionist propaganda, concentrated on this issue, helped to magnify in the public mind the number of escapes, the number of pursuits, and the drama of resistance to the law.

*Chapter Seven*

# THE ROOTS OF A LEGEND

THE LEGEND of the underground railroad began to take form in the period preceding the Civil War. Stories of the exploits of those abolitionists who actually assisted fugitive slaves were repeated by word of mouth and in antislavery publications, often with considerable embellishment. Nevertheless, the existence of such regionally organized assistance did give the legend a basis in fact. Repeatedly described, the exciting incidents seemed more numerous and more significant than they actually were. Distortion entered the picture in the ante bellum period because of repetition and exaggeration rather than pure fabrication of underground railroad adventures.

In addition to actual events, the legend of the underground railroad rests in part on the propaganda literature of the abolitionists and of their southern opponents. Publicity about the mysterious route first appeared in the 1840's and became more frequent in the decade after the passage of the Fugitive Slave Act of 1850. Persons willing to aid fugitives sometimes advertised in the abolition press, and there was little or no attempt to preserve the secrecy which is so often associated with the underground road. Spokesmen for the South found their own propaganda uses for underground railroad material, and their writings also contributed to the development of an exaggerated image of the underground railroad in the minds of many Americans.

As early as 1844, the Chicago *Western Citizen* carried an advertisement for the underground railroad.[1] In it G. W. Burke, who listed himself as "Superintendent," addressed a "Card" to the "friends of the underground Rail Road, in Jersey county, Illinois." Burke pointed out "that the U.R.R. is in excellent order. The station keepers and superintendents are all active and trust-worthy men, [and] *chattels* intrusted to their care will be forwarded with great care, and *unparalleled speed.*" About a month later the same paper published a cartoon captioned "Liberty Line" and showing the underground train with its cargo of happy ex-bondsmen on their way to Canada. Beneath the drawing appeared a humorous description of "the improved and splendid Locomotives" and "best style" passenger accommodations for those "who may wish to improve their health or circumstances, by a northern tour." J. Cross was listed as the road's proprietor. These were only the first of a number of such advertisements for underground railroad stations.[2]

In December, 1850, William Stedman wrote a letter to the editor of the Cleveland *Daily True Democrat* calling attention to the fact that he was the local agent for getting fugitives into Canada. From time to time the underground railroad committee of Cleveland held entertainments and dinners to raise money for assistance to fugitives. These, too, were advertised in the newspapers. Columbus abolitionists also publicized their fugitive aid work. In 1852 a Columbus paper carried a letter stating that the "underground railroad, and especially the express train, is doing a good business just now." It boasted of having "good and competent conductors," and added that it "would not be very safe for slave-catchers to get on the track

---

[1] Chicago *Western Citizen*, December 23, 1842, carried a story from Oswego, New York, concerning a fugitive slave who had escaped, then became ill and returned to the South. He refused to say where he had been, but when tortured, he said "that the abolitionists had a *railroad under ground* and that he started for it; but when he got there the 'trap-door' *was shut.*" Though there may have been earlier uses of the term, this was the earliest found.

[2] Chicago *Western Citizen*, June 6, July 13, 1844.

when the bell rings, at some of the depots in Northern Ohio."
In 1859 Columbus abolitionists openly announced a state meeting of underground railroad workers, which was really a gathering of appointed delegates of various Ohio antislavery societies. In the fall of the same year, eastern abolitionists published
in the antislavery press tentative plans for a national convention of "directors, agents and friends of the Underground Railroad."[3]

Other self-styled underground railroad conductors openly advertised their activity. The *National Anti-Slavery Standard* in
April, 1854, asserted that the editor of the Burlington, Vermont, *Tribune* had been violating the Fugitive Slave Law and
showed no signs of regret. He had published notices of the arrival and departure of fugitives on the "underground" and had
also published information for the benefit of slaveholders to
show that their slaves were safely in Canada. Stephen Meyers,
the "agent" for the underground railroad in Albany, gave information to the *New York Times* that in February, 1858, there
were thirty-six through passengers on the road, and declared
that quite a proportion of the "Southern emigration" was then
stopping in New York instead of going on north.[4] No underground railroad station was more frequently and openly advertised than the one at Syracuse, New York. Shortly after the
passage of the Fugitive Slave Law of 1850, an abolitionist committee in Syracuse announced in the press that the Reverend
J. W. Loguen, who was himself an ex-slave, would devote his time
exclusively to the humane work of helping fugitives and main-
taining the city's underground railroad depot. The committee
asked that all donations of money, clothing, and provisions be
directed to him. Any fugitives going through the city were also
to be sent to him. Loguen published his own fugitive slave nar-

---

[3] Cleveland *Daily True Democrat*, December 20, 1850; Cleveland *Leader*, February 18, August 1, November 8, 1855, December 15, 1858; *Liberator*, October 29,
1852, quoting Columbus *True Wesleyan; National Anti-Slavery Standard*, September 10, 1859.
[4] *National Anti-Slavery Standard*, April 8, 1854; *Maysville* (Ky.) *Eagle*, March 6,
1858, quoting *New York Times*.

rative near the end of the decade, and in it he said that he maintained the underground railroad at Syracuse for a number of years.[5]

Some local newspapers in northern communities from time to time in the 1850's carried descriptive stories about the underground railroad. Such material was dramatic, and its romantic appeal undoubtedly helped to popularize the legend of the underground railroad in the ante bellum era. In the fall of 1852 a Corning, New York, newspaper recounted an incident involving fifteen fugitives and commented: "The underground railroad is in fine working order—rarely does a collision occur —and, once on the track, passengers are sent through between sun and sun." An abolitionist from Columbus, Ohio, published a letter in the New York *Evening Post* telling of Ohio's underground lines that had been "in successful operation for several years." When the routes became known, they were changed, but always kept in operation. Trains usually ran at night and stations were located about ten miles apart. Fugitives were taken through the state "with great speed and safety," and once on the shores of Lake Erie, there was no difficulty getting them passage to Canada. A Cleveland newspaper alleged that the underground railroad was so constructed that it ran on water as well as on land. In 1854 the Chicago *Tribune* boasted that the underground trains ran through the city's streets regularly, and that its passenger business had increased, but that there was no reported speculation in its stock nor opinions as to its dividends. Its business, however, was "increasing at a most astonishing rate." Stockholders had to put out more to increase the running machinery of the road, a "large corps of trusty conductors" had been secured, and the officers and passengers on the road had been furnished with " 'irons' to be used

[5] *National Anti-Slavery Standard*, July 5, 1856, January 22, 1859; *Liberator*, October 26, 1855, July 24, 1857, October 28, 1859; Eber M. Pettit, *Sketches in the History of the Underground Railroad Comprising Many Thrilling Incidents of the Escape of Fugitives from Slavery and the Perils of Those Who Aided Them* (Fredonia, N.Y., 1879) , 54; J. W. Loguen, *The Rev. J. W. Loguen, as a Slave and as a Freeman. A Narrative of Real Life* (Syracuse, 1859) , title page.

against all who may have the audacity to interfere with trains or passengers."[6]

Fugitives were considered underground railroad passengers in these stories, whether they had made good their escapes on their own or with aid from the abolitionists. There was seldom any clear indication of exactly how much and what kind of aid the abolitionists had provided. In the spring of 1854 abolitionists told about a projected plan for an underground railroad from Baraboo, Wisconsin, to a favorable point on the lakeshore. "The road is partly completed, but as yet we have nothing but wooden rails, and our cars are drawn by horse power, as we have not yet procured our steam engine." All this was apparently based upon one incident in which a fugitive from Missouri who had stayed in Baraboo throughout the winter was whisked away to the north when pursuers appeared on his track. The same year an Iowa abolitionist sheet sent word that several of the "mysterious tracks" had already been laid in Iowa and on some of them there had been a brisk business. In 1855 antislavery newspapers reported that a new branch of the underground railroad had been established in Kansas Territory.[7]

Such stories, reprinted as they were in newspapers north and south, could have been of little value to the fugitives. Whatever aid might have been forthcoming from abolitionist organizations was partly abrogated by the publicity. Frederick Douglass voiced strong objections to this kind of propaganda and all exposures of escape plans and fugitive aid. In the pre-Civil War editions of his own memoirs he refused to reveal the escape method which he had used. "I have never approved of the very public manner, in which some of our western friends have conducted what they call the *'Under-ground* Railroad,'" he wrote, "but which, I think, by their open declarations, has been made,

---

[6] *Liberator,* October 22, 1852, quoting *Corning* (N.Y.) *Journal; National Anti-Slavery Standard,* September 24, 1853, quoting New York *Evening Post,* and June 17, 1854, quoting *Chicago Tribune;* Cleveland *Leader,* August 21, 1856.

[7] Milwaukee *Daily Free Democrat,* April 18, 1854; *National Anti-Slavery Standard,* December 23, 1854; Cleveland *Leader,* July 3, 1855.

most emphatically, the '*Upper*-ground Railroad.' Its stations are far better known to the slave-holders than to the slaves." Douglass honored "those good men and women for their noble daring," but he believed that the good resulting from such open avowals was of a questionable character. "It may kindle an enthusiasm, very pleasant to inhale;" he said, "but that is of no practical benefit to themselves, nor to the slaves escaping." Moreover, he maintained, it made escapes even more difficult, since it put the slaveholder on guard and added "to his facilities for capturing his slaves."[8]

But the stories were not meant primarily to help the fleeing slaves; they had, apart from their reader appeal as mildly sensational "revelations," a number of purposes. Some of them were designed to show that even antiabolitionist Northerners would help fugitives. One such person was described as a "theoretical Union-saver, but let a poor fugitive come along, and his hands open wider than any man's in the community."[9] The alleged increase in the number of escapes and the prosperity of the underground railroad also bore out the contention of many abolitionists that public opinion enlightened by antislavery agitation would eventually make slave property untenable, so that abolition would inevitably follow. According to this argument, therefore, it was more important to persuade the public and the slaveholders that many slaves were escaping than it was actually to help them escape. Frequently the antislavery editors congratulated themselves and taunted Southerners with the supposedly large numbers of successful escapes, quoting rather implausible figures for the value of the property which had run away. In 1857 the *National Anti-Slavery Standard* reported the claim of one of the railroad's "directors" that the line on which he was located had, within three years, transported more than a hundred thousand dollars worth "of human bones, as estimated in the Southern market." A Louisville paper reprinted an item from Cleveland which stated that in

---

[8] Frederick Douglass, *My Bondage and My Freedom* (New York, 1856), 323–24.
[9] *Liberator*, October 19, 1855.

a week's time at least twenty thousand dollars worth of property had been carried on the local underground; a Richmond paper took note of a Detroit story telling of ninety-four fugitives who had arrived in one week in Canada, "worth at the present market price the handsome sum of $94,000!"[10]

The fugitive slave and Canadian colonizer Henry Bibb provided in his newspaper *The Voice of the Fugitive* a great many of the underground railroad stories published by other papers. Bibb was especially defiant toward the South, and of course his stories reflected his own stake in Canadian immigration. According to Bibb's accounts, the underground line was always doing a thriving business. "Fugitive slaves are constantly arriving here from all parts of the South," he wrote in 1851. Later that year he boasted, "we can run a lot of slaves through from almost any of the bordering slave States into Canada, within 48 hours, and we defy the slaveholders and their abettors to beat that if they can." He was always glad to note the arrival of fugitives from the "land of whips and chains" in Canada, where "the people are all free, the climate is mild, the soil is rich and productive, and the markets are ready and advantageous to the farmer." "Self-emancipation is now the order of the day," wrote Bibb in 1853. He often addressed comments to fugitives' former owners telling them they "need not spend any more money to employ bloodhounds and negro-hunters" since the ex-slaves were safely in Canada. Letters from fugitives to their former masters were also published in *The Voice of the Fugitive*. Bibb's language was harsh and colorful, and abolitionist editors delighted in reprinting his version of the underground railroad epoch as viewed from Canada West.[11]

Many northern newspapers, of course, were antiabolitionist, but their comments on the underground railroad stories— though unfavorable—were seldom skeptical. Like the south-

---

[10] *National Anti-Slavery Standard*, April 25, 1857; Louisville *Daily Courier*, November 1, 1855; *Richmond Enquirer*, May 13, 1859.

[11] *Voice of the Fugitive*, August 27, November 5, 1851; Milwaukee *Daily Free Democrat*, September 26, 1851; *Liberator*, May 14, November 5, 1852, November 18, 25, 1853; *National Anti-Slavery Standard*, October 7, 1852, September 30, 1854.

ern papers, they made their own contribution to the growing legend. In 1855, when the *Cleveland Leader* published an underground railroad item, the *Indianapolis Journal* remarked that the story would no doubt make the rounds of the abolition papers. "It would seem," ran the *Journal* editorial, "that the editor of the *Leader* is either President, Director, or Conductor of one of the Underground Railroads, and that he and his co-labourers ('in the great cause') are not ashamed to publish their graceless acts to the world." The *Leader's* editor and his coworkers should be kicked over into Canada, grumbled the *Journal.* The *Syracuse Courier's* editor entertained similar opinions. Upon hearing that some prominent citizens of New York were soon to be exposed as freight agents on the underground railroad, the *Courier* commented that such behavior had been overlooked by government authorities. "The so-called 'Agent of the Underground Railroad' not only stalks through our streets in open noon-day," wrote the editor, "but publicly drives along his wagonloads of deluded 'fugitives,' and boastingly appropriates the funds placed at his disposal to pay their way to Canada." They rejoiced at the news of the coming exposés. It was time, said the *Courier,* that the Syracuse City Hall "should cease to be prostituted to the orgies and 'donation visits' of the Rev. Mr. Loguen and his confederates, and that the swindling and treason of these operators, 'conductors' and local agents should be shown up, for the benefit of their dupes, and for the benefit of society." The Cincinnati *Daily Enquirer* told of a slave who had been induced to run away by underground railroad agents, but after disappointment with life "at the hands of the cheese-making fanatics of the Western Reserve," he decided to return to Kentucky. Although it was more difficult to get out of Ohio than out of the South, he finally succeeded in making his way to Louisville. In telling of life in the North, reported the *Enquirer,* the ex-fugitive said "they had treated him as if he was a nigger."[12]

[12] *National Anti-Slavery Standard,* November 17, 1855, quoting *Indianapolis Journal; Liberator,* July 23, 1858, quoting *Syracuse Courier;* Cincinnati *Daily Enquirer,* July 8, 1859.

Early in January, 1860, the *New York Herald* carried a lengthy editorial entitled: "Practical Operations of the Underground Railroad." The *Herald* had sent a special correspondent to investigate conditions among the Canadian refugees. The antiabolitionist investigator found fugitive slaves abandoned, destitute, and miserable, while their rascally agents pocketed most of the money sent to help the new arrivals. The *Herald* tried to prove a connection between John Brown's raid and the Canadian abolitionists. "The underground railroad is no myth," the *Herald* assured its readers. "A regular organization, to which this name has been applied, stretches through every free State in the Union, and has its agents and emissaries on the borders of every slave State and along all the routes travelled by fugitive slaves." It was "a systematized association of negroes and republican abolition whites," with the object of "enticing away of the slave property of the South, and its safe transportation into Canada." There were large stockholders, and among them in New York were "the most prominent politicians in the republican party."[13] The partisan nature of the attack was obvious. The widely circulated rumors of conspiracy were being employed in time-honored fashion to discredit the opposition party. And a great deal of the contemporary discussion of underground railroad activity was little more than that.

Stories of the underground railroad played their part in satirical attacks on the abolitionists and their political allies. An antiabolition novel entitled *Mr. Frank, the Underground Rail-Agent,* by "Vidi," appeared in 1853. It poked fun at politicians who attached themselves to the antislavery cause from expediency yet were at the same time full of race prejudice, and ridiculed the many reforms supported by abolitionists. The writer alluded often to social relations between the races and described a scene involving "several rakish-looking old Quakers, who were situated between buxom-looking negro wenches; and some huge amorous-looking negro-gallants, whom

[13] *New York Herald*, January 5, 1860.

Fate, or their own sense of the beautiful, had thrown amongst exceedingly pretty little country girls." Three years later, *Abolitionism Unveiled* was published. This, too, referred to the underground railroad, to enticing of slaves from the South, and to the vigilance committees that helped them get to Canada. Trickery and rascality were common among its characters. On the eve of the presidential election of 1860 the *Disclosures and Confessions of Franklin A. Wilmot, with an Accurate Account of the Under-ground Railroad!* was published. The book appealed to prejudice against Negroes and abolitionists, but its primary purpose apparently was to vilify Republicans and get votes for Democrats.[14]

This war of ideas had little or no direct relation to the fugitive slave problem or even to the practical problems growing out of slavery itself. Southern propaganda was primarily defensive and based on pride rather than a protection of any vested interest. In 1851 an Alabama clergyman wrote a minister friend, "at this particular time many of our hot-blooded Southerners are very sensitive on the subject of Slavery altho they may not and never will own one."[15] Even slaveowners sometimes talked one way and acted another. Many of them, for example, were unwilling themselves to help "catch other people's negroes," and slave traders were considered outside the ranks of genteel society, but the resistance of Northerners to the recovery of fugitives was no less bitterly resented.[16]

From time to time, and often for political purposes, southern spokesmen bemoaned the extensive losses which they claimed the section had sustained through the slave-stealing activities of the abolitionists. Their accusations seemed to be substantiated by the type of abolitionist propaganda which boasted of the un-

[14] Vidi, *Mr. Frank, the Underground Rail-Agent* (Philadelphia, 1853), 19, 28; Henry Field James, *Abolitionism Unveiled; or Its Origin, Progress, and Pernicious Tendency Fully Developed* (Cincinnati, 1856), 173–74; *Disclosures and Confessions of Franklin A. Wilmot, with an Accurate Account of the Under-ground Railroad!* (Philadelphia, 1860).
[15] James Robinson to Reverend N. M. Gordon, September 6, 1851, Gordon Papers, University of Kentucky Library.
[16] *Daily Richmond Enquirer*, October 9, 1852.

derground railroad's success. Though their motives were very different, propagandists of both sides reinforced one another in fostering a popular belief in the conspiracy of organized slave abductors. The estimates of losses varied considerably, and those who made them overlooked the relatively low monetary value of fugitive slaves and their unreliability as chattels. In 1850, Senator James Murray Mason of Virginia said that his state's annual losses from slave escapes had been estimated at more than one hundred thousand dollars. Several years later, Congressman Eli S. Shorter of Alabama accepted the *New York Times'* statement that since the passage of the Fugitive Slave Law of 1850 thirty-five thousand slaves had fled from the South. He pointed out that this amounted to an annual loss to the border states of four million dollars. In 1856 the Baltimore *Sun* calculated that the alleged thirty-six thousand fugitives then in Canada and the North were worth at least thirty million dollars.[17]

Some Southerners, however, were less eager to believe these charges. When Congressman Thomas L. Clingman of North Carolina estimated in 1850 that the South had lost fifteen million dollars as a result of abolitionist-inspired slave escapes, Edward Stanly, another North Carolina congressman, retorted, "I do not believe my colleague's constituents ever lost a slave by northern Abolitionists." And Henry Clay denied the accuracy of Senator Robert Barnwell Rhett's charge that of fifteen thousand fugitive slaves in the free states only half a dozen had been recovered. "No man knows how many fugitive slaves there are in the North," said Clay. He added that only a few had been returned because in most cases their masters had not taken the trouble to chase them.[18]

The skepticism of Clay and a few others represented a distinctly minority opinion. The prevailing belief in the South

[17] *Congressional Globe*, 31 Cong., 1 sess. (1850), App., pt. 2, 1605, and 34 Cong., 1 sess. (1856), App., 395; Baltimore *Sun*, March 13, 1856; "The South and the Union," *DeBow's Review*, 18:145–54 (February, 1855).
[18] *Congressional Globe*, 31 Cong., 1 sess. (1850), App., pt. 1, 340, and 31 Cong., 2 sess. (1851), App., 321.

that organizations of abolitionists were engaged in running off
slaves in large numbers undoubtedly contributed to the growing sectional animosity as the secession crisis approached. In
1849 John C. Calhoun, while reviewing the grievances of the
South, alluded to indirect violations of the Constitution by the
North and specifically listed organized efforts to "entice, decoy,
entrap, inveigle, and seduce slaves to escape from their masters,
and to pass them secretly and rapidly" into Canada. Other
southern political leaders repeated the same idea, and the Nashville Convention of 1850 affirmed in its report that "organizations were formed to carry off slaves from the South, and to protect them by violence from recapture." In 1857 Edmund Ruffin
mentioned abolition agents active in the South. Ruffin also
called attention to the slave losses around Norfolk, "all of
which were doubtless forwarded by Northern agents, and taken
off in Northern vessels." Less and less distinction was made between abolitionists and other Northerners in southern propaganda. As early as 1851 Senator Robert Barnwell Rhett of
South Carolina posed the question: "What has Congress for the
last ten years been, but a grand abolition convention, preach-
ing and inspiring insurrection amongst our slaves?" In his annual message for 1861 Governor Isham Harris of Tennessee
listed the grievances of the South and described the "anti-slavery
cloud" which covered the North. "It has run off slave property
by means of the 'under-ground railroad,'" said Governor Harris, "amounting in value to millions of dollars, and thus made
the tenure by which slaves are held in the border States so precarious as to materially impair their value."[19]

Southern congressmen made numerous allusions to underground railroad activity during the heated debates in the
Thirty-sixth Congress concerning the choice of Speaker of the

[19] Lexington, Ky., *Observer and Reporter*, February 7, 1849; "Resolutions and
Address of the Nashville Convention," *National Anti-Slavery Standard*, June 27,
1850; *Congressional Globe*, 32 Cong., 1 sess. (1851), App., 44; Edmund Ruffin,
*Consequences of Abolition Agitation* (reprinted from *DeBow's Review*, Washington, 1857), 22–23; *Message of His Excellency Isham G. Harris, to the General Assembly of Tennessee, in Extra Session, January 7th, 1861* (Nashville, 1861), 8.

House. Representative John J. Jones of Georgia objected to a Republican because it was a "notorious fact, that in a good many of the non-slaveholding States the Republican party have regularly organized societies—underground railroads—for the avowed purpose of stealing the slaves from the border States and carrying them off to a free State or to Canada." Arkansas' Congressman Thomas Carmichael Hindman objected to John Sherman, the Republican choice for Speaker, because Sherman had given "full scope and vent to his abolition zeal" and had thereby become "a practical encourager of negro-stealing, and an assistant of the underground railroad." In October, 1860, the *Charleston Mercury* warned Southerners that when a party got in power "whose creed it is, to repeal the Fugitive Slave Laws, the *under*-ground railroad, will become an over-ground railroad."[20] Although these and similar statements may have had an effect in molding popular sentiment toward the North, they are not very sound evidence as to the nature of the subterranean railway itself.

Despite the acrimony of such arguments, however, moderate sentiment continued to be a strong force in the South as in the North. The attempts of such southern leaders as John J. Crittenden, W. C. Rives, Andrew Johnson, and others to bring about a sectional compromise on the eve of the Civil War indicates the existence of such feelings. Moderate southern spokesmen tried to counteract the effect of extremist propaganda, including that concerning underground railroad activity, but even they sometimes echoed the prevailing rationalization of slave escapes. In 1850 a Kentucky newspaper called attention to a Federal court decision which awarded a slaveowner the full value of some slaves who could not be recovered because of mob interference. The editor pointed out that the Federal courts afforded a "peaceful and efficient redress" to Kentuckians in such matters. He contrasted Kentucky's "constant and immove-

---

[20] *Congressional Globe*, 36 Cong., 1 sess. (1860), App., 83, 250; *Charleston Mercury*, October 11, 1860, quoted in Dwight L. Dumond, ed., *Southern Editorials on Secession* (New York, 1931), 179.

able" devotion to the Union with South Carolina's continual "blustering about secession and disunion," even though Kentucky suffered "more every year from the escape of her slaves, by aid of Northern abolitionists," than South Carolina had suffered since the American Revolution.[21]

Stories in the southern press sometimes repeated abolitionist boasts of successful underground railroad escapes as proof of the alleged conspiracy. Should a suspected abolitionist be found in the vicinity, he was held responsible for all slave discontent. In 1848, when six slaves escaped from Cecil County, Maryland, the papers reported, "They were doubtless assisted by Abolitionists, one of whom was seen here about that time." Such reporting was not uncommon, especially when groups of slaves absconded or when no plausible explanation could be offered for an individual slave's escape. When, as infrequently happened, a person with suspected antislavery views was actually caught helping slaves escape, it was reported in the press as unquestionable proof that abolition emissaries were engaged in large-scale organized operations in the area. In the summer of 1845 a Tennessee newspaper commented that Ohio abolitionists were trying to spread their doctrines in that state. The proof lay in the fact that an abolition tract from Ohio had recently been sent through the mails to a free Negro, and at about the same time several slaves in that neighborhood had run away. "These are strong facts," wrote the editor, "indicating clearly an organized plan for inducing slaves to abscond and escape from their owners."[22]

A running fight between two St. Louis newspapers showed that a few remained skeptical about such stories. Missouri slaveholders had the usual problem of runaways, and in the fall of 1854 the St. Louis *Republican* carried a long story about the underground railroad and its organized system of "negro-stealing," with headquarters in Chicago and a regular agency estab-

[21] *Frankfort* (Ky.) *Commonwealth*, August 27, 1850.
[22] *Liberator*, June 16, 1848, quoting *Cecil* (Md.) *Democrat; The Non-Slaveholder*, 4:142 (June, 1849), quoting *Richmond Republican*; Lexington, Ky., *Observer and Reporter*, September 3, 1845, quoting *Nashville Union*.

lished in St. Louis. The charge that some Missouri newspapers
supported such conduct evoked a prompt reply from the editor
of the rival *Daily Intelligencer,* who derided the idea that there
was any such underground agency in St. Louis and suggested
that the *Republican's* editor should turn over to the authorities such knowledge as he claimed to have. The *Republican* replied that the report could be confirmed at the police office,
where they would give facts "which establish the insecurity of
slave property in consequence of the efforts of the Abolitionists
among us." Such statements proved nothing, but helped to give
plausibility to the mass of stories which were eventually to form
part of a favorite American legend.[23]

As that legend became familiar in the South, a number of
local, antiabolition vigilance committees were formed in response to it. Members of such committees passed resolutions
denouncing the abolitionists, suggested laws and measures to protect slave property, and on occasion warned suspected abolitionists to leave the vicinity. They sometimes offered rewards for
the capture of known abolitionists. One Missouri committee
recommended "the propriety of bringing from Illinois, an
Abolitionist for each negro they aid in escaping from Missouri."
Some committees were formed in order to "counteract the
clandestine measures of the Abolition societies." One of the
Missouri committees advocated that the practice of hiring out
slaves be stopped and that free Negroes be forced to leave the
county by a specified date. In 1850 a Virginian suggested a central organization at Washington to assure enforcement of the
Fugitive Slave Law. Owners of fugitives were to give the committee all the necessary information. The committee would
send out agents to recover all fugitives and to "try the great
question who must yield—*the law or the abolitionists.*" A
group of Kent County, Maryland, citizens took action that was
more appropriate though less sensational when they incorpo-

---

[23] Harrison Anthony Trexler, *Slavery in Missouri, 1804–1865* (*Johns Hopkins
University Studies in Historical and Political Science,* ser. 32, no. 2, Baltimore,
1914), 207; St. Louis *Republican,* August 30, September 1, 1854; St. Louis *Daily
Intelligencer,* August 31, 1854.

rated a "Mutual Protection Society" for insuring slave property
and protecting its members from losses through slaves who escaped beyond the state's borders.[24]

Imagined or real, underground railroad activity rendered
slave property insecure and gave those who sold slaves south a
rationalization for such sales. A Delaware newspaper reported
in 1856 that the slaveholders of western Virginia were taking
measures to guard against possible loss by disposing of their
slaves "to those who will carry them beyond the reach of the
underground railroad." For proof, the paper called attention
to a recent sale of fifteen slaves. "The negroes never would have
been sold," ran the story, "had it not been discovered that they
were making preparations to leave for a free territory."[25] A St.
Louis journalist ridiculed the abolitionists for pretending to
"hold in horror the situation of slaves in the South" at the same
time their fanaticism was "driving heretofore kind masters to
risk the future comfort of their negroes by selling them to strangers."[26] It was sometimes argued, too, that such abolitionist interference made the slaveholders crack the whip and maintain
sterner discipline than before. One apologist for slavery asserted that "for every slave the Abolitionists have successfully
run to Canada, thousands who remained behind, have felt their
bonds heavier."[27]

Threats of economic retaliation also grew out of the fugitive
controversy. The *Richmond Enquirer* saw the need for pro-
tective and retaliatory measures in the "riotous demonstration
in Boston" over the rendition of Anthony Burns. "Now is
the time," advised the *Enquirer*, "to break asunder the fetters

[24] *St. Louis New Era,* December 12, 1843; St. Louis *Daily Union,* November 14,
21, 1846; Salem, Ohio, *Anti-Slavery Bugle,* May 15, 1852, quoting *Maysville* (Ky.)
*Eagle; National Anti-Slavery Standard,* December 16, 1852, and November 26,
1853, quoting St. Louis *Missouri Republican; Richmond Enquirer,* November 19,
1850; Jeffrey R. Brackett, *The Negro in Maryland, a Study of the Institution of
Slavery (Johns Hopkins University Studies in Historical and Political Science,* ed.
by Herbert B. Adams, extra vol. 6, Baltimore, 1889) , 91.
[25] Wilmington *Delaware Gazette,* December 31, 1856.
[26] St. Louis *Daily Union,* October 27, 1846.
[27] Nathan L. Rice, *Ten Letters on the Subject of Slavery; Addressed to the Delegates from the Congregational Associations to the Last General Assembly of the
Presbyterian Church* (St. Louis, 1855) , 32.

of commercial subjection, and to prepare for that more complete independence which awaits us." One southern group talked about an "Underground Police Organization" which was to investigate the names of conductors and stockholders of the underground railroad in order to publish their names and spoil their business with southern customers. Cincinnati was especially singled out for this kind of retaliation, and some of the attack against Cincinnati merchants was spearheaded by their rivals in St. Louis, who were quite willing to see the Queen City's rich trade diverted in their direction. Shortly after a violent fugitive rescue in Carlisle, Pennsylvania, a Virginia paper commented, "Our Southern people should mark the town of Carlisle, and be especially careful that none of their sons shall be sent to that place for their education."[28] Even colleges were to be included in the proposed economic warfare to break up the underground railroad.

Some of the southern propaganda seems to have been aimed at the Negroes. Despite legislation restricting the education of slaves, many of them could read, and some of the underground railroad items published in southern newspapers were written, in part at least, for their benefit. Abolitionists were pictured as shysters devoid of principle who would as readily turn a fugitive slave over to the authorities as entice him away from his happy home. They profiteered in the selling of free papers, exploited the fugitives mercilessly, and treated them cruelly. Yet they would waste their funds putting up bail bonds for other abolitionists, who would forfeit the money "rather than do so practical a good as to devote it to the purchase of some of those worthy colored people whose honest efforts to obtain freedom deserve the sympathy and often receive the assistance of slaveholders as well as others."[29]

[28] *National Anti-Slavery Standard,* June 24, 1854, quoting *Richmond Enquirer,* and July 31, 1858; St. Louis *Republican,* March 26, 1855; *Tri-Weekly Maysville* (Ky.) *Eagle,* November 5, 1857; *Daily Richmond Enquirer,* August 23, 1847, quoting Winchester *Virginian.*

[29] Lexington, Ky., *Observer and Reporter,* August 28, 1850; St. Louis *Republican,* August 16, 1855; *Richmond Enquirer,* March 21, 1851, quoting Baltimore *Sun.*

Other stories were designed to convince the slaves that it was difficult if not impossible to escape from the South. After a group of Kentucky fugitives were recaptured, the Louisville *Courier* commented, "They had no chance to get away from the start, as every avenue toward Canada was closely watched." Editors carefully reported instances of recapture in northern states. Another fugitive from Louisville was furious at the Hoosiers because he was captured twice in Indiana. The Hoosiers, reported the *Courier*, "were not such Abolitionists as he imagined. The fact is," the story continued, "since Indiana purged herself of Know-Nothingism, runaway slaves have no chance of escaping through that State."[30] Dire tales of northern and Canadian bestiality also circulated in the southern press, which reported with enthusiasm the voluntary return of fugitives to the South.[31]

Thus southern propaganda contributed to the growth of the underground railroad legend in the pre-Civil War period. There is no doubt that many Americans believed in the existence of a widespread and highly organized underground railroad operated by abolitionists to run slaves out of the South. That the legend was taking form in the ante bellum era can also be established by the numerous descriptions of the underground in contemporary writings. Philo Tower's book *Slavery Unmasked*, published in 1856, described the underground railroad which ran directly through the center of Cincinnati "bearing scores, if not hundreds of passengers, monthly" to Canada. The association was "composed of a set of heroic men and women, ministers and laymen, of noble, moral daring, of the real Jerusalem stock." In a pamphlet by the Presbyterian minister and colonizationist Nathan L. Rice, the underground railroad is described as "a systematic plan to induce and aid slaves to escape from their masters." English travelers in the United

---

[30] Louisville *Daily Courier*, August 20, 1852, August 18, 1853; *National Anti-Slavery Standard*, November 17, 1855, quoting Louisville *Courier*.

[31] Wilmington *Delaware Gazette*, December 23, 1859; Charleston *Courier*, January 18, 1860, quoting *Knoxville Whig*; St. Louis *Republican*, February 24, 1853, July 26, 1859.

States also picked up the popular image of the underground railroad and sometimes included it among those characteristically American institutions which they purported to describe in their travel accounts. Harriet Martineau in 1837 and Joseph Sturge in 1841 both mentioned abolitionist aid to fugitives, although they wrote before the term "underground railroad" was popular and did not use it. James Stirling's book *Letters from the Slave States* informed British readers in 1857 that "already a secret and powerful organization exists, which, under the name of 'The Underground Railway,' facilitates the escape of slaves." Charles Mackay's travelbook described the philanthropic abolitionist railway as an organized system to "shelter and feed the runaway, and provide him with the means of passing from one city to another, until he is safely beyond the reach of all pursuit from the law officers of the Central Government, or from the officious interference of local functionaries or busybodies." Another British author credited the antislavery martyr Charles T. Torrey with being the organizer of the underground railroad to pass the "poor fugitive from one benevolent and trustworthy agent at *stations on the line* to another, so the chain was completed from the slave states to Canada."[32] These and other travel accounts helped to export the developing legend to the British Isles.

So did the Reverend William M. Mitchell's book *The Underground Railroad,* which was published in London in 1860. Mitchell was a free Negro who had been a slave driver and later a minister in Ohio before going around 1855 to Canada, where he served as a missionary among the Negro population. He boasted of twelve years experience as a director of the underground railroad, and wrote his book partly to raise money for

[32] Harriet Martineau, *Society in America* (2 vols., New York, 1837), 2:113–14; Joseph Sturge, *A Visit to the United States in 1841* (Boston, 1842), 233–34; Philo Tower, *Slavery Unmasked: Being a Truthful Narrative of a Three Years' Residence and Journeying in Eleven Southern States* (Rochester, N.Y., 1856), 233–38; Rice, *Ten Letters*, 30–31; James Stirling, *Letters from the Slave States* (London, 1857), 314; Charles Mackay, *Life and Liberty in America: or, Sketches of a Tour in the United States and Canada, in 1857–8* (2 vols., London, 1859), 1:273–74; Eliza Wigham, *The Anti-Slavery Cause in America and Its Martyrs* (London, 1863), 61–64.

a chapel and schoolhouse for the refugees in Canada. Mitchell said the underground railroad had been operating "at least a quarter century" before 1860. He included a version of the frequently repeated anecdote which was supposed to account for the popular name of the institution: A slave who had escaped from Kentucky was hotly pursued by his master, who lost all track of him at the Ohio River. "The d——d Abolitionists must have a Rail-road under the ground by which they run off Niggers," fumed the disappointed slaveholder. Mitchell explained that since the "useful road" was concealed from the slaveholders, it was underground, and since slaves were transported "with such accelerating velocity," it was appropriate to call it a railroad. He defined the underground railroad as a "mutual agreement between the friends of the Slaves, in the Northern States, to aid Fugitives on their way to Canada." They were taken "from one friend to another," only at night, usually for a distance of six to twelve miles. Mitchell pictured a flood of fugitives pouring into Canada by this method. "With the Under-ground Railroad we may safely say that nearly two thousand reach Canada annually," and the number was continually increasing. He alleged that there were forty-five thousand fugitives in Canada, and added that of the "present generation of Slaves 90,000 have attempted to secure their freedom by running away, but only 45,000 have succeeded."[33] He gave no proof for his statistics, and some contemporaries questioned their accuracy. The *Boston Courier,* for example, repeated them and commented, "we cannot but be incredulous as to the amount."[34]

According to Mitchell, the abolitionists played a vital role in successful escapes. "But for the underground-railroad, very few Slaves would be able to reach Canada," he asserted. There were too many proslavery Northerners, as well as a class of men "too lazy to work at respectable occupations," who preferred to

[33] William M. Mitchell, *The Under-Ground Railroad* (London, 1860), 3–4, 5, 71, 113.
[34] *National Anti-Slavery Standard,* March 9, 1861, quoting *Boston Courier.*

obtain a living "by tracking runaway slaves." Mitchell also alleged that there were abolitionists in the slave states who kindly gave the slaves "information as to the direction of Canada, and the Free States through which they must pass to reach it," as well as the names of the important rivers they would have to cross. Besides, there were some "patriotic men, white and coloured," who ventured into the slave states to bring slaves out and deliver them to the conductors of the underground line, who forwarded them to Canada.[35]

William Mitchell's book circulated in England and America. Some of his exaggerations were obvious to his contemporaries, but the book gives a fine description of the underground railroad as it appeared in popular legend by the time of the Civil War. His picture of a well-organized, highly secret system with large numbers of passengers, courageous and efficient operators, and the implication of extensive southern connections are elements in later versions of the legend. So, too, is Mitchell's view of the underground railroad as essential for successful escapes.

Mitchell's work made a late contribution to the ante bellum development of the image of the underground railroad, and that image was already in sharp contrast with such facts as can be ascertained about the activities of Mitchell's abolitionist contemporaries. A great deal of their activity was confined to the verbal level, and much of it brought forth verbal reaction from their opponents. Repetition of charge and countercharge helped popularize the legend in the prewar years, but it was in the period following the Civil War that the legend really gained momentum. Much the greater volume of literature concerning the underground railroad was written long after the events had taken place.

[35] Mitchell, *Under-Ground Railroad*, 13–15, 36, 38–39.

## Chapter Eight

# REMINISCENCE AND ROMANCE

WHEN ASKED by a writer of local history where his mother had obtained her sources for *Uncle Tom's Cabin,* Charles Edward Stowe replied that he did not know. "You know the recollections of old men consist for the most part of Wahrheit and Dichtung," answered Stowe. "Old men dream dreams and young men see visions, and that gets history in a devil of a mess." His mother had insisted, he recalled, that she had heard Lincoln in 1862 give a speech which had not been delivered until several years later. "That," continued Stowe, "is the reason that the historians have to spend so much time hunting around in dark cellars for black cats that aren't there and never were."[1]

Stowe was perceptive. Seldom do historians accept the reminiscences of aged participants without careful evaluation of such material. Yet in the case of the underground railroad, a dearth of contemporary source materials has led a number of writers to rely heavily upon reminiscent material. The postwar flood of underground railroad literature was primarily, though not exclusively, of abolitionist origin. It was this mass of material, written years after the events, that gave the legend form and substance and an enduring place in the story of America's past.

At best, abolitionist sources present only one view of a highly controversial period of history, and their characteristic mode of expression was a language rich in invective and hyperbole but lacking in objectivity and precision. William Lloyd Garrison even wished for a "new and stronger dialect," he said, for the English language was "inadequate to describe the horrors and impieties of Slavery, and the transcendent wickedness of those who sustained this bloody system." Most abolitionists were sure that the tyrannical South was determined to "subjugate the North for the extension and perpetuation of slavery." When the Civil War came, they viewed it as a "contest pure and simple, between *Freedom* and Slavery; between the powers of darkness and the powers of light." To them it was, as Frederick Douglass put it, "an Abolition war instead of being a Union war," and when a northern victory brought an end to the conflict and to slavery, they assumed that it was they, the abolitionists, "who had given the American slaves their freedom." One of their most severe critics, Eli Thayer, said they "never exhibited any diffidence or modesty in sounding their own praises." He accused them of "forming a mutual admiration society possessed by an unusual malignity towards those who did not belong to it." Thayer asserted also that their persecution did not stem from their antislavery principles but rather from their "abusive and insulting manner" and from their support of the "unpopular and unpatriotic doctrines of secession and disunion." As ardent fanatics, the abolitionists met with extreme reaction; they saw no value in moderation, and neither did most of their opponents.[2]

---

[1] W. D. Waldrip quotes the Charles Edward Stowe letter in "A Station of the Underground Railroad," *Indiana Quarterly Magazine of History*, 7:67–68 (June, 1911).

[2] William Lloyd Garrison, "Hard Language," in *The Liberty Bell: By Friends of Freedom* (Boston, 1848); Charles Sumner, "The Struggle," in Julia Griffiths, ed., *Autographs for Freedom* (Boston, 1853), 77; Western Anti-Slavery Society Minute Book, entry for August 24–26, 1851, Library of Congress; Dustin G. Cheever diary, entry for January 1, 1857, Dustin G. Cheever Papers, State Historical Society of Wisconsin; J. Miller McKim to Richard D. Webb, February 17, 1862, William Lloyd Garrison Papers, Boston Public Library; speech of Frederick Douglass in *Proceedings of the American Anti-Slavery Society, at Its Third Decade, Held in the City of Philadelphia, December 3d and 4th, 1863* (New York, 1864), 112; letter from Frederick Douglass, April 3, 1874, in unidentified clipping in scrapbook "Abolitionists' Convention," State Historical Society of Wisconsin; Eli Thayer, *A History of the Kansas Crusade: Its Friends and Its Foes* (New York, 1889), 95–96.

The religious motivation of most abolitionists often produced in them a sense of destiny for their cause. Like the men of the Middle Ages, they saw the hand of God in historical events. An Ohio abolitionist revealed in 1874 that he was thankful he had been an abolitionist "from the start" and had never looked upon slavery as anything but "a sin against God and a crime against man. And the hand of God has never been more visible in human history," he said, "than in its signal overthrow in this country."[3] Few of his friends in the antislavery movement would have quarreled with those sentiments.

Once slavery had been abolished, most Americans north and south accepted the decision. In many circles it was popular in the years after the war to have had a record of antislavery activity, and many people whose timidity had been foremost in the prewar years became ardent abolitionists afterward. This, of course, disturbed the bona fide abolitionists. Furthermore, it was not easy to tell who had been an abolitionist before the war because of the many degrees of antislavery and abolitionist sentiment and the many sectarian splits within the antislavery ranks. Lydia Maria Child was amused to find in 1864 that new antislavery friends were "becoming as plenty as roses in June." She wrote Garrison, "Sometimes, when they tell me they have always been anti-slavery, I smile inwardly, but I do not contradict the assertion; I merely marvel at their power of keeping a secret so long!" The next year an abolitionist wrote that it was "rare to meet one who has ever wished well to slavery, or desired anything but its final abolition." A number of the antislavery workers wrote autobiographical accounts to help set the record straight.[4]

When Professor Wilbur H. Siebert gathered materials in the 1890's for his study of the underground railroad, he wrote let-

---

[3] Samuel Wolcott to the Committee on the Abolitionists' Convention, May 27, 1874, Zebina Fastman Papers, Chicago Historical Society.
[4] Lydia Maria Child to William Lloyd Garrison, *Liberator*, February 19, 1864; "Early Anti-Slavery," *Liberator*, February 24, 1865. For a pre-Civil War example of an individual's claiming a more consistent antislavery record than he actually had, see Merton L. Dillon, "John Mason Peck: A Study of Historical Rationalization," *Journal of the Illinois State Historical Society*, 50:385–90 (Winter, 1957).

ters of inquiry to aged abolitionists and their descendants. Only a few of them denied having recollections of the underground railroad. One informant admitted that he had only a young boy's remembrance and said he could help little, since such information "should be first-hand and accurate." Another said he knew from tradition and personal observation that there was such a road running through Ohio, though he could "recollect but little of the details of its workings." A Granville, Ohio, correspondent revealed that his father and mother had both been antislavery people, always ready "to help in any way in their power to advance that cause," but that the family had had "no immediate or 'official' connection with the 'Underground R.R.' "[5]

An Illinois descendant of abolitionists regretted that he knew so little about the road, since his father had been actively involved in its work. He attributed his ignorance to the prudence of his father. Dr. James C. Jackson of North Adams, Massachusetts, lamented that his extensive collection of abolitionist letters had been destroyed in a fire. Thirty years earlier, he said, he could have written a correct history of the underground railroad from memory, but, he admitted, "it exists in my mind now only as a magnificent dream."[6]

If some of the aged abolitionists were reluctant to offer information which they could not verify, others claimed to have excellent memories. Many reacted in the same spirit as the Reverend H. D. Platt, who answered: "There was a peculiar *fascination* about that 'U.G.R.R.' biz., that *fires me up*, even now when I recall the scenes of excitement and danger." A ninety-five-year-old Pennsylvania abolitionist was "rather proud of be-

[5] Letters to Wilbur H. Siebert from C. F. Atkinson, May 2, 1896, in scrapbook "The Underground Railroad in Massachusetts, vol. 2," and E. S. Shepardson, October 21, 1896, in scrapbook "The Underground Railroad in Ohio, vol. 7," Wilbur H. Siebert Papers, Houghton Library of Harvard University; William Johnston to Siebert, August 23, 1894, in scrapbook "The Underground Railroad in Ohio, vol. 4," Siebert Papers, Ohio Historical Society.

[6] Letters to Siebert from Nathan L. Burton, January 28, 1896, in scrapbook "The Underground Railroad in Illinois, vol. 2," and Dr. James Caleb Jackson, November 20, 1893, in scrapbook "The Underground Railroad in Massachusetts, vol. 1," Siebert Papers, Houghton Library.

ing a son of a Revolutionary soldier, as well as having been both agent and conductor on an Underground Railroad." He claimed that he had helped free nearly a hundred slaves, "taking them at night and on horseback." Another said that he had been an underground railroad agent since 1820 and that he had "enticed slaves away in Louisiana, Missouri and (though they were free) Utah." "The Underground R R was the way we sent fugitives from friend to friend till landed in Canada," said a Michigan veteran of the antislavery movement. Still another aged abolitionist remembered the secrecy and claimed that the underground railroad had had "a regular code of secret signs and passwords by which the members recognized and communicated with each other." Furthermore, he recalled that "each conductor was armed and like the Spartan Soldier never expected to surrender unless mortally wounded." Most of the replies which Siebert received were in general terms, lacking in details. An Illinois correspondent told the eager historian that when he first talked with the aged abolitionists in his neighborhood he thought he would get a great deal of information. But he found "that while they will talk very volubly and at great length what they say, when boiled down so as to get what they *know* shows but little on paper."[7]

Some veterans of the antislavery movement published reminiscences or histories. As with their prewar efforts, these historians continued to work with a sense of mission. One of them detected a hungering "for a greater knowledge and history of the events of the past," insofar as those events had tended to enlighten mankind and raise it to a higher moral level. William L. Cockrum, who wrote an underground railroad history,

[7] Letters to Siebert from the Reverend H. D. Platt, March 20, 1896, in scrapbook "The Underground Railroad in Illinois, vol. 1," and John F. Williams, March 21, 1893, in scrapbook "The Underground Railroad in Indiana, vol. 2," Siebert Papers, Houghton Library; letters to Siebert from H. H. Northrop, May 2, 1896, in scrapbook "The Underground Railroad in Michigan," the Reverend James Lawson, April 22, 1896, in scrapbook "The Underground Railroad in Pennsylvania, vol. 3," and D. J. Murphy, May 7, 1896, in scrapbook "The Underground Railroad in Illinois, vol. 2," Siebert Papers, Ohio Historical Society; E. M. Stevenson to Mr. White, February 24, 1897, in scrapbook "The Underground Railroad in Pennsylvania, vol. 2," Siebert Papers, Ohio Historical Society.

"had no apology to make" for his book. He wanted young people to be informed about "how things were carried on during
the fifties by the pro-slavery people who had control of the government." To Cockrum it was clear that "Hot headed southerners had brought on a war hoping to dissolve the Union."
Zebina Eastman, a Chicago abolitionist and journalist, was also
concerned that the history of the antislavery struggle should
be preserved. "It seems to many of us," he told an abolitionists' convention in 1874, "that this nation cannot afford to have
this chapter blotted out, and the valuable lessons lost upon our
children, who are soon to be followed by other children." The
abolitionists who wrote historical accounts were no more capable of objectivity in the postwar years than they had been in
the days before the war. For documentation they drew mostly
upon their own memories. They repeated the same bitter ha-
treds, the same oversimplified moralistic interpretations, and
even the same loyalty to whatever faction of abolitionism they
had happened to join. In 1892 Frederick Douglass confided to a
friend that the time had not yet come for a "true and impartial
history of the Anti-slavery movement." Differences among abolitionists had "descended from sires to sons and made the task
of writing a true history hard if not impossible for the present." He hoped that at a more distant period the scattered material could be "gathered and the chaff of rivalry, sect and pas-
sion be winnowed out, and the true wheat" saved. As in war,
said Douglass, amid the fire and smoke of battle, "those most engaged see least that is going on over the whole field."[8]

If the abolitionists, as Douglass maintained, were incapable
of making a fair evaluation of the various antislavery groups,
they were even less objective when viewing their role in history
as it related to national events. When writing about what they

[8] Samuel S. Tomlinson to J. J. Janney, June 27, 1892, in scrapbook "The Under-
ground Railroad in Ohio, vol. 7," Siebert Papers, Houghton Library; William L.
Cockrum, *History of the Underground Railroad, As It Was Conducted by the
Anti-slavery League* (Oakland City, Ind., 1915), v; Zebina Eastman's address in
unidentified clipping in scrapbook "Abolitionists' Convention," State Historical
Society of Wisconsin; Frederick Douglass to Marshall Pierce, February 18, 1892,
Nathaniel P. Rogers Collection, Haverford College Library.

considered "the supreme era in American history," the abolitionists were looking back upon a time when they had often been hated and scorned. The Reverend Austin Willey wanted to remind the nation of "the odium, the toil, the sacrifice, the mental suffering, the hate," which the great struggle had cost its noble followers.[9]

Vividly remembering the harsh feelings toward them in the prewar years, the abolitionists wrote about their adventures in a great crusade which had achieved its objective, in a cause that had been vindicated. In part, at least, they wrote in order to secure for themselves a proper place in history.

A number of abolitionist reminiscences and histories contained brief descriptions of the underground railroad. Samuel J. May, a Garrisonian from Syracuse, published *Some Recollections of Our Anti-slavery Conflict* in 1869. In it he described the Syracuse branch of the underground railroad and recorded his version of the rescue of Jerry in that city. James Freeman Clarke's *Anti-Slavery Days* appeared in 1883, the same year that Parker Pillsbury's *Acts of the Anti-Slavery Apostles* was published. Austin Willey's *The History of the Antislavery Cause in State and Nation* came out in 1886.

Henry Wilson's three-volume *History of the Rise and Fall of the Slave Power in America* was one of the most popular of abolitionist histories. Wilson, an ardent antislavery politician who served as vice president under Grant, placed the origin of the underground railroad in the period shortly after the War of 1812. He defined it as the "popular designation given to those systematic and co-operative efforts which were made by the friends of the fleeing slave to aid him in eluding the pursuit of the slaveholders, who were generally on his track." Because of its "timely and effective aid thousands were enabled to escape from the prison-house of bondage." There were, according to Wilson, stations at convenient distances always ready to receive fugitives and house them until they could be sent along the way

[9] Austin Willey, *The History of the Antislavery Cause in State and Nation* (Portland, Maine, 1886), 403.

northward. He pictured the whole of the middle and western states east of the Mississippi as "dotted with these 'stations,' and covered with a network of imaginary routes." The cost, risk, and accomplishments were all great, and the epoch of the underground drama, said Wilson, was one of the brightest pages of American history that had yet to be written.[10]

Each of the volumes of memoirs helped establish the legend of the underground railroad firmly in the minds of Americans. Levi Coffin, Laura S. Haviland, and Robert C. Smedley penned accounts that added substantially to the picture of the underground railroad as a Quaker institution. Others also mentioned the Quakers' contribution. The Reverend Austin Willey emphasized the work of New Englanders in the mysterious institution and the antislavery movement which nurtured it. Marvin Benjamin Butler and William L. Cockrum placed the underground railroad in Indiana, where they had worked. Although the writers did not clearly define the limits of local or regional organization, some of them gave the impression of a nationwide system. According to Eber M. Pettit of Cattaraugus County, New York, the underground railroad was a "spontaneous combination of multitudes of men and women" which extended "from the interior of the slave states to Canada." James Freeman Clarke described a system which "extended from Kentucky and Virginia across Ohio; from Maryland through Pennsylvania, and New York to New England and Canada."[11]

Most of the writers of memoirs emphasized the need for secrecy in their dangerous work, although some of the material

---

[10] Henry Wilson, *History of the Rise and Fall of the Slave Power in America* (3 vols., Boston, 1872–1877), 2:63–69, 85–86.

[11] Coffin, *Reminiscences;* Laura S. Haviland, *A Woman's Life-Work: Labors and Experiences* (Chicago, 1887); Robert C. Smedley, *History of the Underground Railroad in Chester and the Neighboring Counties of Pennsylvania* (Lancaster, Pa., 1883); Willey, *Antislavery Cause;* Marvin Benjamin Butler, *My Story of the Civil War and the Under-ground Railroad* (Huntington, Ind., 1914); Cockrum, *Underground Railroad;* Eber M. Pettit, *Sketches in the History of the Underground Railroad Comprising Many Thrilling Incidents of the Escape of Fugitives from Slavery, and the Perils of Those Who Aided Them* (Fredonia, N.Y., 1879), xiv; James Freeman Clarke, *Anti-Slavery Days* (New York, 1883), 80–81.

in their books reveals quite another picture. Marvin B. Butler, for instance, referred to the underground railroad as a "singular secret, and to many, [a] mysterious mode of transportation," though without "formal organization."[12] Levi Coffin, on the other hand, in his description of the underground railroad in an area where it was unusually active, indicates that the abolitionists practiced a minimum of secrecy.

The abolitionist reminiscences seldom included statistics, but almost all of them gave the impression of a thriving underground railroad corporation, never wanting for business. The Reverend Luther Lee of New York and Syracuse maintained that from "about 1840 to the commencement of the War of the Rebellion the road did a large business." By 1844, according to Addison Coffin, "the Wabash line was in good running order and passengers very frequent." "The Underground Railroad did a large business," wrote the Reverend Austin Willey of Maine.[13]

Stories of high adventure characterized abolitionist accounts of the underground railroad. Most of them had at least one encounter with slave hunters to include in their books. One of the aged conductors who penned a sketch for a county history in Iowa assured his readers that the underground history was one to "thrill the heart and quicken the pulse." It involved "hair-breadth escapes, perilous journeys by land and water, incredible human sufferings," in addition to "all the various phases of misery incidental to an outraged and downtrodden people fleeing from an unjust bondage."[14] William L. Cockrum recounted thrilling stories of his youthful adventures with the Anti-Slavery League of Indiana, which allegedly sent spies to the South, aided fugitives, used a secret code system, kidnapped slaves, and severely whipped slave hunters. Calvin Fair-

---

[12] Butler, *Story of the Civil War*, 179.
[13] *Autobiography of the Rev. Luther Lee, D.D.* (Cincinnati, 1882), 320; Addison Coffin, *Life and Travels of Addison Coffin* (Cleveland, 1897), 88–89; Willey, *Antislavery Cause*, 369.
[14] *History of Clinton County, Iowa* (Chicago, 1879), 413.

bank and Dr. Alexander M. Ross also related incidents from
their dangerous careers as slave abductors.[15]

Although some of the abolitionists told of fugitives who had
escaped alone and unaided, all of them attached great importance to the underground railroad as a device which made
most successful escapes possible. It was the heroism and daring
of the abolitionists to which they called attention. "Considering the kind of labor performed, the expense incurred and the
danger involved," wrote Marvin B. Butler, "one must be im-
pressed with the unselfish devotion to principle, of these men
and women thus engaged." Henry Wilson said that those who
engaged in underground railroad efforts "were generally Christian men and women, who feared God and regarded man."
They undertook such labor because they felt "such service was
but obedience to the royal law 'Thou shalt love thy neighbor
as thyself.' "[16]

At least four writers included different versions of the origin
of the term "underground railroad." Eber M. Pettit recalled
an item in a Washington, D.C., newspaper of about 1839 which
involved a captured fugitive slave who admitted, after having
been tortured, that he was to have been sent north, and that
*"the railroad went underground all the way to Boston."* Pettit
added, "thus it will be seen that this famous thoroughfare
was first called the 'Underground railroad,' in the city of Washington." Levi Coffin recounted a story of a slaveholder who,
after he had abandoned his search for a fugitive, commented
that there must be an underground railroad of which Coffin was
president. Coffin heard the story at a bank directors' meeting,
and it was the first time he had heard the term. Rush Sloane
of Sandusky, Ohio, told a story similar to the one reported earlier by William Mitchell. Sloane traced the term to an inci-

---

[15] Calvin Fairbank, *Rev. Calvin Fairbank During Slavery Times. How he
"Fought the Good Fight" to Prepare "The Way"* (Chicago, 1890) ; Alexander Milton Ross, *Recollections and Experiences of an Abolitionist; from 1855 to 1865*
(2d ed., Toronto, 1876) , and *Memoirs of a Reformer* (Toronto, 1893) .

[16] Butler, *Story of the Civil War*, 180; Wilson, *Rise and Fall of the Slave Power*,
2:85.

dent of 1831, when Tice Davids, a fugitive slave, eluded his pursuing master along the Ohio River near Ripley. Davids swam to the Ohio shore and then disappeared. The master eventually gave up and said the "nigger must have gone off on an underground road." Robert C. Smedley told practically the same story, but placed it near Columbia, Pennsylvania.[17]

The underground railroad reminiscences popularized the jargon of the mysterious institution. "It had, like all other railroads," wrote Eber M. Pettit, "its officers and stations, engineers and conductors, ticket agents and train dispatchers, hotels and eating houses."[18] It also had a full slate of officers. Among those who were listed in the postwar period, either by themselves or others, as president of the underground railroad were Levi Coffin of Cincinnati, Robert Purvis of Philadelphia, Peter Stewart of Wilmington, Illinois, Horace White of Syracuse, and Dr. C. V. Dyer of Chicago.

Reminiscent accounts are bound to be full of inaccuracies. Facts are elusive even to the diligent scholar, but even more so to rambling old folk who are recalling the heroic deeds of their more active days. In 1941, for example, when a local historian in Pennsylvania attempted to get at the facts of the Christiana Riot, he ran into such a confusion of statements that, after weighing the evidence, he concluded that it was "no longer possible to credit any of the local tales" which had been told by participants about the flight of the fugitives from Christiana to Canada.[19]

Two of the most influential underground railroad accounts were those of Levi Coffin and Robert C. Smedley. Coffin published the first edition of his *Reminiscences* in 1876, when he was seventy-eight. He used some letters and other documents to supplement his memory, but the aged reformer admitted that

[17] Pettit, *Sketches,* 35–36; Coffin, *Reminiscences,* 190; Rush R. Sloane, "The Underground Railroad of the Firelands," *Firelands Pioneer,* n.s. 5:35 (July, 1888); Smedley, *Underground Railroad,* 35.

[18] Pettit, *Sketches,* xv.

[19] Joseph Hutchinson Smith, "Some Aspects of the Underground Railway in the Counties of Southeastern Pennsylvania," *Bulletin of the Historical Society of Montgomery County, Pennsylvania,* 3:7 (October, 1941).

errors would appear and asked his readers to pardon them because of his "advanced age and feebleness."[20] Nevertheless, and despite his evident exaltation of his own role as reputed president, Coffin's description of the underground railroad in Indiana and western Ohio is one of the more reliable firsthand accounts; his knowledge of these activities was apparently more extensive and his taste for melodrama was certainly less pronounced than is the case with most of the memoirists.

Vying with Coffin's book for popularity was the *History of the Underground Railroad in Chester and the Neighboring Counties of Pennsylvania,* by Robert C. Smedley. Although apparently he had not been involved personally in the antislavery crusade, Smedley came to be thoroughly sympathetic to the participants while collecting reminiscent material from aged abolitionists and their families. He tried to be "punctiliously exact and truthful," though his bias colored every page of his manuscript. Smedley had originally planned only a newspaper article, but he decided to write a book instead when his inquiries "revealed such well-established and well-conducted plans, such nobleness of purpose, such an amount of charity and unrecompensed labors freely given, that the idea suggested itself that the true Christian principles and commendable works of those noble philanthropists, should not be allowed to die with the times in which they lived."[21] Smedley's became one of the most frequently consulted books on the mysterious institution. Yet many of the stories he related cannot be substantiated.

The pattern of underground railroad reminiscences and histories was remarkably similar in the various published accounts. There were variations, of course, in the details and emphases of some of the reformers. One book, however, was markedly different from the rest: William Still's *The Underground Rail Road,* which was perhaps the most widely read of them all. Still was a Negro who had been secretary of the Philadelphia Vigi-

---

[20] Coffin, *Reminiscences,* ii.
[21] Smedley, *Underground Railroad,* xii.

lance Committee. His nearly eight-hundred-page volume first appeared in 1872. It contained hundreds of anecdotes, excerpts from newspaper articles, legal documents, and letters from former slaves and abolitionists. Numerous illustrations helped to fix the thrilling underground railroad adventures in the minds of Still's readers.

Most of Still's material was culled from his Philadelphia Vigilance Committee records. The committee had seemed to prefer stories about cruel and libertine masters. When describing their masters, the fugitives often used such terms as "very rough," a "very mean swearing blustering man," a "gambler and spree'r," a "free whiskey drinker," and a "notorious frolicker and a very hard master." Such masters delighted in cruel punishment and in whipping naked slave girls. Some accounts were "too harrowing to detail." A few gave different evidence, but the committee found it difficult to accept it. A twenty-one-year-old woman told the committee that she had "always been used very well" and "had it good" all her life. "This was a remarkable case," wrote Still, "and, at first, somewhat staggered the faith of the Committee, but they could not dispute her testimony, consequently they gave her the benefit of the doubt." Occasionally the committee members also doubted stories of excessive cruelty, like the one about a master who "believed in selling, flogging, cobbing, paddling, and all other kinds of torture."

Still referred to the South as "the prison house" and the "hotbed of Slavery," though he stated in his preface that he had taken scrupulous care to furnish "simple facts" and to "resort to no coloring to make the book seem romantic." There is no reason to believe that Still did tamper with evidence, though some of the stories recorded by him for the vigilance committee are obviously exaggerated, probably by the fugitives themselves, who were seeking financial assistance from the committee. Still's preface revealed his own viewpoint: "Those who come after us seeking for information in regard to the existence, atrocity, struggles and destruction of Slavery, will have no trouble in finding this hydra-headed monster ruling and tyran-nizing over Church and State, North and South, white and black, without let or hindrance for at least several genera-tions."[22]

But there is a basic difference between Still's work and other abolitionist accounts. The focus of his book is on the brave fugitives rather than on the abolitionists. Although he did not slight the contribution of numerous white abolitionists, Still's hero was clearly the runaway himself. This was no accidental emphasis. Still's avowed aim was to keep green the "heroism and desperate struggles" of the Negroes; he wanted to make the underground railroad "a monument to the heroism of the bondman under the yoke." Furthermore, he wanted to help prove, by writing a creditable book, the intellectual capacity of Negroes. "We very much need works on various topics from the pens of colored men to represent the race intellectually," Still said. The time had come, he believed, "for colored men to be writing books and selling them too."[23]

Still was a competent businessman who had established a thriving retail coal business in Philadelphia. He used his mer-chandising skills advantageously in promoting his book. Care-fully picked agents were given detailed instructions and ob-ligated to send weekly progress reports to Still. His system proved successful. The agents sold books as fast as they rolled from the press. Still sold books on the installment plan, but he instructed his agents not to deliver the book until the price was paid. Still proudly displayed his volume in the Philadel-phia Centennial Exhibition of 1876. A second edition appeared in 1879, and a third in 1883. No other underground railroad book was so well advertised or systematically promoted.[24] But

---

[22] William Still, *The Underground Rail Road* (Philadelphia, 1872), 3–5, 304, 435.
[23] William Still to J. W. Jones, November 4, 1873, to Dr. Henry Charles, June 6, 1873, to J. C. Price, June 3, 1873, and to W. F. Teister, June 23, 1873, William Still Papers, Pennsylvania Historical Society.
[24] Letters from Still to G. W. Gaines, June 6, 1873, W. H. Jones, June 3, 12, 1873, and E. Sanborn, June 11, 1873, Still Papers; James P. Boyd, "William Still," in Still, *Underground Rail Road*, lxiii.

despite his extremely successful sales technique and the popularity of his book, Still's emphasis has made virtually no impact on the popular legend. For it is not the fugitive whose heroism is given the spotlight, but rather the abolitionist who helped him on his way. Still's book was unique in this sense, but its message has been drowned out by the mass of abolitionist-centered literature published in books, popular magazines, and newspapers.

Not all the postwar accounts of the underground railroad were written by participants. Sons and daughters and more distant relatives of abolitionists loved to hear their fathers and grandfathers relate the thrilling incidents of the underground railroad epoch. After the war, when the antislavery cause had become respectable, these descendants doted on the achievements, heroism, and loyalty of their forebears. In articles, in speeches, and in conversation, the relatives of abolitionists repeated the stories they had heard, sometimes with additional material gleaned from the writings of William Still and Levi Coffin. One elderly lady who deposited reminiscences with a local Pennsylvania historical society could claim to be the descendant of three generations of underground railroad operators. She admitted: "In giving reminiscences one thus environed is likely to hark back to years beyond their time and question whether the earliest of them are memories of things seen, heard and remembered or the echoes of former generations." Another proud daughter of a Delaware Quaker abolitionist claimed that her father was known "to be one of those to whom the terrified black man came to be helped into Pennsylvania and farther north, where he would be free." A Maine college professor recalled that his father's house had been "one of the stations on the underground railroad." An Illinois daughter of an underground railroad operator was "proud to be the daughter of a man whose principles of right and justice were so pronounced."[25] Untold numbers of such family sto-

[25] Mrs. Sarah Louise Oberholtzer, undated ms., "Reminiscences of the Underground Railroad in Chester County," Collections of the Chester County (Pa.)

ries, repeated again and again, helped to fix the mysterious institution firmly in the legendary history of the United States. Often the tradition was based upon a single incident. Although details became hazy and the stories could seldom be verified, there was no doubt in the minds of the second and third generation tellers of such tales as to their fundamental truth.

Local pride in northern communities also contributed to the growth of the legend. Traditional accounts were published in many city and county histories as well as in journals of local historical societies. Every barn that had ever housed a fugitive, and some that hadn't, were listed as underground railroad depots. One local incident sometimes served to create a legend of widespread underground railroad activity in the area. In a pre-Civil War history of Medford, Massachusetts, published in 1855, it was boasted that "Medford was the first town in the United States that rescued a fugitive slave." The postwar histories were full of similar pronouncements. A local historian claimed that "the name of Newport, Indiana, was made hateful to every slaveholder south of Mason and Dixon's line," and another, writing about Columbia, Pennsylvania, said: "The place soon became known to slave-owners, but early experience taught them to give it a wide berth." A local historian in Ohio claimed that "By courageously saving many negroes from the torture of slavery the 'agents' of the Underground Railroad aroused public opinion in Ohio and saved it for the Union; Ohio saved Kentucky for the Union cause; and together they aided in the preservation of the United States Government." Another pointed out that "the citizens of Ashtabula County [Ohio] were worthy sons of the New England fathers" and that a fugitive slave at their doors always found shelter and protection. Often local stations were listed in such histories as

Historical Society; Mary Corbit Warner, ms. address, "An Incident of the Corbit Mansion in the Days of Slavery before the War of 1861–4," Slavery Collection, Delaware Historical Society; "Obituary of Mrs. Frances E. Otwell," *Journal of the Illinois State Historical Society*, 24:166 (April, 1931) ; Emma Julia Scott, "The Underground Railroad," prepared for the Woodford County (Ill.) Historical Society and read at the society's annual picnic, August 30, 1934.

"main depots," or "principal depots," and a number of historians claimed that their respective states were foremost in the antislavery movement. Local stories reflected pride in past achievement but seldom had any documentary basis. When Wilbur Siebert was collecting information for his book, one of his informants admonished him to "pay no attention to county histories as they abound in mistakes and perversions." Even reminiscences could not be trusted. "It is amusing to me," he wrote Siebert, "to hear men, now there is no odium, tell all about the U.G.R.R. system, knowing nothing at all."[26] Undoubtedly, such was the nature of a great deal of the material used by local historians writing after the war.

Local legends seemed to inspire more such legends, and there are few sections in the North that cannot boast at least one underground railroad depot. Stories are still repeated about underground tunnels, mysterious signal lights in colored windows, peculiarly placed rows of colored bricks in houses or chimneys to identify the station, and secret rooms for hiding fugitives. In 1923 an Ohio newspaper item concerning the destruction of an Indiana underground railroad station by fire alleged that the house had "contained secret closets, secret cellars and in the war period a secret tunnel led to the river." Only a few such stories have been thoroughly investigated, and some of those have been found to lack any real basis in fact. A persistent rumor that tunnels for aiding slaves to escape existed under Cleveland's St. John's Episcopal Church led to two investigations by the Western Reserve Historical Society. Despite repeated word-of-mouth legends, both investigations led to the inescapable conclusion that there had never been tunnels under the church. There was a possibility that

---

[26] Charles Brooks, *History of the Town of Medford, Middlesex County, Massachusetts, from Its First Settlement, in 1630, to the Present Time, 1855* (Boston, 1855), 410; Waldrip, "A Station of the Underground Railroad," 64; Theodore W. Bean, ed., *History of Montgomery County, Pennsylvania* (Philadelphia, 1884), 301; Ralph M. Watts, "History of the Underground Railroad in Mechanicsburg," *Ohio Archeological and Historical Society Quarterly*, 43:254 (1934); typewritten excerpts from *History of Ashtabula County, Ohio*, 33-34, and Benjamin D. Blackstone to Siebert, March 3, 1896, in scrapbook "The Underground Railroad in Ohio, vol. 1," Siebert Papers, Ohio Historical Society.

the belfry of the church had at one time been used for housing small groups of people, but there was no basis for the widespread rumor about tunnels. A New Hampshire librarian found only "vague and wholly untrustworthy traditions in some families concerning the 'Underground Railroad,' " but no documented information. There was often "circumstantial evidence" that a particular house had served as a station, but even secret rooms had many other reasons for existence than the hiding of fugitives. Authentic records were exceedingly scarce. A New York librarian sought information concerning an underground railroad in Westchester County, New York. He found a great many people who claimed that stations had been established at various points, but when these statements were "pinned down to matters of historical fact," the evidence was lacking. Tradition told of numerous stations, but there was no clear proof "to establish the authenticity of such traditions."[27]

Reputations of individuals for service in the underground railroad were frequently exaggerated because of some incident in which the person had been involved. When historian Siebert wrote to the Reverend Joshua Young of Groton, Massachusetts, for any firsthand information that he might have, Young replied that there was very little he could tell. "Perhaps, my connection with the U.G.R.R. has been exaggerated," he explained, "owing to the circumstances of my being the only present and officiating clergyman at John Brown's funeral, which gave me some prominence among abolitionists." The underground railroad reputation of Jonathan B. Turner of Jacksonville, Illinois, also rested on shaky ground. Two residents of Jacksonville, who had themselves been referred to Sie-

[27] Columbus *Evening Dispatch*, July 9, 1923; Manuscript no. 2787, regarding attempts to discover evidence of tunnels under St. John's Church, Western Reserve Historical Society; Priscilla Roys to Siebert, April 29, 1935, in scrapbook "The Underground Railroad in New Hampshire," John W. Dow to Siebert, October 28, 1935, in scrapbook "The Underground Railroad in Vermont," Myrtle V. Newton to Siebert, March 19, 1945, in scrapbook "The Underground Railroad in Pennsylvania, vol. 4," and William S. Hadaway to Siebert, January 31, 1933, in scrapbook "The Underground Railroad in New York, vol. 3," all in the Siebert Papers, Ohio Historical Society.

bert as underground railroad operators, denied having had any connection with its doings but referred the historian to Turner, who was supposedly "a station agent." But the aged professor and journalist pointed out that his reputation rested on nothing more than once having helped in the rescue of three women from their pursuers. He had not even been an abolitionist, though he was antislavery in his views. He told the story of taking the women to a Presbyterian elder who was supposedly proslavery and whose home, therefore, was a safe hiding place, then concluded: "And this is all I ever knew about the Underground Railway, or its stations." Yet Turner's biographer describes the professor as "a member of the Underground Railroad" though "never very zealous in its work," and the historian of Illinois College, where Turner had taught, said he "took a very prominent part in the activities of the Underground Railway in Jacksonville."[28] Unfortunately, it is impossible to determine how many other underground railroad conductors have earned the title with no more justification than Turner, who himself denied it.

For many years after the conflict, Republican politicians capitalized on the memories of the war, waving the bloody shirt from hustings throughout the North. Most of the abolitionists who did not renounce political action eventually joined the Republican ranks, and political references occasionally occur in the postwar underground railroad literature. William Still referred to the "Proclamation of Father Abraham." Chauncey C. Olin's underground railroad reminiscences included a story about his being refused service when traveling with a Negro antislavery speaker. He thereupon made up his mind, he wrote, that the hotelkeeper was a "rock-ribbed Democrat of the

[28] Joshua Young to Siebert, April 21, 1893, in scrapbook "The Underground Railroad in Vermont," J. S. True to Siebert, January 27, 1896, Julius F. Pratt to Siebert, January 27, 1896, and Jonathan B. Turner to Siebert, March 6, 1896, in scrapbook "The Underground Railroad in Illinois, vol. 3," Siebert Papers, Ohio Historical Society; Theodore Calvin Pease, *The Frontier State, 1818–1848* (*The Centennial History of Illinois*, vol. 2, Springfield, 1918), 440–41; May Turner Carriel, *The Life of Jonathan Baldwin Turner* (Jacksonville, Ill., 1909), 52; Charles Henry Rammelkamp, *Illinois College: A Centennial History* (New Haven, 1928), 106.

first water." Eber M. Pettit's underground railroad book was more explicit. "But for the Republican party," he wrote, "our own free soil would still be hunting ground for the harrassed fugitive from slavery. This very ground would be cursed with the tread of hunters for human chattels. Such is what the Democratic party would have made our whole country to this day and forever."[29]

The abolitionists' convention held in Chicago in 1874 was primarily a political rally, occurring as it did at a time when Republicans were frantically calling up memories of the war and the antislavery crusade. Governor John L. Beveridge gave the opening address, reviewing the major events in the abolition crusade with special emphasis on the underground railroad, which he called "an instrument in the hands of a just God for the fulfillment of His grand purposes." He reminded the aged reformers that the train finally stood still, the engine fires went out, "and in a day the proclamation of the immortal Lincoln, backed by the War power, perfected the emancipation. 'Hallelujah! de year of jubilee hab come!' " he exclaimed. Other speakers took the cue. Dr. Jonathan Blanchard also pointed out the contributions of antislavery politicians, claiming that Thaddeus Stevens was "an older abolitionist than Garrison, and carried his principles further than any other man, never allowing a fugitive to be taken back if he could get near enough to defend him in court." The whole convention was so politically oriented that Oliver Johnson, a Garrisonian, complained that the meeting seemed "to have been almost exclusively a 'Liberty party' 'Free Soil' affair." He did not detect in the newspaper accounts of the convention "even an allusion to the origin of the great *moral* movement" of the Garrisonian abolitionists. Other abolitionist conventions had a similar focus. A speaker at a commemorative meeting in Philadelphia in 1883 reminded the white-haired and battle-scarred

29 Still, *Underground Rail Road,* 541; Chauncey C. Olin, *A Complete Record of the John Olin Family, the First of That Name Who Came to America in the Year A.D. 1678. Containing an Account of Their Settlement and Genealogy up to the Present Time—1893* (Indianapolis, 1893) , xliii; Pettit, *Sketches,* 173–74.

abolitionists that "if the history of the thirty years before the war was familiar to our young people, the voting now going on would be somewhat different."[30] Political oratory designed to give young people a correct appreciation of the events of the ante bellum period may well have helped to establish the underground railroad tradition in American folklore.

The postwar popularity of underground railroad stories even led a few people to try to make money from them. An aged Indiana abolitionist offered to sell Siebert a full sketch of his part in the stirring movement at the rate of five dollars per thousand words. Friends of the elderly Harriet Tubman raised money to publish and sell her story as a slave abductor and underground railroad operator when earlier pension plans failed to materialize. In California, James Williams sold his fugitive slave narrative for fifty cents a copy. Besides incidents of his own escape and career as an underground railroad conductor, Williams' pamphlet contained a full description of the underground railroad and comments on various topics ranging from Mormonism and spiritualism to a defense of Chinese immigrants, all equally unintelligible. The literate section of the booklet comprised underground tales which were mostly lifted verbatim from William Still's account.[31]

Newspaper and magazine stories, from the Civil War to the present day, have helped to preserve the tradition. Newspapers carried numerous reminiscences of local underground railroad operators and repeated the traditional accounts when abolitionists died. Dwellings reputed to be underground railroad depots frequently furnish material for feature stories; such local legends are often revived when an old building is

[30] Newspaper clippings in scrapbook "Abolitionists' Convention, 1874," State Historical Society of Wisconsin; Oliver Johnson to Zebina Eastman, June 15, 1874, Zebina Eastman Papers; *Commemoration of the Fiftieth Anniversary of the Organization of the American Anti-Slavery Society, in Philadelphia* (Philadelphia, 1884).

[31] J. H. Mendenhall to Siebert, February 5, 1896, in scrapbook "The Underground Railroad in Indiana, vol. 1," Siebert Papers, Ohio Historical Society; Sarah H. Bradford, *Scenes in the Life of Harriet Tubman* (Auburn, N.Y., 1869); James Williams, *Life and Adventures of James Williams with a Full Description of the Underground Railroad* (5th ed., Philadelphia, 1893).

being torn down. Commenting on the death of an Indiana abolitionist who, with her husband, had been connected with the underground railroad, a local newspaper said: "This was an organization of those who believed that slavery was wrong and that laws that protected it were made by scheming and corrupt men and that such laws were contrary to the laws of God." A local paper in Pennsylvania included underground railroad material in a series of historical articles. "In the days of slavery in the South," ran the article, "the slaves fleeing from their masters were helped along the way towards Canada, and freedom by certain persons of this and other counties who sympathized with the slaves; and this route was called the Underground Railroad."[32] Hundreds of such newspaper stories furnished readers with a picture of the underground railroad as an abolitionist institution, dotting the entire North with stations and giving fearless humanitarians an opportunity to strike a severe blow at the wicked slave system of the South. Many of the stories borrowed material from the published abolitionist accounts, and later from Wilbur Siebert's history of the underground railroad. They ran in a clearly defined pattern with little variation. Probably such newspaper items have done as much as anything to keep the legend alive.

Although the underground railroad has not become a major theme of American fiction, writers from the time of Harriet Beecher Stowe's triumph to the present have occasionally found material in it for novels and short stories. In addition, some of the supposedly factual accounts of the institution were highly fictionalized. One such book was H. U. Johnson's *From Dixie to Canada; Romance and Realities of the Underground Railroad*, which was published in 1894. These stories had been published earlier in *Johnson's Lake Shore and Home Maga-*

[32] *Cleveland Press*, February 20, 1932; "Death of Mrs. Sally Towell Thompson," undated item copied from Salem, Indiana, *Republican Leader* in scrapbook "The Underground Railroad in Indiana, vol. 2," Siebert Papers, Ohio Historical Society; "The Under-Ground Railroad," February 23, 1925, unidentified newspaper clipping in Friends Historical Library, Swarthmore College. Numerous other examples of newspaper items on the underground railroad are scattered throughout the Siebert Papers.

*zine.* Johnson claimed personal familiarity with many of the
events he depicted and also said he had gathered information
from others. But according to another Ohio editor, Johnson
"got things all wrong, (that is he filled in the detail) ." Wilbur
Siebert said that while Johnson's tales were based upon research
and included the names of authentic operators and towns, he
had used "the license of the story-teller instead of restricting
himself to the simple recording of the information he secured."[33]

Johnson's book repeated some of the material from Levi
Coffin, Eber M. Pettit, and James Freeman Clarke. He described the underground railroad as a corporation which
lasted twenty years, during which time it "extended its great
trunk lines across all the northern states from Mason and Dixon's line and the Ohio River to the Queen's Dominion, and its
ramifications far into the southern states." It had efficient
officers, "side tracks, connections and switches," and its "station
agents and conductors" were men "undaunted in danger and
unswerving in their adherence to principle." Johnson also pictured a secret code system of "cypher dispatches, tokens and
nomenclature." More than thirty-six thousand slaves secured
their freedom by riding the secret underground line. Johnson
repeated Pettit's story of Washington, D.C., as the place where
the underground railroad received its name. Many of his conductors were Quakers, although he told of a proslavery North-
erner who helped a near-white fugitive girl who had been sold
"to a dealer in the far South for the vilest of purposes." Johnson recounted a story about one Ohio conductor who used
"*railroad* telegraphy" in the form of special songs as signals to
his waiting passengers. Johnson's heroes were the abolitionists
who organized and maintained the railroad to freedom.[34]

Edmund Fuller's *A Star Pointed North* is a fictionalized ac-

---

[33] Undated copy of interview with James E. Chambers, editor of *Northern Ohio
Journal,* in scrapbook "The Underground Railroad in Ohio, vol. 4," Siebert Papers, Ohio Historical Society; Wilbur H. Siebert, *The Underground Railroad
from Slavery to Freedom* (New York, 1898) , 4.

[34] H. U. Johnson, *From Dixie to Canada; Romances and Realities of the Underground Railroad* (Orwell, Ohio, 1894) , 12–13, 147, 181–82.

count of the life of Frederick Douglass which includes scattered references to the traditional underground railroad. The novel refers to the "mysterious routes of the Underground Railroad" with "scattered way stations" in Pennsylvania and New York. Fuller also included a description of the New York Vigilance Committee and referred to Frederick Douglass' work with fugitive slaves. He drew an indistinct picture of the institution, but implied that it had a high degree of organization. Shirley Graham wrote another very popular book about the life of Douglass, entitled *There Was Once a Slave*. This novel places considerable emphasis on Douglass as an underground railroad operator and as an inspiration to those still in slavery and hoping to run away. The abolitionist conductors in this book are often Quakers, who "planned the connections" and added secret hiding places to their houses. The slaves knew of the train and its numerous facilities, which "might be a skiff," a "peddler's cart, an open wagon filled with hay," or simply a "covered-up path through the woods."[35]

Brion Gysin's *To Master—A Long Goodnight* is a novel about the life of Josiah Henson, the supposed model for Harriet Beecher Stowe's Uncle Tom. The book is mostly an attack on "Uncle Tomism," or the attitude of Negroes who accommodate themselves to notions of white superiority, but Gysin also includes material on the underground railroad. He pictures the road as having been organized in the late 1840's and becoming most significant after the passage of the Fugitive Slave Law of 1850. The novel alludes to secret signs on houses known only to members of the underground, and to underground railroad "shepherds" who enticed slaves from the South. The impression is one of considerable organization, with "directors of the Underground" making definite plans to run off slaves.[36]

[35] Edmund Fuller, *A Star Pointed North* (New York, 1946), 249 and *passim;* Shirley Graham, *There Was Once a Slave . . . The Heroic Story of Frederick Douglass* (New York, 1947), 85–87.
[36] Brion Gysin, *To Master—A Long Goodnight. The Story of Uncle Tom, a Historical Narrative* (New York, 1946), 73–76.

*A Clouded Star,* Anne Parish's novel about Harriet Tubman, centers around one of the heroine's slave-abducting trips.
This novel pictures the underground railroad as chiefly Harriet Tubman's organization, but the "stations" as mostly run
by Quakers. Another fictionalized biography of Harriet Tubman, a children's novel by Hildegard Hoyt Swift entitled *The
Railroad to Freedom,* presents a picture which conforms more
closely to the traditional one. The underground railroad is described with all its legendary trappings—secret doors and
rooms, code signals, the grapevine telegraph, and strange and
secret tricks. It was a "mysterious organization whose main
lines and branches stretched like a great network over the country from the Mississippi to the coast," but the number of passengers is placed at only a thousand a year. Harriet Tubman is
clearly the heroine, but assistance from the abolitionist organization was essential to her success.[37]

Another children's book, *Stories of the Underground Railroad,* by Anna L. Curtis, furnishes younger readers with a picture of a well-organized, secret network of routes "northward
to Canada, across all the Northern States, from Kansas to
Maine." The impression is one of a very busy road vitally important to escaping slaves. The stories describe many thrilling
pursuits by slave catchers, who are always eluded by the cunning Quaker or Negro conductors. There are the usual false
partitions and clever hiding places.[38]

The recurrence of underground railroad material in literary
works provides further indication of its widespread familiarity.
No other work using the theme approaches the significance of
*Uncle Tom's Cabin* either as literature or as propaganda. Yet
all the books which contain descriptions of the mysterious institution have helped in some measure to keep the legend
alive for numerous American readers.

[37] Anne Parish, *A Clouded Star* (New York, 1948), *passim;* Hildegard Hoyt
Swift, *The Railroad to Freedom: A Story of the Civil War* (New York, 1932), 94,
211–12.
[38] Anna L. Curtis, *Stories of the Underground Railroad* (New York, 1941), 7
and *passim.*

Historians, too, have tended to accept the traditional accounts as substantially correct, even though most of the source materials were written at least a decade after the events had taken place, and some as much as half a century later. While they have some value in indicating in general that some kind of underground railroad activity did take place, these accounts are useless as sources for such specific questions as how many slaves fled to Canada, or even how many were actually aided in their flight. Probably because of a dearth of contemporary evidence, some scholars dealing with the antislavery movement used these abolitionist memoirs much less critically than would ordinarily have been the case. The abolition of slavery seemed to give new prestige to the abolitionists' pronouncements, and their own view of the crusade was largely accepted.

Some historians close to the events in point of time lowered the numbers of successful slave escapes. Hermann von Holst believed that Senator Andrew Pickens Butler's 1850 estimate of annual loss to the South of $200,000 was "much too high although the traffic on the underground railway was already quite lively." James Ford Rhodes accepted the government census figures of only a thousand slave escapes to the North each year. Writing half a century later, Allan Nevins pointed out that the three major studies of the underground railroad all gave the impression of more organization than actually existed and all exaggerated the amount of active opposition to the Fugitive Slave Act of 1850.[39]

Another scholar who modified the traditional underground railroad history was Edward Channing, who refused to accept abolitionist sources uncritically. He rejected the idea that all the slaves were chafing at their bonds, concluded that most escaping slaves came from the border states, and suggested that the actual number was "very difficult to ascertain." He pointed out that the sight of a fugitive might have aroused humanitar-

[39] Hermann von Holst, *Constitutional and Political History of the United States* (8 vols., Chicago, 1881–1892), 3:552; James Ford Rhodes, *History of the United States from the Compromise of 1850* (5 vols., New York, 1900–1909), 2:76–77; Allan Nevins, *Ordeal of the Union* (2 vols., New York, 1947), 1:384n.

ian impulses in people who were not necessarily abolitionists. Though Channing believed there was some "organized system of relief and evasion," his perusal of original sources "convinced him that there was much less system and much more spontaneity than has generally been supposed."[40]

Much more influential than the works of those who modified the traditional story were the writings of Wilbur H. Siebert, whose first book, *The Underground Railroad from Slavery to Freedom,* appeared in 1898 and was followed by several other books and numerous articles on the same subject.[41] Siebert was painstaking in his methods, copying all material pertaining to the underground railroad that he could find in published sources, and sending out a detailed questionnaire to hundreds of former antislavery workers.[42] He accepted the elderly abolitionists' statements at face value and defended the use of such material on the ground that the memories of the aged were more accurate than those of young people.[43] The romantic stories of the abolitionists were apparently difficult for him to reject, and he did not modify his early impressions in any of his later writings. In a 1923 article he defined the underground railroad as "a vast network of secret routes over which fugitive slaves were passed along, chiefly in the night time, from the Southern States to Canada during a prolonged period before the Civil War."[44]

Siebert believed that historians had previously neglected the underground railroad or had overlooked its real importance,

[40] Edward Channing, *A History of the United States* (6 vols., New York, 1925), 6:103–104.

[41] Siebert's voluminous writings include: *The Underground Railroad from Slavery to Freedom* (New York, 1898) ; *The Mysteries of Ohio's Underground Railroad* (Columbus, 1951) ; "Light on the Underground Railroad," *American Historical Review,* 1:455–63 (April, 1896) ; "The Underground Railroad in Massachusetts," American Antiquarian Society *Proceedings,* n.s. 45:25–100 (April, 1935) ; "The Underground Railroad in Ohio," *Ohio Archeological and Historical Publications,* 4:44–63 (Columbus, 1895) ; and *Vermont's Anti-Slavery and Underground Railroad Record* (Columbus, 1937).

[42] "Inquiry concerning the 'Underground Railroad'" to postmaster at Lawn Ridge, Illinois, April 13, 1896, in scrapbook "The Underground Railroad in Illinois, vol. 3," Siebert Papers, Houghton Library.

[43] Siebert, *The Underground Railroad,* 11–12.

[44] Wilbur H. Siebert, "The Underground Railroad in Michigan," *Detroit Historical Monthly,* 1:10 (March, 1923).

and he was determined to set the record straight. On a map
he located hundreds of underground railroad stations and included in an appendix an impressive list of conductors. The
underground railroad, Siebert concluded, was effective both as
an aid to the fleeing bondsman and as a force for assuring an
eventual northern victory in the sectional struggle; it was "one
of the greatest forces which brought on the Civil War, and
thus destroyed slavery." He depicted it as mysterious and secret in its operations. Although he did not include an estimate of the total number of underground railroad passengers,
he completely rejected the ante bellum census statistics and
implied that the number of slave escapes was very high. He calculated that in a thirty-year period, forty thousand fugitive
slaves rode the underground line in Ohio alone. He tended
to accept at face value the propaganda statements of southern
fanatics and the vague impressions of abolitionists recorded in
publications or correspondence many years after the Civil
War. He also identified more than thirty-two hundred alleged
underground railroad conductors and warned that this was a
minimum figure.[45] It would be difficult to exaggerate the influence of Professor Siebert's work. Numerous graduate students have further documented his thesis, and many writers
and historians have borrowed generously from his monumental
labors. Few writers working since Siebert's book was published have dealt with the underground railroad without consulting its pages, and in most cases his ideas and conclusions
have been borrowed as well. His is the standard work on the
mysterious institution.

Professor Channing believed that Siebert had earned the
"thanks of all students of American history" for his work of
gathering and publishing such a wealth of material, but he also
pointed out that the book was in some places "perhaps a little
credulous, and it is partly based on the recollections of old
men." Few others saw shortcomings in Siebert's writing. One
reviewer of Siebert's first publication saw in its pages a "cate-

[45] Siebert, *The Underground Railroad,* 346, 351.

gorical demonstration that the 'Underground' was in reality a
system' and a far reaching and complex one. The 'Road' soon,
in fact, became the most effective and the grandest protest
that Abolitionism ever made." Another reviewer learned from
Siebert's book that abolitionists, in aiding the fugitives, were
"helping the oppressed, . . . eluding the oppressor," and at
the same time "enjoying the most romantic and exciting amuse-
ment open to men who had high moral standards." A study
of Siebert's volume led Benjamin E. Smith to deplore the lack
of an estimate as to the number of underground railroad passengers, which Smith guessed was not less than a hundred thousand. Quite unintentionally, Professor Siebert had contributed
to the growth of a legend. His work seemed to establish a basis
in fact for the many underground railroad traditions which circulated in the era following the Civil War.[46]

In dealing with history rather than legend, it is necessary
to question the validity of local traditions. Hearsay, rumor,
and persistent stories handed down orally from generation to
generation are not proof of anything. Each local story should
be investigated, the basis for the tradition examined, and the
sources evaluated; if there is no historical evidence, the story
may be considered imaginative rather than factual. The legend and its widespread popularity have made such tales appear
plausible. Each local tradition fits into a general pattern which
in turn seems to prove the truth of the local legend. The further removed people are from the Civil War, the more willingly they seem to accept such tradition as fact.

The characteristic outlines of the traditional version reveal
that it is largely derived from postwar abolitionist reminiscences. The abolitionists' accounts tended to neglect the role
of the fugitive slaves themselves in the escape drama, gave the
impression that all successful escapees were passengers on the
mysterious line, and implied that the "railroad" was a nation-

---

[46] Channing, *History of the United States*, 6:116; clippings of reviews of Siebert,
*The Underground Railroad* in *New York Tribune*, August 5, 1899, *Book News*,
February, 1899, *New York Times*, January 21, 1899, in scrapbook "Publication of
the Underground Railroad," Siebert Papers, Houghton Library.

wide abolitionist organization which operated in secret. In reality, it is probable that fugitive slaves succeeded, if at all, mostly by their own efforts. Such help as they received came sometimes from abolitionists, sometimes from other groups, and was often casual and temporary. In the period of the slavery controversy the underground railroad was more important as a propaganda device than as an aid to the fleeing slave. Far from being secret, it was copiously and persistently publicized, and there is little valid evidence for the existence of a widespread underground conspiracy.

The legend not only distorts the nature of the activity but exaggerates its impact on national events. An abolitionist writer of memoirs said that the underground railroad "did more to hasten the crisis and final clash of arms that resulted in making this a free nation than any other agency." Wilbur Siebert and other scholars, assuming the existence of a widespread and successful conspiracy to transport slaves from the South, have attributed to that conspiracy almost as profound an effect as did the memoirist. Even in a study which gives detailed attention to the fugitive slave controversy appears the statement that "the underground railroad was one of the greatest forces that brought on the Civil War," suggesting an underlying assumption that the "railroad" was substantially the institution described in popular legend.[47]

There is a great deal that will never be known about the underground railroad and its impact on slavery and on the sectional controversy, but there is no justification for accepting at face value the emotional and biased accounts of either the abolitionists or their southern antagonists. Thirty-three years after the war, when the memoir writers were at the height of their activity, an Ohio abolitionist who had himself been prosecuted under the Fugitive Slave Law of 1850 wrote: "It was said by the poet that 'distance lends enchantment to the view'; and in regard to the escape of fugitive slaves by what was called

---

[47] Pettit, *Sketches*, 72–73; Russel B. Nye, *Fettered Freedom: Civil Liberties and the Slavery Controversy, 1830–1860* (East Lansing, Mich., 1949), 213.

the 'Underground Road,' I am convinced that the number passing over this line has been greatly magnified in the long period of time since this road ceased to run its always irregular trains."[48] This was only one man's opinion, but coming from a participant and deviating as it does from the usual pattern of abolitionist reminiscence, it is significant. Other evidence tends to substantiate his conclusion. The greater the distance, the more enchantment seems to adhere to all aspects of the underground railroad, the legend that grew up around it, and its role in America's heritage.

[48] Sloane, "The Underground Railroad of the Firelands," 28.

# INDEX

# Index